GREECE AND TURKEY: ADVERSITY IN ALLIANCE

The International Institute for Strategic Studies was founded in 1958 as a centre for the provision of information on and research into the problems of international security, defence and arms control in the nuclear age. It is international in its Council and staff, and its membership is drawn from over sixty countries. It is independent of governments and is not the advocate of any particular interest.

The Institute is concerned with strategic questions — not just with the military aspects of security but with the social and economic sources and political and moral implications of the use and existence of armed force: in other words, with the basic problems of peace.

The Institute's publications are intended for a much wider audience than its own membership and are available to the general public on subscription or singly.

Other Titles in The Adelphi Library

Arms Control and European Security
  Edited by Jonathan Alford

Nuclear Weapons and European Security
  Edited by Robert Nurick

Security in East Asia
  Edited by Robert O'Neill

Nuclear Weapons Proliferation and
  Nuclear Risk
  Edited by James A. Schear

Regional Security in the Middle East
  Edited by Charles Tripp

Greece and Turkey: Adversity in Alliance

ADELPHI LIBRARY

Edited by
JONATHAN ALFORD
Deputy Director, IISS

Published for
THE INTERNATIONAL INSTITUTE FOR STRATEGIC STUDIES
by
St. Martin's Press, New York

©International Institute for Strategic Studies 1984

All rights reserved. For information, write:
St. Martin's Press, Inc., 175 Fifth Avenue, New York, NY 10010
Printed in Great Britain
First published in the United States of America in 1984

ISBN 0-312-34715-4

Library of Congress Cataloging in Publication Data
Main entry under title:
Greece and Turkey, adversity in alliance.
  (Adelphi Library:)
  Includes index.
  Contents: Greek security / Thanos Veremis – Turkey's security policies / Duygu Bazoğlue Sezer – The Aegean dispute / Andrew Wilson – [etc.]
  1. Greece–Relations–Turkey–Addresses, essays, lectures.
  2. Turkey–Relations–Greece–Addresses, essays, lectures.
  3. Greece–Foreign relations–1974–Addresses, essays, lectures.
  4. Turkey–Foreign relations–1960–Addresses, essays, lectures.
  5. Greece–National security–Addresses, essays, lectures.
  6. Turkey–National security–Addresses, essays, lectures.
  I. Alford, Jonathan.
  II. International Institute for Strategic Studies.
  III. Series.
DF787.T8G725   1984   327.4950561   83-40152
ISBN 0-312-34715-4

Contents

Introduction		vii
1	**Greek Security: Issues and Politics** *Thanos Veremis*	1
2	**Turkey's Security Policies** *Duygu Bazoğlue Sezer*	43
3	**The Aegean Dispute** *Andrew Wilson*	90
4	**Greek Security** *Ioannis Pesmazoglou*	131
5	**Turkey's Security Policies** *Bulent Ecevit*	136
Index		142

Introduction

The papers collected in this volume go some way towards explaining why, of all the internal problems facing the Western Alliance, that between Greece and Turkey appears to be the most durable and intractable. There are both deeply historical origins to the obvious and palpable mutual animosity informing their political relationship and more recent and tangible disputes having much to do with sovereignty, especially in the Aegean. In addition the relationship between Greece and Turkey has been soured by the divided island of Cyprus – the 'Bitter Lemon' of Lawrence Durrell's book. It was not always so. Greeks and Turks alike recall with something akin to nostalgia the period of *détente* and even friendship in the Venizelos-Ataturk years between the two World Wars.

Yet, as these papers make clear, almost everything in the historical antecedents of the two States has been different. Turkey was the colonial power, Greece the colonized. Greece sided with the victorious Western Allies in World War I; Turkey with the defeated Central Powers. Greece in World War II was occupied by Germany; Turkey stayed neutral. Turkey has strong Islamic ties and instincts, despite being now a secular state; Greece is Christian and 'European'. Turkey, uneasily forming a bridge between Europe and the Middle East, claims – sometimes with desparation – to be a European State but is possessed with at best a fragile democracy and a backward and largely rural peasant economy. Greece, while remaining proud of its claim to be the birthplace of European civilization, is currently fostering (under Andreas Papandreou) a distinctively anti-American, anti-NATO pro-Third World image. It too had an uncharacteristic departure from democracy under the Colonels and the possibility of renewing the experience tends to act as a constraint on (and places limits to) the extent to which Greek Governments can follow their inclinations.

On the other hand, the Turkish Armed Forces, although intervening in Turkish politics with somewhat greater frequency, do so as guardians of the Turkish Constitution when consensual politics fail (as they do quite often, breaking down in acrimony and bloodshed) rather than as usurpers of the Constitution.

Thanos Veremis is an historian of modern Greece and describes the security politics of Greece up to and including the first year of Andreas Papandreou's Government. He makes clear the uneasy relationship that Greece has had with NATO in the past and points of the fundamental dilemma that any Greek leader has to face: the Western Alliance cannot (and will not) assure Greece's security *vis-à-vis* Turkey, seen as the main security threat to Greece, yet it is only through the Alliance (and especially through the patronage of the United States) that Greece is likely to be able to acquire the means to confront Turkey by herself with any kind of confidence. In other words, Greece must endeavour to present itself as a loyal ally against a Soviet Threat in order to cope with a Turkish threat but, at least at the present time, the Greek Government has chosen to 'play hard to get' over American bases in Greece in the evident belief that this will bid up the price the United States is prepared to pay. It remains to be seen who holds the higher cards.

Duygu Sezer, who teaches International Relations at the Middle East Technical University in Ankara, argues that Greece is by no means as central to Turkish calculations as Turkey is in Greece's. This is a function of size and the fact that Turkey has both an identity problem and a border with the USSR. She doubts whether, in the last resort, Turkey has anywhere to go but NATO but she unravels some of the neutralist strands in Turkish thinking and indicates just how wide open Turkey has been and is to Soviet blandishment. Turkey, at least as much as the Federal Republic of Germany, welcomed *détente* as a means of resolving her uneasy security dilemma. A poor country, Turkey was forced to profess her loyalty to the Western Alliance (at the risk of offending the Soviet Union) in order to qualify for American aid. Especially over Cyprus, and the maltreatment of the Turkish-Cypriot community by the (larger) Greek-Cypriot community, Turkey was faced with cruel choices. Interference in Cyprus to protect 'her' citizens was bound to alienate the United States and other potential benefactors in Western Europe.

Indeed, as Andrew Wilson points out in his appropriately objective analysis of the disputes between Greece and Turkey, it has been Cyprus, latterly an independent state, almost as much as the Aegean, which has provided the arena in which Greek and Turkish interests have clashed. In 1974 in particular it was the intimate connection between politics in Athens and the Turkish invasion of Cyprus that led to the fall of the Colonels, just as it had been Greek Government's encouragement of and support for the Greek Cypriot community which gave rise to Turkish anxiety in the first place. Yet it is the problems of the Aegean which keep the international community on tenterhooks. While Greece, now that the Turkish Army has become the guardian and arbiter of the Turkish-Cypriot community, can do little to change the *status quo* in Cyprus, the Aegean disputes constantly offer the possibility of Greek initiatives to embarrass or disturb Turkey. Andrew Wilson painstakingly sets out the background, the issues and the legal niceties to the Aegean dispute — over air space, over resources and, above all perhaps, over the question of maritime demarcation. Twelve miles for Greece (in terms of territorial waters) would effectively deny Turkey access to the Mediterranean from her Western ports and especially from Istambul and Izmir. A unilateral extension of her territorial waters to twelve miles by Greece would almost certainly be seen as a *casus belli* by Turkey, to be resolved by force.

The collection is rounded out with two more overtly political pieces, one by John Pesmazoglu, a Greek centrist politician, and the other by the former Turkish Prime Minister, Bulent Ecevit, both of whom have spoken at the International Institute for Strategic Studies. The former piece is distinctly moderate measured by the standards of Papandreou's oratory but it nevertheless gives expression to Greek fears of Turkey and the sense of injustice felt by so many Greeks. Bulent Ecevit's speech — to be expected of a left-of-centre political leader — seems to flirt with unreal notions of Turkish neutralism, never far below the surface in Turkish politics. They are unreal, as Duygu Sezer points out, precisely because Turkey cannot afford, given her pressing security needs, either to pay the price of her own defence or to forego the military assistance offered by the West on condition that Turkey continues to be a loyal member of NATO.

There is a temptation to dismiss this squabbling in the South-East corner of

Europe as unimportant, distracting and even irrelevant. Careful reading of these texts should indicate that this would be a short-sighted view. Much is constructed now on the assumption that Greece and Turkey together block Soviet access to the Mediterranean and the United States in particular is constructing at least part of her future interventionary capability in the Middle East (and especially in the Gulf) on the assumption that Turkey will provide access for American forces. This is not to say that the West should necessarily try to resolve the disputes between them for that way both are likely to shift blame onto the West and NATO for their own shortcomings and political failures but it does mean that the shape of security politics in this area will do much to determine the balance of political and military forces over a much wider region. We do need to try to comprehend the sources, progress and possible outcomes of the various disputes that tend to form the always uneasy and often hostile relationship between two NATO partners.

Jonathan Alford

1 Greek Security: Issues and Politics
THANOS VEREMIS

INTRODUCTION

The security priorities of small states in strategic locations not only concern great powers but are often defined by them. The latter's influence may be exerted either directly or through organizations of collective security, and it is not an uncommon feature of such organizations to equate the interests of its junior members with those of its senior. The equation may rest unchallenged as long as the benefits of the relationship continue to exceed the liabilities. However, when a crisis of incompatibility arises between great-power prescriptions and the perceived interests of the smaller states, the future of the relationship will depend largely on the flexibility of the great-power. It is precisely Greece's attempt to redefine her security priorities and the response of the Western Alliance to such an attempt which are the main themes of this Paper.

Since 1974, Greece has capitalized on the loosening of the international system in order to conduct a more independent foreign policy intended to cope with the perceived threats to Greek security from Turkey and the Warsaw Pact. Problems arise because American and NATO officials would deny the threat to Greece's interests from Turkey and make more of the Warsaw Pact threat, and would seem unwilling to comprehend that Greek threat perceptions are not simply the whim of domestic politics.

The Elections of 18 October 1981 gave the 'Panhellenic Socialist Movement' (PASOK) under Andreas Papandreou a clear mandate. To what extent Papandreou will carry out his promise to revise Greek ties with the European Community and withdraw from NATO remains to be seen, but he has already made it clear that his Administration will not follow in the footsteps of its predecessor.

The United States and NATO rely considerably on bases in Greece for the support of the Sixth Fleet and the US Air Forces. Greece also provides intelligence and communications links between Turkey and Western Europe, nuclear weapons storage, and facilities for exercises and training. The storage of fuel and ammunition for the replenishment of American naval and air forces is important for the functioning of these forces in peace and war. Greece's own security considerations should therefore merit greater Western attention than they have received. However, before analysing recent developments in Greek security politics, a brief historical perspective is necessary to demonstrate the continuity of these policies.

Historical Background

Limited national sovereignty and dependence on guarantor powers were common features of the Balkan states that emerged into statehood in the nineteenth century. Their foreign policies evolved in conjunction with the dynamics of European politics and the security arrangements of the major powers – Britain, France, Russia, Austria and, after 1866, Germany and Italy. Conflicting Balkan claims on the European possessions of the declining Ottoman Empire were also drawn into the realm of international antagonisms.

The two most persistent, but mutually exclusive, Greek security problems have concerned the Turks and the Balkan Slavs. After the establishment of her independence in 1830, Greece did not give up her claims on Ottoman territories with sizeable Greek populations. The welfare and security of these people became a primary concern of the new state, and their discontent was a constant cause of friction between Greece and the Ottoman Empire. After 1869 the Ottomans embarked on a policy of exploiting the inherent rivalries among the Balkan claimants for their European possessions. By the end of the nineteenth century, the religious struggle between adherents of the autonomous Bulgarian Exarchate Church and the followers of the Greek Patriarch in Macedonia developed into a covert conflict between Greece and Bulgaria.[1] The major predicament of Greek foreign policy at the beginning of the twentieth century became to adjudicate priorities between her two major, and often conflicting, security concerns – the liberation of Greek populations from Ottoman rule on the one hand, and preventing the Bulgarians from dominating Macedonia on the other.

The Balkan Wars of 1912–13 and World War I (which did not end for Greece until 1922) resolved most of the outstanding differences between the Balkan participants. The Treaty of Lausanne, signed in 1923, ended the era of Greek irredentism and signified the beginning of Greece's internal development. One and a half million refugees from Asia Minor descended upon a country of less than five million as a consequence of Greek defeat by the Nationalist Turkish forces, and this had a direct impact on the country. The urban refugees provided cheap labour for the growing industrial sector and brought skills useful for the development of the economy. The rural refugees settled mostly in Macedonia and Thrace and promoted the linguistic and ethnic homogeneity of these regions after the voluntary exodus of Bulgarians and the compulsory exchange of the Macedonian Turks.

The power vacuum in the Balkans and the Eastern Mediterranean created by World War I gave Italy the opportunity to pursue her interests in that region without opposition, but the improvement of relations with Italy in 1928 gave Greece some respite to deal with her other Balkan concerns. In 1930 an Accord was signed by Kemal Atatürk and Prime Minister Venizelos which settled outstanding matters between Greece and Turkey and began a tacit relationship which lasted longer than any other in the inter-war period in the Balkans.

In February 1934 a Treaty was signed between Greece, Romania, Yugoslavia and Turkey. This was heralded as a triumph of Balkan co-operation, though, because it was shunned by Albania and Bulgaria, the Treaty did not secure the signatories from external threats but virtually invited the European powers to involve themselves in Balkan disputes. Venizelos, whose policy had been to ensure Greece's integrity in case of any international conflagration, was critical of the multilateralism of his successor, P. Tsaldaris. Venizelos' main concern while in office had been to avoid a war with Italy if the latter attacked Yugoslavia through Albania. His fears were not unfounded. The rift between Britain and Italy after the Abyssinian Crisis of 1935 and Greece's willingness to attach herself inextricably to British interests (in spite of Britain's reluctance to provide guarantees of alliance) had paved the way for the Italian attack of October 1940. Ioannis Metaxas, appointed Dictator by King George II in 1936, displayed a constancy towards Britain which was only rivalled by that of his anglophile royal patron.[2]

In the Winter of 1940 the Greek army repelled an Italian surprise attack and, after a successful counter-offensive, pinned down the Italian forces deep inside Albanian territory. Between 5 April and the end of that month, German armoured divisions, coming to the help of the Italians, overran Yugoslavia and Greece. The King and his Ministers, along with what could be salvaged of the armed forces, were evacuated to Crete, and after that island also fell a government-in-exile was established in London and Cairo.

Greece's resistance to invasion, and the subsequent British presence in that country forced Hitler's Germany to embark on a Balkan campaign, thereby disrupting the timetable of her attack on the Soviet Union.[3] The Greeks were proud of their contribution to the Allied cause, but the terrible price they were subsequently forced to pay fuelled their resentment of a royalist regime which had long denied them their political rights. For many, resistance was a war against both occupying forces and authoritarianism in general. The reluctance of the exiled Government to recognize the extent of anti-monarchist sentiment in Greece increased the influence of the Communist-led broad-based resistance movement EAM–ELAS and precipitated a devastating conflict between royalist and anti-royalist officers in the Greek Army in the Middle East and North Africa.

An aggressive EAM-ELAS policy of monopolizing the resistance, and the incompatibility of Communist political goals with British commitment to the constitutional monarchy, brought about an internal confrontation after the German withdrawal during which some of the smaller Republican resistance groups sided with the repatriated Government and the British against the Communists.

In 1946 the first elections for ten years were held in circumstances hardly conducive to parliamentary politics. The KKE (Greek Communist Party) abstained, thus ensuring victory for the right-wing parties – which promptly conducted the plebiscite which brought back King George. The disorientated liberals, increasingly isolated in the middle of a polarized political scene, threw in their lot with the royalists in the civil war which broke out between right-of-centre nationalists and Communists. This armed conflict, which continued from 1946 to 1949, inflicted the worst punishment on the country since the War of Independence. Its legacy in material loss was no less appalling than its long-term effect on Greek society and politics.

In 1947, Stalin, who had until then honoured his 1944 agreement with Churchill to allow Britain a free hand in Greece, demanded the withdrawal of British troops. He also sought revision of the 1936 Montreux Convention, which defines the regime of the Dardanelles, and raised claims over the Dodecanese Islands which were ceded to Greece in 1947.[4]

Between 1946 and 1948 British influence gave way to US influence in Greece. In March 1947 the Truman Doctrine declared US intentions to prevent Greece and Turkey from passing under Soviet control. For the US, Greece became the first testing ground – and indeed the first battle-ground – of the Cold War Doctrine. Besides military aid, the US supplied military advisers and formed a joint General Staff with the Greek Government to conduct operations. In the UN General Assembly, Albania, Yugoslavia and Bulgaria were condemned for aiding the Communist forces, but in fact it was Tito's break with the Cominform in 1948 which deprived the Greek Communist forces of their strategic exit to Yugoslavia and of Yugoslav support. By the Autumn of 1949 the Government forces held the field.

War, enemy occupation and civil strife had brought Greece disaster to a degree hardly paralleled elsewhere in Europe. Central and local administration was paralyzed; the economic infrastructure was shattered; inflation was out of control. As Campbell states, 'Dependence on great powers which had characterised Greece's history since the establishment of the modern states was never more evident than in her reliance on the American presence during these years to preserve the Greek version of parliamentary government and free economy'.[5]

I. THE CONDITIONS OF GREEK SECURITY

The Region

The Mediterranean, extending from Gibraltar to the Dardanelles and the Suez Canal, covers 1.5 million square kilometres. It connects three members of the Southern Region of NATO, which is the largest area in Allied Command Europe, 4,000 km from East to West and some 1,400 km from the Alps to the coast of Libya.[1] About one tenth of the world's population resides in the states bordering the sea – on which 1,500 ocean-going ships and some 5,000 smaller craft travel on an average day. The Mediterranean is also the junction of three Continents, three major religious communities (Christian, Moslem and Jewish), two major military and ideological blocs and a number of non-aligned states. It is also an important route for west-bound Middle East oil pumped to Eastern Mediterranean pipeline terminals, as well as for oil exported to Europe from North African producers.[2]

Europe and the United States have a vital interest in maintaining the *status quo* in the Mediterranean and especially in its more troubled eastern part. The priorities of the West in the region include the protection of oil interests, the prevention of a crisis over

Israel which might endanger relations with Saudi Arabia, and the containment of Soviet influence and incursion. The Sixth Fleet and American bases in various littoral states are both political instruments and a deterrent against the Soviet Union. The Fleet normally comprises two aircraft-carrier groups and some fifteen surface combatants, varying from cruisers to escorts, and one main amphibious unit – although recently one carrier task force has been on temporary duty in the Indian Ocean. The aircraft carriers each have eighty to ninety combat aircraft, some of which have a nuclear strike role. These aircraft have a combat radius of 600 to 800 km, thus covering land targets in the southern Soviet Union. NATO tactical air units, nuclear stockpiles and communication networks also contribute to the Western military presence in the region.[3]

The major installations used by the United States in Greece include the Hellenikon air base in Athens, the Nea Makri communications station near Marathon, the Iraklion air station and the Suda Bay complex in Crete. Other US communications facilities and five NATO Air Defence in the Ground Environment (NADGE) sites are spread throughout the country, mainly in the north of Greece. There are also nuclear weapons and storage sites dating from the 1960s. The missiles are held in Greek bases with the warheads under US control.

The most important of these facilities is generally acknowledged to be the Suda Bay complex, which houses fuel and ammunition for use by US and NATO naval forces. The Bay provides port facilities, an anchorage which can accommodate most of the Sixth Fleet if necessary and an airfield for use by American military reconnaissance aircraft. The NATO missile firing range at nearby Namfi, where training and testing exercises are conducted, is associated with the Suda complex.

The Iraklion air station supports reconnaissance flights and the refuelling of US aircraft. Also associated with Iraklion is an electronic surveillance station manned by the US Air Force Security Service (USAFSS). This listening post monitors Soviet activities in the eastern Mediterranean.

The Hellenikon air base serves as a headquarters and provides support for other US Air Force Europe (USAFE) facilities in Greece. Electronic and photographic reconnaissance missions are mounted from this base, which is also the staging point for air transport operations of USAFE, and it also provides support for the US Military Airlift Command (MAC).[4]

Nea Makri houses a major communications centre which is part of the global US Defense Communications System (DCS). The centre is tied into the Licola terminal at Naples, Italy, and the Morón terminal in Spain. The Kato Souli terminal near Nea Makri is linked with the Sixth Fleet and with bases in Naples and Spain. Mount Pateras, 20 miles West of Athens, is believed to connect Greece with the Yamanlar terminal near Izmir, Turkey, and provides a link between North-east Crete, the island of Lefkas in the Ionian Sea and a terminal in southern Italy.[5]

The Soviet Threat and NATO

In strictly regional terms, the Soviet Union appears to be more interested in diminishing the threat posed to her own security than in competing with the United States for supremacy. Through 'carrot and cannon tactics' the Soviet Union has secured passage by way of the Dardanelles into the Mediterranean. The Soviet naval squadron based at Sebastopol on the Black Sea is deployed in the Mediterranean, spending much of its time at deep water anchorages near choke-points of the Mediterranean, and it also has use of port facilities at Tartus and Latakia (Syria) and limited repair facilities at Tirat (Yugoslavia). The rapid growth of the Fifth Escadra during the past ten years has reflected a general Soviet projection of power at sea. The Escadra comprises up to 15–20 major surface combatants, amphibious landing craft and auxiliary vessels. Its nuclear and diesel-powered submarines (up to 10) come from the Soviet Northern Fleet. To compensate for lack of regular access to ports, Soviet warships make extensive use of shoals in international waters where the sea is shallow enough to permit the anchoring of large vessels and the rendezvous with oilers and supply ships.[6] The Soviet Union has established anchorages and maintenance facilities ten to eleven miles from the low tide-mark off the coasts of Anticythira, St Eustratios and Crete. An extension of Greek territorial waters will require Graeco-Soviet consultations leading to one of two possible solutions: either the Soviet facilities will remain in operation within Greek territorial waters and thus will be regarded as foreign military installations, or these facilities will have to be removed. It is safe therefore to assume that the Soviet Union would oppose such an extension, unless she were given guarantees of uninterrupted tenure. In case of such a development it would be expected that the US and NATO would react adversely to an official 'co-existence' of their bases along with Soviet facilities in Greek territory.[7]

In spite of the expansion of Soviet naval presence in the Eastern Mediterranean between 1970 and 1980 the USSR continues to lack significant sea-based and land-based air power. This obstacle has been partly overcome by the appearance of naval *Backfire* bombers, based in the Crimea, which can cover most of the Mediterranean basin. The introduction of this aircraft has increased the importance of the number and quality of Greek and Turkish air defence fighters.

The Warsaw Pact has also expanded and modernized its land forces facing NATO's Southern Flank. Some 33 Warsaw Pact divisions are deployed on the Graeco–Turkish borders against a total of 25 Greek and Turkish divisions. The Pact possesses an advantage of three-to-one in terms of mechanized and armoured capability.[8] The Soviet Union has also deployed intermediate-range ballistic missiles (IRBM), including the SS-20 with three multiple independently targetable re-entry vehicles (MIRV), in the Crimea and in the Northern Transcaucasus.[9] As part of NATO's Theatre Nuclear Force (TNF) modernization, ground-launched cruise missiles (GLCM) are to be deployed at Comiso in Sicily in the mid-1980s.

Turkey
Greece's post-war defence was primarily directed against both an internal and external Communist threat. Her northern borders with Albania, Yugoslavia and Bulgaria originally attracted the almost exclusive attention of military planners and, through her association with the United States and NATO, Greece's security concerns were incorporated into the larger scheme of Western collective security. However, the Graeco–Turkish dispute over Cyprus, compounded in 1974 by the Turkish invasion of the island, drastically altered Greece's security orientation. Besides the Cyprus issue, three other critical questions have given rise to serious tension between the two NATO allies: *1)* Turkey's demands over the Aegean continental shelf; *2)* the air-space dispute; and *3)* the reallocation of operational responsibilities of the Aegean sea and air space. These are discussed below.

At the centre of Greek concern over Turkish claims in the Aegean is the security of the islands formally ceded to Greece in 1923 and 1947. Turkey, while facing the Greek islands with the second largest fleet of landing craft in NATO and a newly constructed Fourth (Aegean) Army, accuses Greece of violating articles of the Lausanne and Paris Treaties by militarizing her islands off the coast of Asia Minor. Prominent Turks, such as former Defence Minister Sancar, former Prime Minister Demirel, former Minister of Foreign Affairs Esenbel and former Vice-Premier Turkes, have made undisguised references to Turkish 'rights' and claims on the Greek islands. If Turkey eventually succeeded in controlling contiguous Greek islands, her strategic value would be increased, and, with control of the entire sea approaches to the Dardanelles, her bargaining position *vis-à-vis* the two superpowers would be considerably enhanced. Greece's current security concern is to safeguard her sovereign island territories.

More than any other country in the region Greece's economy is dependent on the sea. Half her population of nine million live in three major Mediterranean ports – Athens (Piraeus), Thessaloniki and Patras – and most of their inhabitants are employed directly or indirectly in trades connected with the sea. Greek concern over the welfare of the islands should not be underestimated. Moreover, the prospect of a Turkish population of about 70 million by the end of the century adds to Greek anxieties.[10]

5

II. GREEK SECURITY PROBLEMS AND POLICIES

There is a historical continuity to Greece's security problems which is underlined by her geopolitical significance. Although World War II altered the social regimes of her northern neighbours, some of the issues which have traditionally caused strife among these states themselves and between them and Greece are still active today. However, the intensity of conflict has depended on the condition of Soviet–American relations. The era of detente improved relations between Greece and her Balkan neighbours, but it was ultimately disillusionment with United States policy during the Junta period and the subsequent conflict with Turkey that was to bring about a partial emancipation of Greek foreign policy.

Relations with the Balkan States

The issue of the ethnic balance of Greek Macedonia was resolved with the exchanges of populations between 1920 and 1923.[1] The overwhelming preponderance of the Greek element in Macedonia, enhanced by 700,000 Greek refugees from Asia Minor, could not be disputed, yet the KKE – badly split over the issue – was forced by the Comintern during the Sixth Balkan Communist Conference in 1924 to underwrite the Bulgarian slogan for a 'united and Independent Macedonia and Thrace'.[2] This policy, which amounted to the ceding of Greek Macedonia to a state under Bulgarian influence, was abandoned in 1935 but caused irreparable damage to the image of the Communist Party at home.

After German occupation, Bulgaria in practice incorporated most of Eastern Macedonia and Western Thrace without the formality of declaring war on Greece. In Western Macedonia the German authorities gave the Bulgarians a free hand in propaganda and intimidation of the local population. Greek resistance forces were confronted with a double struggle, against the occupying army as well as against the parliamentary Bulgarian nationalist battalions (Ohrana). In 1943, at a conference between Yugoslavia and Greek partisans, Tito's representatives for the first time used the term 'Macedonian nationals' and sought EAM–ELAS co-operation in order to win Bulgarian collaborators back to the 'Macedonian' ideological camp. Although ELAS refused the Yugoslavs the right to organize Greek Slavophone resistance groups, they agreed to include them in their resistance movement and later granted them the option of forming their own units of the Slav Macedonian National Liberation Front (SNOF) under ELAS command.[3]

Yugoslav plans to form a Macedonian state under Yugoslavian dominance, to include the Bulgarian Pirin Macedonia (and the Greek 'Aegean' Macedonia), were naturally not welcomed by the Bulgarian Communist regime after World War II, but the relative weakness of the Soviet-liberated country, as opposed to the triumphant partisan regime of her neighbour, did not permit overt opposition. Until Tito's break with the Cominform in 1948, Yugoslavia enjoyed a period of unqualified preponderance, and Tito's 'Macedonian' policy was to a considerable degree accepted by the Dimitrov regime in Bulgaria.

Discussions of a South Slav Federation between Yugoslavia and Bulgaria were concluded in the Bled Protocols of 1947, the high point in the co-operation between the two states. It was implied in the Agreements that the Pirin Macedonians (as well as their Aegean 'brethren') would be granted cultural autonomy as a first step towards their incorporation in the People's Republic of Macedonia. The Bulgarians reluctantly kept their side of the Agreement, but the Greek Communists were in no position to agree to such decisions, and the Greek Government had by then severed its communications with the Communist states.[4]

Until 1948 the Bulgarian Government kept a low profile on the issue of Greek Macedonia, reiterating its claims to Western Thrace and demands for an exit into the Aegean. These claims had been supported at the Paris Peace Conference of 1946 by both the Soviet Union and Yugoslavia. However, the clash between Stalin and Tito had a profound effect on the entire nexus of Balkan politics. Yugoslavia terminated her support for the Greek Communist guerrillas who continued to keep faith (though inconspicuously) with the Cominform. Seeking a way out of isolation and encirclement by hostile Communist states, Tito signed the death warrant of the 'Greek Communist Democratic Army' and proceeded to improve relations with the Greek Government.

The KKE split badly over Yugoslavia's rebellion. Zachariades, the powerful Chairman of the Greek Communist Party, upheld Cominform orthodoxy and cashiered his Commander-in-Chief, taking over his office while pro-Yugoslav elements and certain other Slav-speaking groups fled to Yugoslavia. At the fifth plenum of its Central Committee in January 1949 the leadership of the KKE endorsed the new Cominform policy for the establishment of an independent Macedonia within a Balkan Federation. This return to the 1924 position remained the party line until it was officially abandoned in 1956. In August 1949 the 'Democratic Army' was heavily defeated and, along with Slavophone supporters, sought refuge first in Albania and then in other Communist countries.

The Bulgarian Government was quick to repudiate the content of the Bled Protocols and declared that their Pirin district was part of a Bulgarian-sponsored autonomous Macedonia. The teaching of the Macedonian dialect was banned, and all traces of Yugoslav propaganda among the Macedonians were eradicated. By 1952 Bulgarian claims on Greek Macedonia were once again being pressed hard. As Bulgarian propaganda intensified, so Greece was pushed closer to Yugoslavia, and Yugoslavia was drawn closer to Greece as her fears of Soviet-Bulgarian-Albanian encirclement mounted. In 1953 a Treaty of Friendship and Co-operation was concluded in Ankara between Greece, Yugoslavia and Turkey, and in 1954 the Treaty was complemented by a Military Alliance signed in Bled.[5]

The dispute over Greek Macedonia continued among the KKE leaders in exile. Zachariades, who had already in 1949 declared his sympathy for the emancipation of the Slavophones, declared unmistakably in his 'Ten Years of Struggle' that he supported the political autonomy and self-government of the Macedonian Slavs, thus making life exceedingly difficult for his fellow Communists in Greece[6]. Because there was an implication in his statement that he favoured a Bulgarian-orientated but independent Macedonia – and not the Yugoslav variety – he was condemned by both Moscow and Sofia. Partsalides, a member of the Central Committee (and a revered figure of the internal KKE after 1960), heavily criticized his leader's separatist pronouncements as reviving a mistake that had plagued the KKE during the inter-war period.

With Stalin's death in 1953, relations between Belgrade and Moscow improved, leading to a Yugoslav-Bulgarian *rapprochement* in 1955. However, the suppression of the Hungarian uprising in 1956 brought about another deterioration, lasting until 1960. In 1959 Greece and Yugoslavia agreed on free border traffic, but this was denounced by Greece in 1962 after renewed hostility over the issue of Macedonia. A new period of understanding between the Soviet Union and Yugoslavia began in 1962, but also foundered – this time as a result of Soviet intervention in Czechoslovakia in 1968.

The see-saw of improvement and deterioration in Yugoslav-Soviet-Bulgarian relations had a marked impact on Greece. Every normalization of relations among the three countries meant that Yugoslavia would revive her accusations that Greece was depriving her alleged Macedonian minority of its cultural heritage. The standard Greek reply amounted to a denial of the existence of such a minority.

From the end of World War II Greece's primary concern over Macedonia was to maintain the territorial *status quo*. It was assumed that occasional Yugoslav statements supporting the rights of the alleged minority in Greece were stimulated by both pressure from Skopje (the centre for Macedonian nationalism) and the need to confront Bulgarian arguments with a principled position on the identity of the Macedonian Slavophones. Greek tactics with respect to such intermittent Yugoslav and Bulgarian claims were to respond to, rather than to initiate, verbal aggression and to try to play down what was considered an artificial issue.

Graeco–Romanian relations from 1957 to 1959 were highlighted by the Stoika Plan to ban nuclear weapons from the Balkans. This Romanian proposition was adopted by the left-wing coalition party EDA and was extensively employed during electoral campaigning.

Improvement of relations between Greece and her Communist neighbours was initiated by the dictatorship in 1967 because the regime was experiencing political if not economic isolation from Western Europe. Bulgaria's favourable response to Greek overtures indicated Soviet willingness to exploit Greek isolation, but it could also be seen in the wider context of global detente. The Soviet intervention in Czechoslovakia had an adverse effect of Tito's relations with Bulgaria, and the Greek Colonels had no desire to alleviate Yugoslavia's problem. Irritated by criticism from Yugoslavia in 1967 over the arrest of political dissidents, the Colonels denounced the 1959 Agreement concerning frontier traffic. Relations with Yugoslavia improved after 1970 on the Greek Government's initiative.[7]

Greece and Albania resumed diplomatic relations in May 1971. These had been severed during the War, and Greek claims on territories and war indemnities were excluded from the negotiations – which were thus about trade and cultural exchanges only.

Since the restoration of democracy in 1974, as a result of the tensions over Cyprus and the Aegean, Greece has consistently pursued a comprehensive Balkan policy to secure her northern frontiers by improving relations with all her Communist neighbours. This *rapprochement* can also be viewed as a necessary and overdue adjustment to bring Greece into the era of detente and Eurocommunism. To quote an apt comment, 'If we were to compare the growth of East–West trade and the volume of scientific and technological exchanges between the industrial West and the developing East with Greece's timid initiatives during the 1960s, we would find that the country's foreign policy was in disharmony even with that of its NATO partners'.[8]

Besides her importance in providing the most accessible land-route to Western Europe, Yugoslavia's influence among the non-aligned countries was considered useful in the Cyprus dispute. Greece and Yugoslavia agreed to relieve their mutual borders of a concentration of troops and to divert them to other areas vital for their respective national defences. Old problems such as the free zone at Thessaloniki were settled, and trade between Greece and Yugoslavia grew from $120 million in 1975 to $250 million in 1980. Greek entry into the European Economic Community (EEC) and restrictions on trade with non-members reduced this figure to $208 million for 1981 and turned the balance in Greece's favour. A pipeline to bring oil from the Aegean to Skopje is being constructed, and goodwill visits were exchanged between Karamanlis and Tito, as well as between other members of their respective Governments. The death of Tito has somewhat numbed the initiative of his successors but has not altered the friendliness of relations between the two nations. Yugoslavia's backing of Skopje's claims over the alleged Macedonian minorities is basically aimed at Bulgaria, but the matter is also of concern to Greece and so causes irritation in Athens. The difference of view however, between the central Yugoslavian Government and 'Macedonian' Skopje is that Skopje considers the recognition of a 'Macedonian minority' a precondition for any further improvement in Yugoslav–Greek relations, whereas the Government in Belgrade believes that friendly relations between Greece and Yugoslavia will also promote a solution to the Macedonian problem. It is logical to assume therefore that any future weakening of Belgrade's control over Skopje will rekindle friction between Greece and Yugoslavia.[9]

Relations with Albania – improving steadily since 1971 – reached a high point after Hoxha's break with China. Visits of a commercial and cultural nature were exchanged starting in 1977, and trade amounting to a total of $21 million was exchanged. A regular air link between Athens and Tirana was inaugurated in 1978. Hoxha himself took a friendly stance towards the Greek minority in his country (estimated by a Western source to amount to anything between 40,000 and

80,000), the status of which constituted the most serious obstacle in any Graeco–Albanian *rapprochement*. Besides stressing the need for closer relations with Greece, the Albanian leader has extolled the importance of preserving Greek language, culture and tradition among the Albanian Greeks.[10]

The opening towards Bulgaria was mainly the result of a personal initiative by Karamanlis and his individual style of conducting foreign policy. After visiting an enthusiastic Nicolae Ceaucescu in Romania in May 1975 and visiting Yugoslavia in June of the same year, he was received by Todar Zhivkov of Bulgaria on 2–3 July. Although Graeco–Bulgarian relations have been troubled in the past, Karamanlis' direct appeal to Zhivkov eventually made an impression on Bulgarian reluctance to enter into a multilateral relationship even on a limited basis. Initially Bulgaria attempted to enlarge Balkan multilateral initiatives to include other East European nations. Following a Greek initiative, however, an inter-Balkan Conference of Deputy Ministers of Planning (or Undersecretaries for Co-ordination) took place in Athens in February 1976. Although Bulgaria opposed Balkan multilateralism in principle, she nevertheless attended the summit to avoid discouraging the two NATO participants – Greece and Turkey – from their dialogue with the East. A renewed effort by Karamanlis to give the Summit Meetings a regular and substantial character was politely rebuffed by Bulgaria, reflecting perhaps Soviet fears that institutionalized Balkan co-operation might adversely affect the cohesion of the Warsaw Pact. That fear may be diminishing. At the April 1979 Corfu meeting with Karamanlis, President Zhivkov appeared to have overcome his inhibitions, and he then agreed to multilateralism in specified fields.[11]

Considering the strains of the past between the two nations, Graeco–Bulgarian relations are now uncommonly good. No territorial or minority claims marred the exchange of visits between Karamanlis and Zhivkov. It can be anticipated that Papandreou's Government will press further. Commerce increased from $104 million in 1978 to a total of $157 million in 1980,[12] while industrial co-operation, the linking of electrical grids, access to the 'free port' of Thessaloniki and the expansion of vital land communications have been agreed.[13]

Despite a generally encouraging trend in Greece's relations with the other Balkan states, the Soviet Union can still threaten to exploit latent discontent among ethnic groups and differences over contested territories. Either or both could destabilize the present delicate balance. The Macedonian dispute, which is now mainly between Yugoslavia and Bulgaria, may return in the 1980s, initiated possibly by Belgrade (to appease Skopjean nationalism) or by Sofia (whose old claims on what is today Yugoslav Macedonia may be encouraged by Moscow to embarrass Yugoslavia). Yugoslav apprehensions, which subsided after Tito's death, were rekindled at the beginning of 1981 when Bulgaria celebrated 1,300 years of statehood.

Her position as an outsider to these quarrels among Communist states has enhanced Greece's credibility as an honest broker in the Balkans. The efforts of Karamanlis were initially blunted by Bulgaria, and Greece was also faced with Turkish fears that a Balkan Pact might contribute to Turkey's isolation. However, most Balkan leaders have taken care not to offend Turkey and, according to Stavrou, even Yugoslavia, 'usually a trustworthy friend of Greece, has had to reconcile any response to a Greek–Turkish dispute with its role in the non-aligned movement and with its national interest'.[14] Greece's major objective in the Balkans has not been to secure allies against Turkey but rather to relieve her own borders from tension in case of any attack from the East.[15]

In short Greece has to a quite satisfactory exent established both bilateral and multilateral relations in the Balkans after decades of mutual distrust. Since his electoral victory, Papandreou has furthered his friendly policy towards Communist Balkan states by receiving Ceaucescu in Athens and visting Belgrade and Sofia.[16]

Graeco–Turkish Relations

The favourable trend in Graeco–Turkish relations created by the 1930 Accord and the 1933 and 1938 Treaties of Military Co-operation was interrupted by the outbreak of World War II. In 1939 Turkey concluded a Trilateral Treaty with Britain and France, undertaking the obligation to 'lend them all aid and assistance' in case any of the signatories was involved in war with a European power in the Mediterranean.[17] Her subsequent failure to enter the war affected Greece badly, since she was under very great pressure from Axis forces. Furthermore, a Turkish capital tax (*varlik vergisi*), which operated between 1942 and 1944, caused considerable hardship to the ethnic minorities of Istanbul, and in particular to Turkish citizens of Greek, Jewish and Armenian origin.[18]

By 1951, however, Greece and Turkey had resumed friendly relations in the face of a common Soviet threat. Both were recipients of aid under the Marshall Plan, and both were formally admitted into NATO on 18 February 1952, at the height of the Cold War. A year later they signed, together with Yugoslavia, a Treaty of Friendship and Co-operation followed by a formal Alliance. The Alliance, which might have served as an indirect link between NATO and Yugoslavia, foundered on the improvement of Russian–Yugoslav relations in 1955 as well as on the Cyprus issue, which for almost a quarter of a century has been the major source of tension between the two NATO allies.

The Cyprus Problem

Cyprus was occupied by Britain in 1878 and became a colony in 1925. Her mixed population (80 per cent Greek and 18 per cent Turkish) and her position as an important strategic location in the Eastern Mediterranean meant that the island soon became a bone of contention between states of the Western Alliance. The Greek-Cypriot claim for self-determination in order to unite the island with Greece – a mixture of traditional irredentism and contemporary anti-colonialism – was initially confronted by Britain's reluctance to abandon her position in the Eastern Mediterranean; and later the same mixture served to inflame nationalist feeling in Greece and Turkey, and to erode their respective relations with the United States. NATO became implicated in the dispute in the 1960s. The Organization was designed to provide a defence against the Soviet Union, and it operates on the assumption that the notion of collective security supersedes all other local priorities. It was therefore ill-equipped to resolve local disputes between its members.

In January 1950 a plebiscite of Greek Cypriots was organized by the Orthodox Church. This yielded a 96 per cent vote in favour of unification (*enosis*) with Greece, and revived old pressures on Greece to take up the issue with Britain. Greek Governments since 1931 had carefully avoided claims that would cause friction with Britain, and the Liberal Coalition Government of 1951 was no exception to that rule. Yet the United States was all the while assuming a dominant position in Greece, and in consequence Greek inhibitions towards Britain gradually diminished. In 1954 the Conservative Government of Marshal Papagos, strongly committed to the United States, embraced the cause of the Greek Cypriots.[19]

When Archbishop Makarios, then political and spiritual leader of the Greek-Cypriot community, began to steer the question towards the United Nations, Britain decided to introduce Turkey (hitherto apathetic about the conflict) into the matter, to provide a counter-weight to Greek demands. The Turkish Government assumed responsibility for the welfare of the Turkish Cypriots and eventually control over their affairs. Thus the foundations of the future intercommunal conflict were laid, and what began as an anti-colonial struggle gradually developed into a confrontation between Greek and Turk.

Relations between Greece and Turkey deteriorated in September 1955 when a mob in Istanbul, demanding the annexation of Cyprus by Turkey, attacked and destroyed Greek houses, shops and churches.[20] By 1959 the Cyprus issue had become such a liability for Greece's relations with Britain and the United States that Prime Minister Karamanlis felt compelled to seek a speedy solution to the problem. Makarios in the meantime had retreated from the *enosis* aspiration, for this provoked Turkish demands for the partition of the island. He adopted instead his platform of Cypriot independence. Finally Britain came to realize that to retain control of Cyprus in opposition to the Greek Cypriots was becoming too expensive. She sought a way of reconciling the retention of sovereign base rights with Cypriot independence.

In 1959 the Greek Prime Minister Karamanlis and the Turkish Prime Minister Menderes drafted an agreement in Zurich for the creation of an independent Cyprus. This plan was duly presented to the leaders of the two communities. The agreement provided for the British sovereign military bases in the island and an independent republic for the Cypriots. The integrity and constitution of the state were to be guaranteed by Britain, Greece and Turkey, and the latter two states would contribute contingency forces of 950 and 650 respectively. A Greek-Cypriot President and a Turkish-Cypriot Vice-President were given veto power over vital legislation, and the Turkish minority was represented in the Government and in the Civil Service to a greater extent than numbers demanded. The leaders of the two communities, who had played no part in the drafting of the Zurich Agreement, affixed their signatures to the document in London.

After the electoral defeat of Karamanlis in 1963, the Centre Union coalition under the ageing George Papandreou was faced with a new phase in the Cyprus entanglement – the protracted struggle between the ethnic groups of the island. Confronted with a deadlock in the passing of vital legislation, President Makarios proposed to Dr Kutchuck, the Turkish-Cypriot Vice-President, thirteen amendments to the 1960 Constitution. The veto powers of both the President and (more important to the Turks) the Vice-President would be abolished, and the number of Turkish Cypriots in the Administration would be diminished. Turkey, followed by Dr Kutchuck, rejected the proposals, and fighting broke out between the two communities which lasted well into the Summer of 1964 and caused considerable hardship for the outnumbered Turkish Cypriots. It was only after US President Johnson's personal warning to the Turkish Prime Minister Ismet Inönu that a Turkish invasion of Cyprus was warded off during the Summer. An uneasy peace was restored by a UN peacekeeping force (UNFICYP), but mutual hatred continued to smoulder.

General Grivas, already head of the most active anti-Communist band when the German forces pulled out of Greece, had become leader of the guerrilla EOKA movement in Cyprus which harassed the British forces between 1955 and 1959. A champion of *enosis*, he strongly disapproved of the Zurich Settlement and of Makarios' policy of pursuing independence rather than unification with Greece. In November 1967 Grivas, now commander of the Greek-Cypriot National Guard, attacked Turkish-Cypriot villages, thus provoking a new threat of Turkish invasion. This threat was once again averted by American and NATO intervention, leading to the removal both of excessive Greek forces and of General Grivas from the island. Grivas, however, returned to Cyprus secretly in 1971 and eventually founded the EOKA-B organization, which became an agent of destabilization of the Archbishop's Government and undermined the progress of intercommunal talks.[21]

EOKA-B shared the conviction of the Greek military regime (which took power in 1967) that Makarios, with his alleged Communist sympathies, jeopardized both the prospect of eventual *enosis* as well as the position of the Western Alliance in the Eastern Mediterranean. Furthermore, they believed that *enosis* (with attendant concessions to Turkey) had been blessed by the United States as the best way of bringing the island into NATO, and they also saw *enosis* as a way of getting rid of a neutralist Makarios. It was on the basis of these assumptions that the Greek military regime (Junta) launched the coup against the Archbishop in July 1974 which led to Turkey's occupation of the northern part of the island.

The Junta's interest in Cyprus was believed to run parallel to that of the United States. Turkey, already on bad terms with the Greek Junta because of disputed claims over the Aegean continental shelf, was in no mood to compromise over Cyprus. Furthermore, US–Turkish relations had changed since the Johnson era, with Turkey becoming more assertive. Prior to the coup against Makarios, Ankara had informed Washington that it would not restrict opium production, thus asserting Turkey's interests in the face of American pressure.

Although Turkey did not react to the coup against Makarios immediately, this was soon seen as a golden opportunity to exercise the right of intervention which they argued had been conferred on them by the 1960 Treaty of Guarantee.[22] International detente had considerably reduced the possibility of effective Soviet reaction, and the Junta's choice of an old enemy of the Turkish community, Nicos Sampson, to replace Makarios sealed the fate of the island. In the words of an important Turkish diplomat in Washington, 'The Greeks committed the unbelievably stupid move of appointing Sampson, giving us the opportunity to solve our problems once and for all. Unlike 1964 and 1967, the United States leverage on us in 1974 was minimal. We could no longer be scared off by threats of the Soviet bogeyman'.[23]

American Undersecretary of State Joseph Sisco was sent to Ankara to mediate, but there he met an adamant Prime Minister Ecevit, who, ironically, put forward the very demand that Makarios had put to Athens, namely the removal of the Greek officers serving with the Cyprus National Guard.[24] Ecevit also demanded the establishment of a federal state with Turkish and Greek components with permanent access to the sea to permit forces to intervene. When Sisco conveyed these terms to the military regime in Athens he was confronted with incredulity and confusion. The Junta acted as if they had never anticipated the possibility of a Turkish invasion.

When the Turkish forces landed near Kyrenia, the Junta hastily ordered a chaotic general mobilization, which betrayed the regime's total unpreparedness for such an eventuality. According to an account by a Greek official who had access to classified records of the invasion:

> Even as the Turkish ships were steaming towards the shore, the Greeks had no orders from their commanders to shoot. The national guard was sending messages: 'the ships are coming, there are planes overhead, but we have no orders to fire'. It was only when the Turkish paratroopers began landing over Nicosia that a reaction was ordered by the Greek commanders.[25]

In a matter of days the Junta disintegrated. On 23 July it handed power hastily to a civilian government under Karamanlis – who was summoned back from Paris after an absence of eleven years. Although Turkey had agreed to a cease-fire, she continued to land troops and supplies and extended her control in breach of the agreement. At the conference held in Geneva, Turkey refused to accept the Greek plea for the removal of her forces or, later, to withdraw her advancing troops to the cease-fire line established on 30 June. Two plans were handed over to the Greeks. The Turkish-Cypriot leader, Denktash, asked for a bizonal federation with a demarcation line running across the island through Nicosia and Famagusta, with the northern part for the Turks. The Turkish Foreign Minister, Gunes, submitted a plan for six autonomous Turkish cantons. Both plans involved 34 per cent of Cyprus passing under Turkish-Cypriot rule. A request by the Greek and Greek-Cypriot representatives for thirty-six hours to consult with their Governments was refused by Turkey, and the second phase of her invasion – known as Attila II – was put into effect on 14 August. By 16 August 37 per cent of the island had come under Turkish control and 200,000 Greek Cypriots (roughly a third of the island's population) had been displaced from their homes and had flocked into improvised refugee camps in the southern part of Cyprus.

Since the *status quo ante* had been restored during the first days of the invasion, Attila II had no legal basis or other purpose except to consolidate the position of Turkey on the island.

According to Nancy Crawshaw, 'From now on considerations of strategy took priority over the obligations imposed by the Zurich Treaties, which specifically precluded partition and the division of Cyprus into separate states'.[26] Turkish Cypriots from the South and immigrants from Turkey were settled in the North of the island to fill the vacuum that the flight of the Greek-Cypriot refugees had created.

Following the second Turkish offensive, Karamanlis dispelled any doubt that Greece might come to the rescue of Cyprus. The general shock at what was considered to be NATO's apathy over Turkey's determination to impose her own solution on the island was expressed by the Greek withdrawal from the military arm of the Alliance. Although of questionable strategic good sense, the decision was justified as the only alternative to war with Turkey (for which Greece was quite unprepared). Karamanlis also pointed out the decline in credibility of the Alliance during the preceding seven years.

The only moral consolation for the Greek Cypriots was the UN General Assembly's unanimous Resolution 3212 of November 1974, urging a withdrawal of all foreign troops from Cyprus and the return of all refugees to their homes in safety, as well as the endorsement of this Resolution by the Security Council in December. In April 1975 intercommunal talks were resumed in Vienna under the auspices of UN Secretary General Kurt Waldheim, followed by a meeting between Karamanlis and Turkish Prime Minister Demirel which endorsed the talks. During the third round of talks in Vienna, the Greek-Cypriot negotiator, Glafkos Clerides, agreed to allow the passage of 10,000 Turkish Cypriots to the north, but comprehensive proposals promised by Denktash failed to materialize, and all but 2,000 Greeks were expelled from their homes in the North in spite of an agreement to safeguard their position. At the end of the year the Greek and Turkish Foreign Ministers sought resumption of the intercommunal discussions with the aim of formulating a package deal in an agenda covering territorial matters, the features of a federation and the competence of the central Government. In February 1976 both sides agreed to produce proposals within six weeks. On 6 April Greek-Cypriot territorial and constitutional proposals were submitted to the UN Representative. The Turkish-Cypriot plan of 17 April for bizonal federation, however, included no territorial proposals. By September the discussions reached a dead-end as the Turkish Cypriots refused to commit themselves to further proposals. In January and February 1977 Makarios met Denktash and agreed with him on the guidelines of a settlement. In March the sixth round began in Vienna, with the Greek Cypriots handing in a plan for a two-region federation, leaving 20 per cent of the island under Turkish administration. No Turkish-Cypriot territorial proposals appeared.[27]

On 3 August 1977 Makarios died. In view of the *de facto* partition of Cyprus, some of the critics of the Archbishop's non-aligned policy were compelled to admit that it was only through his diplomatic skill that the territorial integrity of the indefensible island had been preserved for so long. His gravest errors had been his refusal to safeguard the needs of the Turkish-Cypriot minority and his failure to realize in time the implications of detente for the fate of the weaker non-aligned nations. However, his evaluations of Turkish strategy and American priorities in the Mediterranean were vindicated.[28]

At the beginning of 1978 Ecevit's return to power and his favourable disposition towards a speedy solution of the Cyprus issue took into account the US Administration's willingness to link the lifting of an arms embargo imposed on Turkey by Congress with progress in Cyprus. On the initiative of the Turkish Prime Minister, Karamanlis and Ecevit met at Montreux in March 1978 'in order to create a climate of confidence'. In April, however, the US State Department announced its decision to back the lifting of the arms embargo, and the Greek Government was faced with criticism at home for allegedly promoting Turkey's peace-loving image. The long-awaited Turkish-Cypriot proposals, delivered to the UN Secretary General on 13 April, were such a disappointment to the Greek Cypriots that all efforts at finding a solution halted. The British *Guardian* newspaper criticized the proposals as 'the most marginal surrender of land [and] an appallingly weak federal government'.[29]

Although there were no signs of a solution to the Cypriot deadlock, the United States lifted the arms embargo on 14 August on the following conditions:

1) That the President would provide Congress with regular reports on the progress of a solution in Cyprus;

2) That no provocations would be made either in the Aegean or in Cyprus;
3) That the balance of military strength as it stood in 1978 be maintained.[30]

On 9 November the UN General Assembly passed a resolution to remove Turkish forces from the island and insisted that the Security Council implement it. On 29 November a 12-point US–Canadian–British 'framework for a Cyprus settlement' was released at the United Nations. The framework was rejected by both sides. In his report to the US Congress of 29 January 1979 President Carter wrote: 'the government of Turkey has taken a constructive attitude towards efforts to bring about a resumption of the intercommunal negotiations'. The Reuter News Agency, however, was not of the same mind on 7 February: 'There is an air of pessimism as sources on both sides admit serious differences remain. At the heart of the problem are conditions which the Turkish-Cypriot leadership has set in return for their agreement to return to the negotiating table'.

Efforts by Dr Waldheim brought about the arrangement of a summit meeting between Kyprianou and Denktash, and an agreement was reached on 19 May towards the resumption of the intercommunal dialogue. The common views of the two sides were incorporated in a joint document. The UN Resolution, which Denktash recognized for the first time, was included with the Makarios–Denktash guidelines as a basis for future negotiations.[31] At the beginning of the Summer of 1979 the talks broke down once more, with the Turkish Cypriots refusing to discuss Varosha (Famagusta) first, as agreed, and insisting on amendments to the 19 May Agreement which introduced new terms to the negotiations. In December 1979 the UN reiterated its previous resolutions and set a deadline for positive development in the intercommunal talks, after which a committee would be sent to the island for mediation. Before the deadline expired furious efforts were made to revive the talks. These bore fruit in September 1980 and averted action by the UN and a new appeal by the Cypriot Government. The talks limped on through 1981 after Denktash proposed that only a limited number of inhabitants of Varosha would return to a section of their town which would remain under Turkish arms. The much-acclaimed Turkish proposals of August 1981, although more comprehensive than those of the past, constituted a poor basis for negotiations. The terms amounted to a 4 per cent territorial concession, an upholding of the Confederate system and restricted freedom of movement. In late February 1982, the new Greek Premier, Andreas Papandreou, paid a state visit to the island and declared his solidarity with the cause of an independent Cyprus and asked for the withdrawal of all foreign troops from the island. He offered to finance a larger UN peace-keeping force on the island.

The entire history of post-1975 intercommunal talks was summed up in a memorandum conveyed by Greek-Cypriot Foreign Minister Rolandis to Dr Waldheim in 1979. According to the document, each time the Greek Cypriots made moves to accommodate a Turkish position, the Turkish side has taken a step back, first from 'federation' to 'federation by evolution' and then to proposals for the creation of two virtually separate states.[32]

Besides the Cyprus issue, three other critical questions have given rise to serious tension between Greece and Turkey: 1) the Aegean continental shelf; 2) control of the air traffic over the sea; and 3) the allocation of operational responsibility of the Aegean and its air-space within the framework of NATO.[33]

The Continental Shelf
Concerning the first issue, Turkey considers her continental shelf to be an extension of the Asia Minor land mass into the sea to the west of certain Greek islands, to which she denies possession of a continental shelf. It follows that the islanders can only exploit the sea-bed of their islands within the territorial sea limit of six miles. Greece, while referring to the Geneva Convention which recognizes the right of islands to a continental shelf, also reserves her right (following general world practice) to extend her territorial sea limit to twelve miles. Such a decision would automatically solve the continental-shelf con-

troversy in Greece's favour but would, according to Turkey, constitute a *casus belli* because it would limit Turkish access to international waters.[34] Retreating from an earlier commitment, Turkey has insisted that the question of the continental shelf should be solved through political negotiations between the two interested parties, while Greece, although submitting to negotiations, believes that the dispute necessitates a settlement by international legal arbitration[35]. The advantages of such a solution are obvious. International arbitration will save the politicians of both countries from loss of face and a decision made by the International Court of Justice will be easier to accept.

Throughout the Summer of 1976 the Turkish ship *Sismik* conducted seismic research in areas of the Aegean shelf appertaining to Greek islands. Because of bellicose opposition at home and the danger of an armed confrontation with Turkey, the Greek Government appealed to the UN Security Council and simultaneously sought arbitration unilaterally by the International Court of Justice. The Security Council did not attempt to deal with the substance of the dispute but tried to lessen the tensions by asking both sides to abstain from hostile acts. On 11 September 1976 and 19 December 1978 the International Court indicated its inability to come to a decision on the substance of the Greek application.

Since the 1978 Karamanlis–Ecevit meeting in Montreux, however, tension on this specific issue has considerably declined. Both sides agreed to discuss the problem and to abstain from activities (such as magnetometric studies for discovering oil in disputed areas) which would cause friction between them. Although bilateral discussions have not led to a solution so far, they have at least excluded the possibility of recourse to violence. Turkey continues to reject the median line between the islands and the mainland and insists on her formula of equity, but she has refrained from pressing the continental shelf argument.

Air Traffic Control
While refusing to accept an extension of Greece's territorial waters, Turkey points out that the existing six-mile limit should set the standard for Greek air space, which since 1932 has extended four miles beyond the limit of Greek territorial sea. By constantly violating the ten-mile limit of Greek airspace with her fighters, Turkey has since 1974 embarked on the dangerous practice of unilaterally redefining Aegean air-space. This systematic testing of nerves may easily lead to tragedy.

A regional convention of the International Civil Aviation Organization (ICAO) in Paris decided in 1952 that the Aegean controlled air-space (except the band of Turkish national air-space off the coast of Asia Minor) should form part of the Athens Flight Information Region (FIR) for air traffic control purposes. All planes flying west (civil or military) were required to file flight plans and to report positions as they crossed the FIR boundary after leaving the coast of Turkey. Planes coming from the opposite direction were required to report to the control centre in Istanbul as they entered the Turkish FIR. As Andrew Wilson has pointed out: 'To have placed the FIR boundary further to the west would have obliged Greek aircraft to pass through a Turkish zone of control on flights to the Greek islands. To this extent the arrangement was consistent with geography and seems to have worked well for 22 years'.[36] On 6 August 1974 the Turkish Authorities issued NOTAM 714 (notice to ICAO for transmission to air users) demanding that all aircraft reaching the median line of the Aegean report their flight plan to Istanbul. Greece refused to accept this contravention of ICAO rules and, on 14 August 1974, issued NOTAM 1157 declaring the Aegean area of the Athens FIR dangerous because of the threat of conflicting control orders. All international flights in the Aegean between the two countries were suspended. On 22 February 1980 Turkey withdrew her claim to air-traffic rights in the eastern half of the Aegean, and the air corridors were subsequently reopened.

The NATO Framework
The third issue concerning operational responsibilities in the Aegean will be treated in the following section in some detail. It will be

sufficient here to note that, as far as Turkey is concerned, the matter of restructuring responsibilities in the Aegean is now under consideration. The reintegration of Greece into the military structure of NATO in October 1980 was achieved after Turkey was persuaded to postpone her revisionist claims on the operational *status quo* in the Aegean. The PASOK Government seems resolved not to discuss any modifications which may impinge on the safety of the Greek islands, but Andreas Papandreou, in his interview with the *Financial Times* (24 February 1982), admitted that, as Turkish pressure had diminished since the advent of military rule in Ankara, Greece might perhaps exchange her right to extend her territorial waters for the withdrawal of Turkish objections to the pre-1974 operational responsibilities of Greece. Such operational arrangements that exist within the NATO framework, however, are without international legal status, and if Greece chose to withdraw from the structure or to ignore Turkish demands there is nothing that Turkey could do to impose her claims short of war.[37] The problem is not therefore of a legal but rather of a political nature. Since Greece has chosen to pursue her security interests through her membership of NATO, she will be faced in the coming years with the difficult task of constantly assessing the advantages against the liabilities of her choice. What appears to be clear at this point is that no Greek Government can accept arrangements that would affect the air-space of the Greek islands.

In his September 1979 Harvard speech, George Rallis (then Greek Foreign Minister) expressed his country's fundamental concern over the Aegean problem in the following terms: 'Claims that could result in the enclavement of the Greek islands of the Eastern Aegean in a Turkish continental shelf and in a Turkish controlled air-space are obviously unacceptable to Greece, all the more so since such claims have no basis either in International Law or in International practice'.[38]

Greek Relations with the US and NATO

Victory against the Communist forces in the Greek civil war was secured through American aid and commitment. The war-ravaged country was not only made safe for the western democratic system but was also given vital transfusions of economic support. A large section of the population considered the Marshall Plan to be manna from heaven and American generosity the epitome of benevolence and altruism. There were, however, three points which invited American penetration of the Greek policy-making process: strategic concern over a Soviet and Balkan threat; the sorely needed economic aid to finance reconstruction; and the political weight that American approval carried in the 1950s. Such approval, whether of a party or a government, carried with it the active promise of support and the passive guarantee of a term in office unobstructed by foreign interference. The mythology of American omnipresence as well as the perpetuation of the Communist scare, which Cold-war politics, eager politicians, administrators and officers encouraged, explain some of the effectiveness of American influence in Greek affairs.[39]

Between 1947 and 1950 American foreign policy in Greece favoured centrist rather than conservative political formations and leaders. This policy was based on the assumption that Greece could face the Communist threat best if social reforms were promoted. In the 1950s, however, the United States became convinced by the Korean War 'that the danger of Soviet expansion was strictly a military one, and that it could be resisted not by political and economic reforms achieved through the democratic left and centre, but by reliance on military elements not merely in strictly military matters but in politics as well'.[40] Ambassador Peurifoy's involvement in Greek politics was so direct that few had doubts in 1951–2 as to which party the Americans favoured. Through his influence, the life of the centre-coalition Government under General Plastiras was shortened, and the simple majority system, endorsed by Peurifoy as a guarantee of stability, facilitated the electoral success of Marshal Papagos (Commander-in-Chief of the Government forces in the civil war), whose conservative party secured some 80 per cent of the seats in Parliament with 49 per cent of the vote. Papagos' success perhaps proved somewhat greater than the Ambassador had anticipated. Staunch in his friendship towards the United States and his anti-Communist sentiments, he was also a nationalist, and he pursued the unification of Cyprus with Greece in spite of the damage it caused in his relations with the other NATO members. Although it is alleged that Papagos' unification policy was not initially opposed by the United States, his stature within the conservative camp made him less manoeuvrable than his weak predecessors. His successor, Constantine Karamanlis, was more concerned with maintaining good relations with NATO and the United States than with pursuing an independent course over the Cyprus issue. American influence, although not American popularity, did not diminish during or after Papagos' term in office. Decisions concerning the economy, the armed forces and the gendarmerie were profoundly affected by American advice and instruction. The reduction or termination of aid and the refusal of loans to correct disequilibria could bring pressure to bear on rare occasions of Greek obstinacy.

The difference between conservatives and liberals on security issues and NATO was one of degree rather than kind. Both sides basically agreed that Greece's main security lay in her northern borders, that Communism threatened mutually cherished values, that NATO was indispensible for the defence of the country and that America was Greece's natural ally and guarantor. The 1953 Greek–American Agreement to provide bases and other facilities for the United States within the framework of NATO was, in general terms, accepted not only by the conservatives but by the more prominent liberals as well. The latter only registered their opposition to the high level of military expenditure and, in 1958, to the installation of American nuclear weapons on Greek soil. They agreed that concessions on that issue could be made in a package deal which would include a favourable settlement of the Cyprus question, or if all other NATO members accepted nuclear bases on their own soil.[41]

The issue which posed the greatest threat to the association of Greece with NATO was that of Cyprus. It has been pointed out that the discussions of the 1956–8 and 1963–4 periods illustrate 'the significantly leftward changes in the positions of the non-Communist political movements in Greece generated by this dispute'.[42] The conservative Government strove unsuccessfully to secure self-determination for the island through the UN. The cool or negative reaction of most NATO members to the Greek cause came as a blow to the conservatives – who were then faced with the predicament of deciding the relative priorities of Greek national aspirations and their dedication to the Western Alliance. The latter prevailed in determining the Government's ultimate disposition towards a speedy settlement in 1959, but NATO lost its initial attraction even to the conservatives, let alone the liberals. The Centre Union exhibited its full support for Cypriot independence after the conclusion of the Zurich–London Agreements. George Papandreou, in line with Makarios, made it his Party's policy to reject NATO involvement in Cypriot affairs and favoured arbitration by the General Assembly of the UN over the crisis that flared in 1963–4. American officials were clearly not pleased.

The exclusive relations between the Americans in Greece and the ruling conservative party throughout the 1950s and early 1960s estranged them from liberal politicians waiting in the wings. The rise of the Centre Union Coalition under George Papandreou coincided with President Kennedy's policy for reform as a deterrent to Communist influence. Although lacking in precision, Papandreou's platform for 'democratization' was charged with the rising expectations of a Greek society experiencing a significant improvement of its standard of living in the early 1960s.[43] Implicit in the notion of 'democratization' was a promise of autonomy in the conduct of Greek foreign policy. Henry Labouisse, Kennedy's Ambassador to Greece, was a choice in keeping with the US Administration's progressive ideas, but he could not dispel the growing strains between American officials in Greece and the Centre Union Government. When the son of George Papandreou, Andreas, attempted as Minister to the Prime Minister, to check CIA and USIA activities in Greece, the Government's relations with the United

17

States deteriorated even further. The Cyprus dispute, however, became the most serious source of mutual irritation. According to Maurice Goldbloom (Labour Information Officer at the US Economic Mission in Greece 1950–51), 'From the American point of view, the crucial thing about the quarrel was not the rights and wrongs of the two communities on the island, but the damage it did to relations between Greece and Turkey, both allies of the United States'.[44]

This quarrel furthermore acquired a special significance for the US position in the Eastern Mediterranean when President Makarios joined the non-aligned movement, a policy which required the maintenance of good relations with potential enemies of the United States. Seizing the opportunity, the Soviet Union declared her support for the integrity of the island and, in 1964, issued warnings that she would not remain passive in case of foreign intervention. Bringing Cyprus under the NATO umbrella by way of *enosis* with elements of partition became, therefore, an option of American policy in 1964. According to the Acheson Plan, the island would be united with Greece; Turkey would acquire a sovereign military base; two Turkish cantons would be formed, exercising local autonomy; and the Greek island of Kastellorizo would be given to Turkey. This plan was rejected by both Greeks and Turks, but the die-hards of *enosis* on the one hand and of partition on the other drew their separate conclusions about American designs on the island – conclusions which precipitated the developments of 1974.

Identification with the right-wing and the throne after 1965 limited the flexibility and scope of American policy in Greece. Throughout the conflict between Papandreou and the King over what the latter felt was a struggle for the control of the armed forces, American officials could not conceal their anxiety over the future of the Monarchy. The coup of 21 April 1967, which averted a likely Papandreou victory at the impending election, was greeted with mixed feelings by the United States, including a certain amount of relief. The Colonels, who had staged the coup over the heads of their superior officers, were extreme right-wingers who had, in the early 1950s, identified with Papagos in his quarrels with the throne. Their credentials included little else besides skills in matters of intelligence and propaganda, and the instant justification of the coup was apparently its mission to prevent a (fictitious) Communist takeover.

The Junta went out of its way to encourage the allegations of American complicity, thus assuming the legitimacy that partnership with the United States provided. Although there was no concrete evidence to support these claims, it was true that the US had not denounced the regime and limited her options even further by dissuading King Constantine from attempting to dismiss the Colonels at the outset. No dilemma over recognition arose since the Ambassador was accredited to the King, and, when the latter fled Greece after a belated attempt to overthrow the Junta in December 1967, normal relations of the US Embassy were continued with the Regent.

The tedium of rationalizations and false hopes employed by American policy-makers to justify their attitude towards the Junta disappointed many of those parliamentarians in Greece who favoured the United States and who had hoped that the US Administration would see through the inherent limitations, let alone the brutalities, of the unpopular regime. An embargo on heavy weapons (although not spare parts) imposed on Greece in April 1967 was suspended in October 1968 following the strain that the Soviet invasion of Czechoslovakia caused in the Balkans. It was re-imposed briefly in the early days of the Nixon Administration. Members of Congress, as well as high-ranking officials, made negative appraisals of the regime's value to the United States; yet the Administration chose to formulate the ambiguous dilemma of 'how to deal with an ally with whose internal order we disagree yet who is a loyal NATO partner.'[45] In fact the dilemma did not exist. Since no possible parliamentary alternative in Greece would have upset the *status quo* in Greek–American relations, America's credibility suffered a steep decline – especially after the National Security Council in 1970, under the direction of Henry Kissinger, advised restoration of full-scale military assistance to the dictatorship. Such official visits to Greece as those by Commander of NATO forces General Goodpaster, Secretary of Defense Melvin Laird, Secretary of State William Rogers, the President's brother Donald Nixon, Secretary of Commerce Maurice Stans and, finally, Vice-President Spiro Agnew, did more for the regime than any lifting of the embargo.[46]

In the case of short-term gains, the United States relationship with the Colonels was rewarding. American bases in Greece and Greek territory and air-space remained available to the US during the June 1967 War and the September 1970 crisis in Jordan. In 1971–3 the Nixon Administration negotiated important home-porting privileges for the US Sixth Fleet in the Piraeus and Elefsis area. Papadopoulos – the initial strongman of the Junta – not only displayed his loyalty to NATO but also held secret talks on the Cyprus question with Turkey and tried to bring the 'renegade' Archbishop into line. Failing that, the Junta then orchestrated a series of abortive attempts against Makarios' life. With respect to Cyprus, the Colonels combined the irredentist line of Papagos with the conviction that the United States was willing to bring the island into the fold of NATO and to remove Makarios' dangerous influence by supporting its unification with Greece.[47] The Junta felt that the obvious price for such a prize was the removal of Makarios – an all too happy prospect for Ioannides (who had overthrown Papadopoulos in November 1973) who shared American fears of the Archbishop's initiative towards Moscow but was mainly enraged over his alienation from the principle of *enosis*. Far from being the 'Castro of the Mediterranean', Makarios was a political conservative and a traditionalist, practising tactics of balance-of-power diplomacy to avoid partition of Cyprus – an eventuality which ultimately he was unable to forestall.[48]

Interpretations of the developments in Athens during the crisis of July 1974 are based on educated guesswork and logical deduction rather than on confirmed evidence. Ioannides' supporters claimed that their leader had assurances through the CIA that Turkey would welcome Makarios' removal and that intervention would be averted if the rights of the Turkish minority were guaranteed. Some attributed the subsequent disaster to Makarios' escape; others add American duplicity to the interpretation.[49]

Once the Turkish troops had landed on the island, Ioannides gave the Greek Armed Forces orders to counter-attack, but he was faced with the reluctance of his superiors in military rank to follow orders. Given the state of the Greek forces after seven years of mismanagement and the purges of able officers, the decision of the Generals to summon the politicians and seek an armistice appeared to be the most sensible course of action. There were allegations, however, that the American intelligence establishment in Athens – who wanted at all costs to avoid a war between Greece and Turkey – was encouraging the Generals to revolt against Ioannides. His collapse was precipitated by an ultimatum from General Davos, Commander of the Third Army Corps in Macedonia. Be that as it may, the problems of Greece received scant American attention throughout the period of the Colonels' rule and a surprising lack of attention on the eve of the events of July 1974. In May 1974 the Greek-Cypriot and Turkish policy desks were transferred from the office of Near East Affairs to the Office of European Affairs – an office which apparently possessed little experience in Eastern Mediterranean problems. Secretary Kissinger's alleged inaction during the crisis – attributed to his concerns with major developments within the United States – was interrupted only in one instance. On 23 July 'strong representations were made with the Colonels in Athens . . . with respect to a possible counter-offensive against Turkey in Thrace.'[50]

Kissinger maintained guarded optimism over the outcome of the discussions in Geneva, even though the terms of the cease-fire agreement were constantly being violated, and he failed to support British efforts at conciliation. It was becoming increasingly obvious that the United States was prepared to let events run their course in Cyprus, and that she would only assume an active role if the two NATO allies were actually at war. After the Turkish invasion the fate of Cyprus had been sealed and, to the United States, partition emerged as the only credible solution.[51] Constant involvement and intervention had characterized US relationships with others for at least twenty-eight years, so that abstention from action could only be viewed as an equally potent instrument of foreign policy. Greece responded by withdrawing from the military branch of NATO and cancelling the home-porting rights of the US Sixth Fleet.

When the United States arms embargo on Turkey came into force in February 1975 after a heated battle between members of Congress and the Ford Administration, Kissinger saw it as Congressional intrusion into his realm of making foreign policy. He attacked the punitive legislation for being a product of a 'Greek lobby' in the United States and implied that the strings were being pulled by the Foreign Ministry in Athens. These claims notwithstanding, the author had ample opportunity throughout the embargo's duration to observe the total disinclination of the Greek Foreign Ministry and Government to involve itself in what was considered to be an internal American affair. The mood of Congress against the Secretary of State had already been shaped, it appeared, by his record in Chile, by the war in Vietnam and Cambodia and by his position *vis-à-vis* the Greek Junta. However, the Congressional backlash can best be explained by post-Watergate hostility towards the President and determination to assert the authority of Congress against the Administration by upholding US Law, i.e., the Foreign Assistance Act of 1961 and the bilateral agreements of 1947 and 1960 between Turkey and the United States.[52]

On 27 March 1976 the United States Administration signed a Defence Co-operation Agreement (DCA) with Turkey providing about one billion dollars worth of military aid over four years in return for the use of 26 installations on Turkish soil. The document rekindled the Greek Government's fears that the military balance with Turkey would be upset in favour of the latter, and the Greek Foreign Minister was quick to initial an Agreement with the United States for military aid to the value of $700 million over four years in return for facilities at four NATO/US bases whose legal status was being renegotiated. The Agreement was never implemented because the DCA with Turkey failed to go into effect; but it did establish the 7:10 ratio by value of military aid which the Greeks hold dear.

Although both the Turkish and the compensatory Greek Agreements were subject to Congressional ratification, Karamanlis was criticized by the opposition, which chose to interpret his action as indirect approval of US military aid to Turkey. On 6 October 1976 the renegotiation of some forty earlier bilateral agreements with respect to the American and NATO military presence in Greece was concluded, but the ratification was witheld pending US negotiations of similar matters in Turkey – and Greece's return to NATO. The new agreement provided that the Suda Bay and Iraklion bases in Crete, the Hellenikon air base and the Nea Makri base near Athens would acquire a Greek commander, and Greek permission would be required for their operation in time of war. As noted earlier, the two bases in Crete are of particular concern to NATO because they facilitate monitoring of Soviet activity in the Eastern Mediterranean as well as storage for the sea mines and nuclear warheads.

President Carter's promises of justice for Cyprus had raised Greek hopes that an equitable solution would be promoted by the new Administration after 1977. American popularity in Greece improved markedly during the first months of the new Administration, but the subsequent efforts of the President to lift the embargo without any substantial evidence of improvement of the situation in Cyprus was seen by the Greeks as yet another display of American *realpolitik* – in which Greek concerns had a low priority.

Ironically it was her anxiety over what she perceived as the threat from a NATO ally, and not the original *raison d'être* of NATO (i.e., the Soviet danger), which compelled the Greek Government in June 1977 to table a proposition for a special military relationship with the Atlantic Alliance. The proposition involved the reintegration of the Greek Armed Forces into the Alliance in case of an East–West conflict, together with the establishment at Larissa of a regional NATO headquarters under Greek command. On matters of operational responsibilities in the Aegean, Greece asked for a return to the *status quo ante* (i.e., before her 1974 withdrawal from the integrated military structure). An understanding along those lines was reached in February 1978 between the Supreme Commander of NATO (then General Haig) and the Commander-in-Chief of the Greek Armed Forces, General Davos, which was accepted by all NATO members except Turkey.

However, a second formula appeared in Greek newspapers in May 1979. This caused embarrassment to the Greek Government which was accused by the opposition of negotiating vital issues of national defence in complete secrecy. The new set of proposals, which General Haig produced after consulting Turkish officials, included articles which revised the *status quo ante* 1974. The points criticized by the Greek press can be summarized as follows: Greece would forfeit operational responsibility over the air-space of her eastern islands; the Larissa Headquarters determining questions of Aegean defence would be placed under NATO command; and areas of the Aegean sea vital for Greek security would be entrusted to the care of an *ad hoc* NATO task force. This set of proposals was promptly rejected by the Greek Chief of the General Staff, and this was followed by Haig's final proposals to SACEUR, including a plan to commit responsibility for the largest part of the Aegean to a NATO commander. The November 1979 proposals by General Rogers (who became SACEUR in June 1979) attempted to reduce the problem of Greek re-entry into a Graeco-Turkish dispute.

Although it was through SACEUR's decision in 1964 that the operational responsibility for the Aegean air-space assigned to Greece would coincide with her FIR, the Haig and Rogers Plans were justified on the basis that changes had taken place since 1974 which posed obstacles to a return to the *status quo ante* concerning Greek and Turkish areas of operational control. It is therefore necessary to examine these changes in order to verify the basis of such a claim.

Until 1974, an American COMLANDSOUTHEAST (Commander Allied Land Forces South Eastern Europe), based at Izmir, had co-ordinated both Greek and Turkish land forces – each possessing operational responsibility within its sovereign territory. An American COMSIXATAF (Commander 6th Allied Tactical Air Force), also based in Izmir and subordinate to COMAIRSOUTH in Naples, co-ordinated Greek and Turkish Air Forces, each maintaining responsibility within the zones coinciding with the outer limits of their sovereign air spaces. Pending Greek re-entry into the military command of NATO, the two Izmir HQs were reconstructed to operate under Turkish command while separate headquarters were to be set up in Greece (in Larissa) under Greek command.

The reconsideration of operational responsibilities did not appear to many Greeks to be the logical outcome of the separation of commands. In other words, the fact that Greeks and Turks could not continue to operate in joint headquarters did not necessarily entail a restructuring of zones of operational responsibilities. Turkey argues that she had in fact sought a revision of the operational *status quo* prior to 1974 and that she had registered with NATO her opposition to the 1957 and 1964 decisions. Her demands therefore (as reflected in the Haig and Rogers proposals) focus on a westward extension of her Air Force's operational responsibility over an Aegean archipelago studded with Greek islands, and they do not appear to be matters to be resolved between Greece and Turkey. General Rogers, however, implied during the discussion of his November 1979 proposals with General Davos that Greece and Turkey should examine bilaterally the issue.

With respect to Naval Forces, until 1974 COMEDEAST (Commander Eastern Mediterranean) was – according to the 1957 NATO decision – the Greek Chief of General Naval Staff. COMEDNOREAST (Commander Northeast Mediterranean, covering Turkish territorial waters and the Black Sea) was a Turkish Admiral based in Ankara. Both Commands were subordinate to COMNAVSOUTH (Commander Allied Naval Forces Southern Europe) and ultimately to CINCSOUTH (Commander-in-Chief Allied Forces Southern Europe) in Naples and were not connected with whatever changes occurred in the Izmir

21

land and air headquarters of NATO. After Greek reintegration, the Command of the Eastern Mediterranean should therefore revert automatically to its pre-1974 status.

The question of the future status of the American military bases in Greece, established under the terms of a bilateral agreement signed by the United States and Greece in 1953, is probably one of the most sensitive to be faced by the Papandreou Government. Having originally promised to dismantle the installations, the new Premier is now considering the practical aspects of such a decision. The bases, and particularly the ones in Crete, have been a subject of heated debate since the Cyprus crisis of 1974, because many Greeks believe that they played a role in Turkey's seizure of northern Cyprus. Furthermore, an investigation published in the daily *To Vima* in the Autumn of 1981, suggested that Herakleion and Hellenikon also have a strategic role by helping to determine the complex flight patterns followed by the fleet of strategic nuclear bombers the US Air Force keeps airborne at all times. The report also indicated that, in the event of war, Herakleion can be used, in co-operation with other bases, to fix a target and direct nuclear missiles against it. These activities, the report suggested, could make the bases likely targets for nuclear retaliation. If the bases are dismantled, however, Papandreou must face the cost of replacing through Greece's own means an infrastructure worth hundreds of millions of dollars, as well as the relative strengthening of Turkey's position in NATO.[53]

There has been no conclusion to date of the discussions concerning the US–Greek Defense Co-operation Agreement (defining the status and operation of US bases on Greek soil) which was initialled in July 1977. The deadlock in the negotiations dates from mid-June 1981 and was due to American refusal to accept some of the more important Greek demands. These include the amount of military aid and weapons systems required by Greece, a US guarantee that the 7:10 ratio between Greece and Turkey in terms of arms supply will be maintained in future, a guarantee that no act of armed aggression between the two will be tolerated, and – more important for the US – the demand that the terms which govern the operation of the bases under joint control should include the prerogative of the Greek Government to limit or suspend their activities under special circumstances.[54]

The victory of PASOK in the elections of October 1981 appeared to alter the basis of negotiations. The new Prime Minister asked the United States to guarantee Greek security against an attack from Turkey, since NATO was prevented by the Turkish veto from considering such a demand. The discussions on the future of the bases, however, are not encouraged by circumstances. PASOK cannot bring itself to admit to its public the vagaries of international politics nor to face the fact that the US has become a tougher negotiator. The Americans, on the other hand, do not appear to be in a hurry to reach a new agreement, since the bases continue to operate under favourable terms.

By May 1982 the Greek Premier initiated an opening towards the West, accentuated by a corresponding deterioration of relationships between PASOK and the Moscow-orientated KKE. Greek ratification of Spanish entry into NATO, Secretary Haig's visit to Athens and Greek willingness to participate in a NATO exercise led by a Turkish Commander constituted the highlights of this impressive change of stance. Concerning the status of the bases, examined in October, Papandreou appears to insist on three demands: the preservation of the balance of power in the Aegean; an 'adequate contribution' to Greece's military needs; and control of operations so that the bases might not be used against friendly countries.[55] Violations of Greek air-space on 26 May by Turkish fighters obliged Greece to withdraw her forces from the NATO *Deterrent Force 82* naval exercise in the Eastern Mediterranean and to file strong protests with Turkey and NATO. Turkey refused to accept the Greek *démarche*, stating that she did not recognize the ten-mile limit of Greek air-space, and she simultaneously declared her intention to extend the limit of Turkish territorial sea beyond six miles.[56] This development may have served as a reminder to the Greek Prime Minister that Turkey was still able to call the tune in the Aegean.

III. DOMESTIC FACTORS

PASOK

The elections of 19 October 1981 gave a Socialist party an absolute majority of seats in Parliament for the first time in Greek history. The Panhellenic Socialist Movement (PASOK) under the leadership of Andreas Papandreou had made great strides, winning 13.5 per cent of the votes in 1974, 25.3 per cent and 48.1 per cent (with 172 deputies in Parliament) in 1981. The party's leader, the charismatic Andreas (as he is widely known) commands unquestioned authority over a compliant party apparatus, and he personally determines most of its activities. PASOK was founded in 1974 as a continuation of his Panhellenic Liberation Movement, which operated during the Junta period, and, unlike most traditional Greek political formations with the exception of the Communist Party, it has become a mass party with a formidable grass-roots organization and regional committees, relying on influential professionals rather than on local bosses and patrons for its regional representation.

A former Berkeley professor of economics, Andreas Papandreou has in the past drawn on his American experience to criticize the United States in terms which often sounded deliberately simplistic. In doing so, however, he has effectively capitalized on the ill-feeling generated in Greece by American foreign policy during the Junta period and the Cyprus crisis.

National independence, popular sovereignty and social liberation constitute the main points of PASOK's ideology – which has been described as populist leftist, combining national pride with faith in the people's infallibility. In spite of its claims to Marxist authenticity – which, incidentally, have not been reiterated after the elections – the party extends its appeal to the disaffected of all social classes and holds a promise for every Greek except the agents of 'foreign imperialism'. In practical terms PASOK draws the bulk of its constituents from those who feel that they have missed out on the development boom of the late 1960s and 1970s. Although the Greek farmer of today has little in common with his isolated and impoverished counterpart of the past, PASOK has successfully exploited the grievances of the peasants and those who have crowded into the cities.

The realization of popular sovereignty and social liberation, depends, according to PASOK, on the achievement of national independence, since the relation between these three fundamental goals is seen as a 'linear succession of stages'.[1] The party's most important source of political capital stems directly from the resentment that the average Greek feels against dependence on Great Powers. According to Papandreou, Greece belongs to the Third-world periphery which is exploited by the capitalists of Western Europe and the United States. Critical of the United States for sharing world domination with the Soviet Union, he is an exponent of non-alignment on the model of Yugoslavia and certain Arab states. In his evaluation of detente, peaceful co-existence and the post-Helsinki 'competitive co-existence' between the super-powers, he claims that the initiative has always been with the US because it is in the nature of capitalism to expand or perish. Thus it is the contraction of profit margins which has led the US to greater exploitation of the Third World, and to search for investments in the USSR and China.[2]

According to Papandreou, the Middle East and the Persian Gulf occupy a top position on America's list of priorities because of her need for Arab oil to supplement her own production. Makarios' neutralism and Arab connections, as well as the proximity of Cyprus to Israel, have been a source of constant US anxiety. The incorporation of the island into NATO, either through unification with Greece (an option of the past) or through domination by Turkey (a post-1974 option), has been a US imperative since the late 1950s. The malleability of the Greek Junta and its oafish foreign policy paved the way for the ultimate 'solution' of the Cyprus problem.

Andreas Papandreou rejects the evolutionary tactics of Social Democracy and considers Western tolerance of Euro-communism as an effort of the industrial north to pacify its own working class. He calls on all 'non-aligned' Mediterranean countries to join forces against great-power influence, and he maintains that Greece should pursue her own self-interest and disassociate herself from foreign patrons. He considers Turkey and Israel to be the two pillars of American policy in the Middle East, and he expects Greece to stand no chance in competition with Turkey either in the bilateral context with the US or in NATO if Turkey persists with her demands in the Aegean. He argues that the Turkish barrage of claims are aimed at subverting Greek sovereignty over the islands close to Asia Minor. With a Turkish continental shelf that will encircle these islands, and foreign control of their air-space, either their populations will be forced to abandon them or else Turkey will raise her old contention that Greece is not capable of defending them effectively. Papandreou has accused the previous New Democracy Government of conducting discussions and negotiations that would have compromised sovereign Greek rights, and he has pointed out that since Turkey makes these claims she should appeal to the International Courts for arbitration.[3]

During his electoral campaign in 1981 Papandreou played down his opposition to the EEC and promised to submit the question of membership to a plebiscite. His shift towards legitimacy was accentuated by PASOK's invitation to European Socialist Party leaders to gather in Corfu during the Summer of 1980, there to discuss problems of socialism. Since most of the leaders present did not oppose either the EEC or NATO, Papandreou appeared by implication to have reconciled his party with Greece's dual membership. The rift between the more radical Executive Bureau of the party and its moderate parliamentary representatives has underlined the party's predicament – caught between radical purism on the one hand and the need to modify its position to gain wider support among liberal and even conservative sectors of the electorate on the other. Throughout the Winter and Spring of 1981 Papandreou had conducted a low-key campaign against the Government, hoping perhaps to reconcile PASOK to a constituency disappointed by the performance of the ruling party but which was still sensitive to the possibility of social upheaval.

Papandreou's interview to the daily *To Vima* on 26 April 1981 sparked off a debate which may well continue. PASOK's leader covered the most important domestic and foreign policy issues in this interview. He distinguished between 'socialization' as advocated by PASOK and 'nationalization', which he thought was already excessive and inefficiently carried out by state employees. 'Socialization' would involve state encouragement to agricultural co-operatives and an extension of bank credit to competitive firms and to those that provided services to society and control of the key industries. Concerning defence and foreign policy issues, Papandreou maintained that Greece had the capital and knowledge to set up an advanced arms industry, that he would seek the removal of all nuclear weapons from the country and discourage participation in 'cold war blocs'.

On the timing of withdrawal from NATO, Papandreou promised to take into account the country's need for military equipment as well as the existing balance of power in the world (especially in the Balkan region). He also insisted that as long as US bases remained in operation they would have to be under effective Greek control. Their future would depend on American willingness to supply the Greek armed forces under terms as favourable as those granted to Turkey.

Finally, he dismissed suggestions that PASOK's ultimate objectives had changed since the party was established in 1974. 'A party which is close to assuming or has assumed power', he said, 'has several intermediate objectives which are not determined only by its ultimate goals, but also by the strength of the prevailing winds'.[4]

On 20 October 1981 he gave an interview to the American ABC network in which, as the new Prime Minister, he gained the esteem of large sections of the Greek public. Both political friends and enemies welcomed his candid appreciation of Greece's position with respect to the West and Turkey. By identifying Greece's primary security consideration as Turkey, he respected public opinion on that issue, but he also thereby created a significant diversion of attention from the economic problems faced by his Government. His subsequent performance in the November

1981 EEC meeting in London, and in the early December NATO meeting of Defence Ministers in Brussels (Papandreou had retained the defence portfolio), irritated some of his Western colleagues, but on the whole it drew praise at home. Less popular, however, was the Government's reluctance to take a firm position against the military coup in Poland and against the role of the Soviet Union in its perpetration. A timid official amendment came somewhat too late to be convincing.

Papandreou's most substantial departure from his predecessors' line was his opening towards Iraq and the Palestine Liberation Organization (PLO). His refusal to endorse the despatch of an EEC peace force to the Sinai in November, the welcome afforded to Yasser Arafat on his December visit to Athens, and Greece's February 1982 vote in the UN against Israel's annexation of the Golan Heights, signify an altogether new Greek stance with respect to the Middle East. Most recently, Libya's President Gaddafi was invited to Athens, and Arafat visited Greece immediately after his expulsion from Beirut.

The New Democracy Party

The 'New Democracy' Party can trace its origins with little effort. General Papagos' right-wing Greek Rally and its subsequent offshoot, the National Radical Union under Constantine Karamanlis, practically shaped political life in post-war Greece. After the fall of the military dictatorship, Karamanlis, heading New Democracy, won both the 1974 and 1977 elections with 54.3 per cent and 41.8 per cent of the vote, respectively. In May 1980 he was elected President of the Republic by parliament and was replaced as head of the Party and as Premier by George Rallis. The latter was the more moderate of the two candidates for succession, the more conservative candidate being the Defence Minister, Evangelos Averof. This orderly change of leadership, effected through the party mechanism without rupturing its ranks, is quite unusual in Greek party politics and can be seen as a further step towards Westernization, pursued by the Administration since 1974.

Karamanlis' own political transformation following his defeat and departure from politics in 1963, have determined New Democracy's general orientation. A staunch anti-Communist and a strong supporter of NATO in the 1950s and early 1960s (although he had considerable personal admiration for De Gaulle), he has, since his triumphant return in 1974, reflected accurately the change of mood in his public. In terms of policy, this has implied the following: a shift of emphasis from loyalty to the United States and NATO to closer ties with Western Europe and the EEC; improvement of relations with the Communist Balkans and the Soviet Union; and greater tolerance of parliamentary and press opposition, highlighted by the 1974 legalization of the Greek Communist Party. More than two decades of consistent anti-Communism without a serious corresponding challenge to Greek internal or external security, has desensitized the public to invocation of the 'red peril'. A feature of this new state of affairs is the eclipse of anti-Communism, not as a political position but as a repressive, all-encompassing state ideology.

Between 1974 and 1980 foreign policy formulation was the exclusive prerogative of Karamanlis, aided by hand-picked professional diplomats. He took pride in the consistency of his policy, and his yearly evaluations of security issues in Parliament differed only marginally. Entry into the European Community, realized in January 1981 after tortuous negotiations, was the hallmark of his dogged pursuit of an 'organic Greek presence in the West'. A guarantee of parliamentary democracy and a peaceful deterrent to counter Turkish intransigence were, in his estimation, the most important by-products of membership of the EEC. His Balkan multilateralism and his 1979 trip to Moscow were to a great extent motivated by concern over Turkey. His own solution to some of the problems between Greece and Turkey includes mutual submission to international legal arbitration, while on the issue of operational responsibility in the Aegean – a matter to be settled between NATO members – he has held steadfastly to the position of upholding the *status quo ante* 1974.[5] Although he claimed that Greece had no choice in 1974 but to assume full control of her armed forces, he recognized the value of

NATO and pursued Greek re-entry so as to avoid the isolation of Greece when Greek sovereign rights were threatened. Karamanlis also acknowledged the importance of sustaining friendship with the US, and he insisted that facilities for the United States in Greece should be governed by considerations of mutual advantage.

The change of leadership in New Democracy and in the Government in 1980 did not alter the principles of foreign policy set by Karamanlis, but the mechanism of implementation changed significantly. Joint sessions between the Prime Minister, the Minister of Defence and the Foreign Minister became instrumental in decision-making. The new Foreign Minister, C. Mitsotakis, initiated an opening towards Turkey which bore – in public estimation at least – his personal stamp. After April 1981 this opening foundered on what were widely regarded in Greece as hostile Turkish acts.

In spite of New Democracy's efforts to modernize its stance from paternalistic conservatism to moderate liberalism, the last elections proved that PASOK was the more successful of the two in seeking out the uncommitted centre vote. The association of New Democracy's political predecessors with the side that won the Civil War not only secured them the conservative and nationalist vote but also the support of those who were afraid to antagonize the state. Ruling party and state went hand in hand, and it was New Democracy's own repudiation of repressive measures against urban and rural opposition groups that in fact encouraged more voters to try their luck with PASOK. Furthermore, the latter's nationalist platform outflanked New Democracy's position as the sole guardian of nationalist orthodoxy.

The electoral defeat of October 1981 – although in no sense abject since the party won 35.9 per cent of the vote – generated a minor panic in its ranks which led to another change of leadership. The choice of Averof as Party leader may add zest to the performance of the major opposition party but it may also impede its efforts to win back the more liberal of its voters who deserted to PASOK. The overall performance of New Democracy in opposition has so far been unimpressive.

The Centre Union Party
The Centre Union Party was reconstituted in 1974 by former deputies who had supported George Papandreou during his 1965 conflict with the Palace, and a coalition of social democrats and resistance fighters against the Junta. The Centre Union–New Forces combination entered the election of 1974 with the reputation of possessing candidates of the highest calibre, but the overwhelming presence of Karamanlis in the New Democracy Party limited the Centre Union–New Forces to 20.42 per cent of the vote.[6] The elections of 1977 dealt a heavy blow to the party, which then secured only 11.6 per cent of the vote. Badly split even before the elections, members of the New Forces formed an independent grouping and others left EDIK (the name of the party since 1976) after the original leader, George Mavros, was replaced by John Zigdis. The New Democracy Party – with its opening towards the centre – attracted some wayward EDIK deputies – while others joined John Pesmazoglu's Social Democratic party (KODISO) which aspired to create a modern alternative to the expiring Centre Union. The elections of October 1981 eradicated centre parties from Parliament altogether, although Pesmazoglu won a seat in the European Parliament. The greatest percentage of former Centre Union votes went to PASOK, thus moderating its constituency.

The Communist Party
The Greek Communist Party (KKE) was legalized in 1974, and it entered the elections of that year with a unified list of candidates, though its ranks had split into a segment loyal to Moscow (known as the 'Exterior' by its opponents) and one of Eurocommunist orientation, called the Greek Communist Party of the Interior. In the 1977 elections the 'Exterior', which inherited the bulk of the party membership, voters and newspaper circulation, outnumbered the 'Interior' five-to-one. It won 9.3 per cent of the vote while the 'Interior' – part of a coalition with four socialist and progressive groupings – shared only a 2.7 per cent with its partners. The foreign policy of the 'Exterior' is almost totally in line with that of the Soviet Union and is therefore opposed to the EEC and, of

course, to NATO. The 'Interior' abandoned the concept of the 'dictatorship of the proletariat', adopted democratic pluralism and favoured Greek entry into the EEC. An influential spokesman for the 'Interior', Leonidas Kyrkos, evaluated the Cyprus issue from the angle of American interests in the Middle East and considered that a war between Greece and Turkey would increase the dependence of both on the United States, as had been the case with Israel and Egypt after 1973. In the elections of October 1981 the 'Interior' failed to elect a deputy to Parliament, but Kyrkos won a place in the European Parliament. The 'Exterior' added 2 per cent to its previous performance and became the third party in a Parliament now of three parties. Given the adverse economic prospects and PASOK's inability to make all its promises true, the KKE may play a more active role in the coming years.

The Role of the Armed Forces
Greek security is naturally in part defined by the state of the armed forces, in terms not only of physical readiness but – perhaps more important – of the willingness of officers to restrain themselves from playing politics and to confine their activities to the protection of the homeland. The seven years of military dictatorship caused serious damage to the capabilities of the Greek forces. The mobilization of the Summer of 1974 revealed the degree of deterioration of discipline and morale as well as of equipment. Five years after the fall of the Junta, the Greek Army now appears to be free of the problems associated with its recent history. In terms of leadership, unity and equipment, it has probably never been in a better position to defend the homeland. Yet the obvious question in everyone's mind is whether civilian supremacy over the military has been firmly established, or whether a future political crisis will set the tanks rolling once again. A look at the background of post-war developments in the Greek officer corps may help to answer the question.

The Post-War Period
The officers of the post-war period possessed none of the ideological pluralism that their colleagues had shown in the inter-war years. The abortive coups of 1935, 1943 and 1944 had resulted in a clean sweep of anti-monarchical and left-wing officers, and the victory of the nationalist forces during the civil war determined the orientation of the post-war Army. The military after 1945 professed anti-Communism and exclusive allegiance to the King and, unlike officers of the past, they showed considerable social and educational homogeneity. Moreover, they were under the continuous influence of American military missions after 1946, due to their contribution during the Civil War. Although constitutionally under civilian control, the military soon found ample opportunity to develop independence from Government as a result of the autonomy permitted them. Military intrigue was often mistaken for patriotic zeal, and officers who strayed were merely admonished by the Government with fatherly understanding.

The official status of the Armed Forces was defined by a series of 'compulsory enactments' issued by the Sophoulis Government in December 1945. The Supreme Council of National Defence (ASEA), which included the three War Ministers, the Chiefs of the three branches of the Armed Forces and the Chiefs of the British Missions (without a vote), was chaired by the Prime Minister. ASEA dealt with the general orientation of defence, the appointment of the military high command and the allocation of military expenditures – thus confirming the supremacy of the civilians over the military.[7]

However, 'the institutional affirmation' of the tendency towards the autonomy of the military occurred in January 1949, with the appointment of General Papagos as Commander-in-Chief of the Armed Forces. ASEA was replaced by a War Council with purely decorative functions, while the Commander-in-Chief acquired complete authority over all military matters.[8]

His suggestions, which could even include the imposition of martial law, were binding for the Minister of Defence. Papagos' extraordinary powers, which were given to him due to the emergency conditions caused by the Civil War, concentrated authority over military decisions and facilitated the establishment of American influence, unhindered by political opposition.

Although the post of Commander-in-Chief was abolished after Papagos' resignation in 1951, a precedent of institutionalized military autonomy had been set up and a group of officers had found a new patron in the person of the honoured Commander-in-Chief.

The Civil War ended in September 1949 but it became a point of reference which continued to live on, and it had brought into being a segment of the military with an excuse to covet its aspects of autonomy throughout the 1950s and 1960s. This was not an army of state-builders or modernizers but rather the trump card of the state against the 'internal enemy'.[9]

The most active post-war clandestine association of officers was founded in the Middle East in 1943 and assumed the initials IDEA (most probably in 1945) which stood for 'Holy Bond of Greek Officers'.[10] The foremost objective of the organization was to purge the armed forces of elements that failed to conform to its own high standards of nationalist purity, so that the military would serve 'the nation rather than political parties'.[11] Despite the sonorous language of its charter, the organization gradually became a pole of attraction not for the military establishment, which enjoyed royal favour, but for a less distinguished group of somewhat disgruntled officers. Papagos, a national symbol by 1950 and a threat to the royal monopoly of influence in the Armed Forces, became, perhaps unknowingly, the natural leader for this breed of right-wingers who felt that their advancement was blocked by a political and military establishment with intolerably liberal and leftist sympathies.[12]

The abortive coup of 31 May 1951 was launched by the IDEA conspirators in order to forestall Papagos' resignation from the army, which had been brought about by his clash with the monarchy. The failure of this coup and the punishment of its protagonists were more apparent than real. As matters turned out, its objectives were better served by its failure. Papagos, whose timely intervention stopped the half-baked conspiracy in its tracks, emerged as the only figure who could exert influence on all levels of the military structure. Once he became a popularly elected Prime Minister, he not only reinstated most of the dismissed members of IDEA but he also tolerated the foundation of a parallel military establishment, rival to the Throne, which would in the future threaten the very regime it was supposed to be guarding. Papagos merely averted a schism which reappeared sixteen years later. By postponing it, he in fact made it more dangerous.

Intervention in Politics

The reasons that brought about the 1967 military intervention were varied. Detente reduced the importance of the army as guarantor of internal order. The furious efforts of the military regime in 1967 to rekindle the 'red peril' were not only an exercise in self-deception and rationalization but also the last attempt of the Junta to preserve unity among military networks that had ceased to be of the same mind.

The second important reason for intervention was the conflict between the Throne and Parliament which flared during the Papandreou years. The main cause of the dispute was the control of the armed forces, but it resulted in the emancipation of certain military networks from both political and as royal tutelage. It was these networks, with a marked contempt for politicians as well as for the Court, that sought to save Greece from 'chaos'.

The least discussed cause of the 1967 coup, but a vital one nonetheless, was the professional grievances of a certain segment of the officer corps. The sudden expansion of the army during the Civil War and reduced opportunities for promotion afterwards caused congestion in the middle ranks. The traditional pyramid of promotions (whereby one third of the officer corps advances in rank, one third remains stationary and the last third is retired) was further undermined by political and royal favouritism, so that most officers were retired in the rank of Brigadier. This practice undermined the advancement of able officers and preserved the least qualified (who would otherwise have been retired). It was officers of the latter type who became willing clients of the 1967 regime.

The anomaly of 1967 created vacancies in the army which were filled not on merit but rather according to loyalty to the regime. Although favouritism had never been absent from promotion, the insecure dictatorship surpassed all precedent in its exercise of nepotism. Some 3,000 officers were retired or dismissed between 1967 and 1972, and they were replaced by friends of the Junta.[13] Since military men involved in politics rarely have time to improve their professional skills, the promotions of 1967–72 seriously undermined the competence of the army. Furthermore, congestion of the middle ranks reached an absurd level. In 1974 officers between the ranks of Lieutenant and Captain formed 43 per cent of the entire officer corps, while those in the ranks of Major and Colonel amounted to no less than 54 per cent.[14]

The institutional structure of the armed forces was also significantly transformed by the Junta. Before the conspirators firmly established themselves in power, the Armed Forces were governed by Law 2387 of 1953, according to which each Chief of Staff (Army, Navy and Air Force) was separately responsible for his own service to the Minister of Defence who was vested with the highest authority over military matters. The General Staff of National Defence co-ordinated the activities of the three services without in fact having any authority over them.[15]

Papadopoulos created the position of the Chief of the Armed Forces, thus depriving the Minister of Defence of his authority and the Chiefs of Staff of any autonomy within their separate branches. By concentrating power, the dictator was in a better position to control it. This concentration of military authority, which, among the other NATO members, exists only in Turkey, ultimately contributed to the decline in morale and initiative of the separate Service Staffs.[16] Their performance during the Cyprus crisis of 1974 leaves little doubt about the failure of the system. The institution of the General Staff, however, was highly praised by American military experts, despite the fact that such an institution is prohibited in the United States by the National Security Act of 1947.[17]

After the Junta
The Act of August 1977 determining the present structure of command in the Armed Forces did away with the innovations of the Junta. According to Act 660, the Government alone is responsible for national defence. The Supreme Council of National Defence (ASEA) is made up of the Prime Minister, the Deputy Prime Minister, the Ministers of Defence, Co-ordination, Foreign Affairs, Public Order and the Chief of the General Staff. Besides drafting defence policy, it appoints the Chief of the General Staff and the Chiefs of Staff and it makes most other important military appointments.[18] The decisions of ASEA are based on the recommendations of the Defence Minister who is in turn advised by the Chief of the General Staff. Since the Minister has no direct experience of the problems in the Armed Forces, his decisions are obviously influenced by his military advisers, that is by the Chiefs of Staff.[19] This state of affairs is seen by some as creating separate areas of autonomy for the military which may prove dangerous for future parliamentary regimes.[20] Others, who fought for the dissolution of the Junta's military institutions, have argued that areas of autonomy for the branches of the Armed Forces will guarantee the development of a more professional mentality among officers and will act as a deterrent against joint conspiracies.[21]

Be that as it may, institutional measures are rarely of value if they are not accompanied by the officers' personal concern for the advancement of their professional competence and backed by a civilian culture which frowns upon the politicization of the army. Preventing partisan views from entering the Armed Forces, however, is one thing; isolating the forces from any public scrutiny is quite another. According to Article 68, Paragraph 2, of the 1975 Constitution, Parliament can form Committees of Enquiry after a two-fifths vote in the Assembly on all matters except those of a military nature – which require an absolute majority.[22] Withholding information and creating a *cordon sanitaire* around the Armed Forces can be as counterproductive as the tendency to absolve the officers from all responsibility during the seven years of military dictatorship. During the electoral campaign of 1977 only N. Konstantopoulos of the 'Alliance' (a coalition of left-wing groupings) spoke his mind about the Greek Military. Other parties, including PASOK, bypassed the issue or simply attributed the entire responsibility for the military dictatorship to politicians who had allegedly undermined discipline in the Army before the Junta seized power.

There is at present a consensus in Parliament on military issues. With the exception of occasional references to an incomplete purge of Junta elements, the officer corps is rarely criticized. The seizure of power by the Junta is attributed in somewhat simplistic terms to a 'conspiracy of a few fools' (*afrones*), and the former Minister of Defence often reassured Parliament that civilian supremacy had been firmly established. Questions regarding the military budget are usually settled by general agreement, and the opposition does not now press for military cuts.

Although little information is available concerning the present state of mind in the Armed Forces, there is no indication that the Greek officers corps is not happily occupied with the exclusive task of protecting the homeland from external threats.

There is no way of predicting future developments, but there are ways of preventing the future from evolving in the wrong direction. An effective democratic education at the Military Academy, coupled with skills allowing middle-ranking officers to face retirement without alarm, could certainly work to minimize conspiratorial thoughts. Other prescriptions for a lasting 'cure' of the Greek military could include autonomy within their own sphere of professional expertise, freedom from political pressures and the abolition of activities outside their main line of interest.

Internal and external security considerations are intertwined. The events of the Summer of 1974 give ample proof of the outcome when the internal and the external fronts are challenged simultaneously.

Economic Aspects of Greek Security
It has been said that Greece fits the description neither of an under-developed nor of a peripheral economy. Between 1962 and 1978 an average growth rate of 6.6 per cent per year was achieved despite economic turbulence. Productivity grew by 7.3 per cent per year and *per capita* income reached $US 3,000. During the same period industrial production rose by 9 per cent per year, industrial employment by 3.3 per cent (agricultural labour constitutes only about 20 per cent of the total labour force) and agricultural production by 4.2 per cent. Unemployment declined to the lowest level in Europe and the return of guest workers from Germany did not alter the picture.

Industrial production forms 60 per cent of Greece's total exports in value, one third of which goes to the Middle East and North Africa.[23] Diversification of trade precludes dependence on a single market, while production has generally overtaken demand. Dependence on external energy sources has somewhat diminished. In 1978 foreign capital inflows constituted only 20 per cent of the $US 3 billion invested in the Greek economy. Some Greek economists suggest that in strictly financial terms Greece therefore is now very much less dependent on foreign capital. Such dependence as remains, they claim, is due to political constraints of the past rather than to the nature of the Greek economy. Finally, the size of the Greek-owned merchant fleet is yet another factor which may contribute to greater economic independence.[24]

Other evaluations, however, point to contrary conclusions. Economic growth is seen as import-based, constantly inflating the foreign trade deficit. This deficit is covered by immigrant and merchant marine remittances, tourism and foreign loans.[25] Should one or more of these sources of foreign exchange decline and inflation continue to grow, the positive picture of the economy may well be reversed. The emigration of labourers in the 1960s is seen as a mixed blessing. A potentially cheap input in production (labour) was unwisely replaced by the importation of expensive foreign capital. Industrial growth was therefore to a large extent based on foreign capital and knowledge, especially in those sectors concerned with higher levels of technology. Domestic investment has been concentrated more in light industries and in the less productive sectors such as construction.[26]

Moreover, there has been a negative trend in Greek economic affairs since 1979. The data for 1980 presented by the Governor of the Bank of Greece pointed out that inflation (running at 26 per cent) and stagnant production were the chief economic problems facing the Government (and this is still the case). Gross domestic product at constant prices in 1980 rose by only 1.9 per cent compared with 3.7 per cent in 1979. Gross investment also dropped in that year due to reduced activity in the construction sector and to reductions in public expenditure. Despite the slowing down of economic activity, the rate of urban unemployment remains low, and the official estimate of the rate of unemployment in 1980 was 2.5 per cent compared with 2.2 per cent in 1979. Present domestic and international economic conditions would appear to rule out the possibility of overcoming the recession by the adoption of expansionist policies. Predictably the New Democracy Government pursued a restrictive set of economic policies, but efforts to restrain the growth of money supply met with only partial success. By the end of 1980 the balance of payments deficit was $US 2,217 million, compared with $US 1,882 million the previous year. The oil import bill alone increased by $US 947 million over the same period. High interest rates continued into 1981 as well as efforts to restrain the growth of money supply, but it did not appear that monetary measures alone could cope with the economic situation.

Shortly before the elections, Papandreou told an American journalist: 'They [the New Democracy technocrats] believe Greece is a capitalist country, but it is really on the periphery of capitalism, and has many pre-capitalist characteristics, our huge underground economy being one example. This means that huge doses of Government intervention and planning will be needed to bring Greece up to par with the developed capitalist nations'.[27]

The state has played a paramount, if not always efficient, role in Greek economic development. Besides contributing its own resources, it has provided the infrastructure and the legislative pre-conditions to encourage the private sector. It was also responsible for negotiating the major foreign investment deals which were often heavily criticized. PASOK's moderate doses of state intervention, however, are producing little result in curbing inflation, improving the balance of payments or increasing national productivity. At the end of 1982 Papandreou is still faced with most of the economic problems he inherited from the previous Administration. In spite of an extensive change of guard in public positions and a reshuffling of the civil service, PASOK has yet to produce a visible alternative to the familiar recipes of anti-inflationary and austerity measures. With public consumption further restricted by the impact of such measures, and a fall in private investment for the third consecutive year, Papandreou realized that much of what he had hoped to achieve would have to be deferred. The July 1982 Cabinet reshuffle indicated that the foreign-based technocrats of the party carried the day. Gerassimos Arsenis, a former director of UNCTAD who was PASOK's Governor of the Bank of Greece, became the Minister of National Economy (a newly created post), and it may be predicted that he will attempt to reduce the budget deficit inherited by the previous Administration and to ensure implementation of austere budgetary and monetary policies. Although 'socialization' of key industries amounted to establishing supervisory committees with representatives of employees, management and local government, the ultimate role of the state in the economy is still to be resolved.[28]

Membership of the EEC was seen by Karamanlis as a kind of insurance against such internal anomalies as the coup of 1967 and perhaps Turkish demands on Greek sovereignty. Whether this appraisal is correct remains to be seen, but the economic implications of being a member of the Community have become the object of much discussion in Greece. Somewhere between the enthusiastic supporters and the emotional opposition are those who see it as the least evil of the possible alternatives. Membership may provide security for certain spheres of economic activity (agriculture in particular) but at the price of possible damage to others (such as industry). To some, Europe appears to offer a genuine alternative to submission to exclusive US influence, and these would even predict a future economic conflict between the US and the EEC.[29] To others, Europe is as dependent on the US for defence as Greece, and so the EEC does not offer genuine emancipation from the influence of the US.

At present the European Economic Community possesses no instrument of crisis management, and, with the exception of Ireland, its members rely on NATO for their own security. The leading economic power in the EEC, West Germany, has attached great importance to the efficient functioning of the Alliance and has often given the matter priority over other considerations. While aiming at a renegotiation of the original agreement of accession, Papandreou has retreated from his original promise to submit the future of Greece's membership of the Community to a plebiscite.

IV. THE NATURE OF GREEK SECURITY IN THE 1980s

The Link with the West and Turkey

On 18 October 1980, George Rallis' Government announced its decision to bring the country back into NATO's military arm. The Alliance had previously overcome Turkey's insistence that Greek reintegration should be preceded by a reconsideration of operational responsibilities in the Aegean. The decision was received with relief by NATO members, but it generated mixed feelings in Greece. Criticism of the Atlantic Alliance, which was once confined to the left of the Greek political spectrum, became widespread during the Junta period, and especially after the Turkish invasion of Cyprus in the Summer of 1974. Voices of caution pointing to the practical advantages of membership were drowned by the moral tone of the opposition. The chief objection to re-entry was one of principle, namely that the reason for withdrawal – the military occupation of 40 per cent of Cyprus by Turkey – had not been resolved.

On a more practical level, Turkey's decision of 22 February 1980 to withdraw her six-year-old claim to air-traffic-control rights in the eastern half of the Aegean marked an improvement of relations which continued until April 1981. At the beginning of March 1981, the Greek Foreign Minister, K. Mitsotakis, announced a series of modifications to the air-traffic arrangements within the Athens FIR designed to facilitate the movement of Turkish aircraft in the Aegean airspace. These included a reduction by approximately one half of the extent of the Terminal Control Area of the airport on the island of Lemnos and various adjustments to the upper and lower altitude limits of several Aegean air corridors.[1] These unilateral measures made in good faith were criticized by the opposition in the Greek Parliament but were welcomed by the Turkish Foreign Ministry as 'gestures of good will'.[2] However, while Graeco–Turkish discussions over questions of the Aegean air-space were taking place, Greek sovereign air-space was repeatedly violated by Turkish aircraft during April 1981.[3]

Violations of Greek air-space and territorial waters also occurred in May, and these were interpreted as Turkey's way of registering her opposition to the ten-mile limit of Greek air-space and served to remind her allies that the question of operational responsibilities was still unresolved. The latter issue has acquired a certain urgency in view of the impending assumption of operational responsibilities by the Larissa NATO headquarters. NATO authorities urge Greece to consider the question of responsibilities *after* the Headquarters become operational, but Turkey will not even agree to an interim arrangement whereby the pre-1974 *status quo* would remain in force, let alone to recognize a permanent state of affairs along those lines.[4] Since Greece considers this an issue of cardinal importance to her security, there is no apparent way out of the impasse.

Although Greece has often complained that the United States and West Germany have been partial towards Turkey, it is ultimately Greece's own traditional compliance in the face of Western pressure that accounts particularly for her disadvantageous bargaining position within the Alliance. The reasons for this compliance are to be found in the foundations of the modern Greek state as well as in its subsequent development and dependence upon foreign powers. During World War II Greece joined the Allied cause (without even being granted a treaty of alliance) and suffered occupation and civil war. The fact that a great power became instrumental in resolving her internal problems determined Greece's post-war diplomacy as well as her defence policy.

The entire post-war orientation of Greek defence was based on the American belief that Greece's main security concern was of an internal rather than an external nature. According to a National Security Report of 1949, Greece was to have 'a military establishment capable of maintaining internal security in order to avoid Communist domination, while Turkey was designated with a military establishment of sufficient size and effectiveness to insure her continued resistance to Soviet pressures.' The Greek army was therefore primarily supplied and organized to face the internal Communist threat. A modification of the original report, appearing two years later, included an external operational assignment for the Greek forces, but it made clear that Greece would not be supplied with the necessary materiel to repel a foreign attack and, furthermore, that the United States could make no commitment to come to the aid of her ally if the latter were faced with an external attack. Greece was nevertheless expected 'through certain limited accessories to cause some delay to Soviet and satellite forces in case of global war.'[5]

Given the allocation of defence roles between Greece and Turkey, it is not difficult to assess the implications of their joint entrance into NATO for the former's security. Whereas Greece was primarily geared to face an internal threat and ill-equipped to resist a Soviet attack, she was nevertheless expected to aid Turkey, which was presumably the primary target in the Balkans, and so ran the risk of attracting enemy reprisals.

Of course Greece is no longer divided by civil strife, her economy has made important strides since the 1950s, and her defensive position was transformed after 1974. She continues, however, to lag behind Turkey in US estimation of her comparative strategic importance (for reasons which are obvious).

On the other hand, since Atatürk, Turkish diplomacy has pursued a successful course of non-involvement in international conflicts. Although Turkey signed a Treaty of Affiliation with Britain and France in October 1939, she kept out of World War II and, with the exception of the Cold-war period, retained her relative independence in international politics. With the emergence of detente and the relaxation of tensions between the super-powers, some of the urgency which governed relations between Turkey and the United States disappeared. Refusing to forfeit the tangible benefits deriving from her value to the Western Alliance, Turkey resumed her traditional independent posture, constantly reminding her allies that she could either seek solutions to her problems elsewhere or, more simply, that she could still prove a significant liability if she refused to play her part as host to American bases. The loss of Iran and her own internal misfortunes have enhanced Turkey's importance for the United States.

Since 'loss' of Greece has never entered into American calculations, it is ultimately the thought of Turkey neutral or on the enemy side which haunts the American military establishment. It is not without some justification that Greece fears that she will be asked to pay the price of an effort to reinforce Turkey's faith in the Western Alliance. It is therefore to Greece's advantage to seek maximum autonomy within the NATO framework.

In spite of differences on the security level, there is considerable Greek admiration for Turkey's ability to maintain an autonomous stance in her relationships with the West and the Great Powers. Flexible diplomacy and Turkish patriotism have won the country sixty years of uninterrupted peace and, except for the Cold-war period, a prudent relationship with both the super-powers. Turkey's Western commitment in the 1950s should not be attributed to American penetration but rather to the goals set and the decisions taken by Turkish policy-makers based on wide domestic support. Furthermore, no national division on the scale of the Greek Civil War has so far encouraged foreign powers to intervene directly in Turkey's internal affairs.

Some Greek politicians also tend to compare Greece's rather ineffectual withdrawal from NATO in 1974 with Turkey's reaction to the American embargo. Instead of leaving NATO in high dudgeon, the Turks at the end of July 1975 suspended the operation of all but one of their American bases and then successfully renegotiated their defence agreements and ensured the lifting of the arms embargo.

European Community membership may well benefit Greece on certain fronts, but it will probably disappoint those Greeks who believe that it will also constitute a guarantee against future Turkish aggression. As noted earlier, the EEC possesses no instrument of crisis management and, excepting Ireland, its members belong also to NATO. West Germany, moreover, considers Turkey vital for the defence of NATO's south-eastern flank. In 1978 Germany exerted considerable pressure on the United States to lift the arms embargo imposed on Turkey after the 1974 invasion of Cyprus, although she has also been in the vanguard of those urging a return to democratic rule in Turkey. Furthermore, Western Europeans have already taken measures to avoid the Graeco–Turkish dispute spilling over into the EEC and to mitigate the political effects of Greece's accession on their own relations with Turkey.[6]

Membership of the EEC and NATO will also entail fashioning Greece's relations with the United States with reference to that larger context.[7] Greece may support European efforts at preserving detente and arms control by offering her services in the Balkan region, where she now enjoys good relations with her Communist neighbours.

European attitudes towards the US, however, have changed in two important respects during the past seven years: confidence in American leadership has been shaken; and America's economic problems have had political implications in her relations with her allies. Europeans now believe that they are entitled to 'more attention, consideration and consultation than in the arrogant days of unlimited and undisputed American world power'.[8] Greece also shares those European attitudes *vis-à-vis* the Eastern Bloc which have caused American discomfort.[9] Most European countries have neutralist and Communist sections of public opinion to placate, and they have tried to take advantage of detente and to avoid involvement in wider super-power disputes.

It is in this wider context that the electoral outcome of 18 October 1981 in Greece must also be assessed. Besides the residual tensions in US–Greek relations arising from American support for the Junta and for the Turks over the subsequent Graeco–Turkish problems, European and American security perceptions no longer appear to be wholly compatible. Economic recession, which drives both Western and Eastern Europeans into closer co-operation, and the controversy over the need to deploy new nuclear weapons to counter Soviet superiority, have not left Greek politics unaffected. The non-aligned tendencies of the Papandreou Government, which would have been unthinkable in the past, do not provoke serious criticism from the Greek opposition. Notwithstanding Papandreou's current suggestion that the terms of Greece's entrance into the EEC should be revised, it is likely that his Government will in fact tend to align itself with a European policy that seeks a more autonomous relationship with the East.

Developments in the Aegean and Cyprus will largely determine the future of Greece's relations with NATO and the United States. Given the division of PASOK into moderate and radical wings, moderation on the foreign policy front may be essential to offset the radicalizing effect of a declining economy on politics. Thus if the United States and Turkey prove less understanding of Greece's position, the anti-American tendencies within PASOK will prevail, encouraged by the traditional nationalism of the liberal right. External pressures promote consensus at home, and only a relaxation of tension would allow the opposition to resume an effective stance towards the foreign policy of the Government.

The Soviet and Communist Threat

For the past fifteen years the Soviet Union has taken care to avoid provocative gestures that might encourage dissension between Greece and Turkey. Predictably, she has followed an opportunistic policy in the dispute between the two NATO allies. Although championing Cypriot integrity throughout the 1960s, the Soviet Union not only remained passive during the 1974 invasion but also invited Turkish Foreign Minister Erkin to Moscow at the end of October 1974. A year later, at the opening ceremony of the Soviet-financed steel mill at Iskenderun, the two countries agreed to 'draw up a political document on friendly relations and co-operation'.[10] Furthermore, during the NATO Summit of May 1977 in Washington, Turkish Prime Minister Ecevit declared that his country felt no threat from the USSR and should therefore reconsider her obsolete defence policy.[11] A year later, while the fate of the arms embargo on Turkey was being discussed in Congress, Ecevit visited Moscow and an agreement between the two states was signed and entitled 'The Principles of Good Neighbourly and Friendly Relations.'[12] Today Turkey ranks as the largest recipient of Soviet aid among the developing countries.

Spurred on by the Soviet-Turkish *rapprochement* and by her problems with NATO, Greece has sought a way out of her impasse with the Soviet Union (which lasted for 50 years). Contacts were initially established in such fields as industry, shipping, commerce, tourism and sport. In January 1977 a long-term trade accord was concluded, and two years later Greece secured the supply of 1.2 million tons of Soviet oil. The visit of Foreign Minister Rallis to Moscow in 1978 was followed by the establishment of Consulates in Thessaloniki and Odessa, intended to facilitate mercantile marine co-operation between the two countries. This Graeco-Soviet thaw was highlighted by two events, both of which caused considerable speculation in the West during the Autumn of 1979. Three weeks before Mr Karamanlis visited Moscow in October 1979, an agreement was concluded between a private Greek company and the Soviet Union which offered the latter shipyard repair facilities in the Neorion docks on the Aegean island of Syros. Although it was explicitly stated that armed ships were excluded from the deal, the agreement raised protests from the US State Department which, in turn, provoked bitter statements from even the pro-Western Greek press to the effect that Greece was free to conduct her own trade policy and resented foreign interference.[13] In 1981, presumably under pressure from the United States, the Greek Government obliged the firm to alter the terms of the agreement. While the yards remained opened for the repair of merchant ships, they were closed to auxiliary units of the Soviet Mediterranean Fleet.[14] After the accession of the PASOK Government, however, the firm was allowed to proceed with the original agreement. The Greek Government pointed out that the Soviet repair orders rejected by the Greek firm had been placed with French shipyards.

The state visit of Karamanlis to the Soviet Union of 1–5 October 1979, although not intended to explore possibilities of a fresh alignment with the Soviet Union, did produce a considerable relaxation of tensions between the two countries. Continued improvements in Graeco–Bulgarian relations have made the potential Soviet threat even more remote.

Whether their evaluation of Soviet intent is correct or not, the fact remains that both NATO allies of the Southern Flank consider the Warsaw Pact threat as one which is not of immediate concern. Turkey is currently preoccupied with her internal problems and with the resurgence of Kurdish nationalism, which has been reinforced by the breakdown of central authority in Iran and the subsequent war with Iraq. The Soviet Union has not tried to make political capital in Turkey either by encouraging left-wing activities or by condemning the military regime which took over in September 1980.[15]

Greece, on the other hand, is mainly preoccupied with what is perceived as a threat from Turkey. Greeks of all political shades are convinced that, although the Turkish regime is incapable of offensive action, due to its present economic and social problems, it has nevertheless staked its claims for future demands on Greek sovereign rights.[16]

Neither Athens nor Ankara believes that NATO considers the Eastern Mediterranean theatre to be as vital as that of Central Europe. It appears that most scenarios of conflict drafted by NATO and the US place more emphasis on the Central European Front and consider the Flanks of secondary importance.[17] Be that as it may, the somewhat relaxed attitude would be bound to change if a crisis in Yugoslavia brought a pro-Soviet leadership to power, or if Albania were to invite the Soviet Union to return the naval base at Vlöne which she was forced to abandon in 1961. A Soviet foothold on the Adriatic could make communications between the Southern Flank of NATO and its Central Command much more difficult. Equally, if Greece were lost to NATO, the movement of war materiel by sea to Turkey and Italy in wartime would be hopelessly disrupted.[18]

In the event of war between the two Blocs, Soviet *Backfire* bombers and SS-20 missiles (as well as the Soviet 5th Escadra) will prove serious threats to the American fleet in the Mediterranean. Greek and Turkish aircraft would be expected to intercept Soviet aircraft flying out of the Crimea, and therefore airfields in both countries would probably come under attack. With or without Turkish approval, the Americans will almost certainly mine the Dardanelles to prevent further deployment of Soviet vessels into the Aegean. Aircraft from Sixth Fleet carriers could deliver nuclear weapons on Southern Soviet bases as, in future, could ground-or sea-launched cruise missiles. With nuclear warheads stockpiled in Italy, Greece and Turkey, these countries may expect to suffer counterstrikes or even pre-emptive attack.

If Greece were incapacitated or neutralized, Turkey would be isolated from the nearest friendly land border by 700 miles of inaccessible terrain. Warsaw Pact thrusts from Bulgaria could then be directed against the Straits without fear of a flank attack. NADGE sites which provide warning of air attacks on Italy, Turkey or the Sixth Fleet would themselves be attacked, and sea communications between the Western and the Eastern Mediterranean would become a great deal more difficult.[19] If, on the other hand, Turkey was incapacitated or chose to remain neutral, Greece's eastern flank would be exposed to Soviet naval and air attacks and Warsaw Pact forces would attempt to reach the Aegean through the narrow strip of Western Thrace, again without fear of flank attack from the east. The Soviet forces already in the Mediterranean would, however, still be faced with a Greek archipelago in which naval, air and missile forces might be hard to silence.

In peacetime, Soviet interests in the Eastern Mediterranean are somewhat different. Turkey's agreeably loose interpretation of the Montreux Treaty allows a steady flow of Soviet vessels into the Aegean, from where Soviet ships must follow a careful course through the Greek archipelago in order to reach North Africa, the Middle East or the Atlantic.

From February 1982, the Soviet press (*Pravda*, *Izvestia* and *TASS*) inaugurated a new policy towards Greece which is not confined simply to bilateral issues. The Soviet Union addressed Graeco–Turkish issues in terms favourable to Greece. It is not without significance that this 'opening' has more or less coincided with the renewal of US–Greek discussion (in May 1982) on the future of American bases in Greece.

Future Prospects and Security Options for Greece

Whether or not PASOK fulfils its promises to pursue a policy of non-alignment to a much greater extent, it is clear that Greek policy towards the Western Alliance is entering a new phase. Although speculation about the degree of change is hardly consistent, there is little doubt that Greece will attempt to assert her independence from foreign influence considerably more than she has done.[20]

In a country where foreign policy issues tend to play a decisive role in the outcome of elections, the erosion of US and NATO credibility during the last thirteen years has paved the way for PASOK's rise, first to influence and now to power. The problems of the economy notwithstanding (and these have become more serious recently), it has been the marked commitment of the Reagan Administration to Turkey and the failure of the moderate tactics of the Karamanlis and Rallis Administrations to achieve a *rapprochement* with Turkey that have convinced even right-wing voters to support the more nationalistic and activist PASOK.

Although he condemns power blocs in principle, Andreas Papandreou will not fail to exploit the opportunities afforded him by operating within the Western Alliance, and he will make full use of the rights afforded Greece by her NATO membership in order to safeguard Greek security. For instance, Greece will want to ensure that Spain's entry into NATO will not alter the operational responsibilities in the Eastern Mediterranean in any way that might affect Greece's interests. She has bargained her compliance in the matter of Spanish entry for a formula that will protect all NATO countries from predator members (but with a particular, if undeclared, eye on Turkey). Germany and Italy appear to be interested in leading the search for such a formula.[21] It is precisely such practical concerns and pragmatic policies which may irritate PASOK's left wing. Papandreou may find it hard to contain the kind of nationalistic left-wing fervour that his campaign undoubtedly released as he moves carefully into dialogue and compromise with Turkey.

Although reintegration into the military structure of NATO was decided in October 1980, there is as yet no sign that an agreement will be reached concerning Turkey's demands for the reconsideration of operational responsibilities in the Aegean. Neither Greece nor Turkey seem likely to move from their positions on the matter, but it is ultimately the United States which will play the decisive role in concluding the conflict.

Some Greek analysts question the validity of the American view that Turkey offers comparative advantages as an ally over Greece; others, however, accept American appraisals at face value and point to the implicit danger of relying on a biased mediator and ally. NATO and the US clearly view the dispute between the Southern Flank states as a nuisance which must be solved in an equitable way. The future significance of the problem tends to be played down and, in somewhat simplistic terms, is attributed mainly to historical and emotional factors which were allegedly used by politicians and journalists to serve political ends. However, the fact that the issue has been extensively exploited by political parties underlines its importance for both countries. For Turkey, extended control over the Eastern half of the Aegean would enhance the strategic value of her territory. Her strategic location has already been more effective than any other factor or asset in securing foreign aid and loans. For Greece the alienation of her Eastern islands would amount to loss of sovereign territory and be a major blow to her economy.

Greek interpretations of Turkish motives abound. The least sophisticated emphasize the technique of 'distraction' allegedly employed by the Turkish Government to divert public discontent from internal social issues to external adventure. Others would point to rapid population increase and the declining economy as leading to a revival of Turkish expansionism. The third, and perhaps most convincing, interpretation focuses on Turkey's evolving relationship with the West and the United States. Developments in Iran have tended to increase Turkey's geostrategic importance in American eyes, not least because Turkish air bases could become of crucial significance for any attempt by US tactical aircraft to interdict any Soviet move to the Upper Persian Gulf. Greece fears that Turkey is trying to maximize her bargaining power to secure a firm foothold in the Aegean.

Regardless of interpretations, Greece is bound to pursue a number of objectives to ensure both the independence of her national security from external constraints and a continuous supply of military hardware. The latter objective is being pursued by improving the domestic arms industry and maintenance facilities. Recent developments include a rifle assembly plant (destined shortly to go into full production), ammunition factories, facilities to upgrade elderly tanks and the production of communication systems. The core of Greece's defence industry consists of the $300 million plant of the Hellenic Aerospace Industry located at Tanagra. It can overhaul, repair, modify and convert military and commercial aircraft, accessories, engines and electronics. It aspires to service commercial and military airfleets and to manufacture some air-frame spares. The Hellenic Shipyard near Piraeus has been building a series of ten fast patrol craft for the Navy and Coast Guard as well as six *La Combattante II* fast missile craft. There are reports that the shipyard is also laying the keel of a frigate for the Hellenic Navy. The Government-owned firm Steyr Hellas is expected to receive an order for $500 million worth of equipment including 3,500 heavy-duty military trucks and engines.[22]

In parallel with expansion of domestic procurement, Greece is also seeking to diversify her sources of military supply to avoid the foreign policy constraints imposed by reliance on a single provider. The current and prospective scale of Turkey's power may, however, require a more drastic solution. Given the Turkish rate of population growth and the increasing US military aid to Turkey,[23] Greek policy-makers cannot exclude the option of developing nuclear weapons. While still a member of the opposition, Papandreou mentioned the nuclear option (especially since rumours held that Turkey was co-operating with Pakistan to develop her own nuclear weapons) while simultaneously commiting himself to a nuclear-free zone in the Balkans.[24] Although the number and location of US and NATO nuclear weapons based in the Balkans is classified, it can be assumed that they are antiquated and incapable of striking targets deep in Soviet territory. As Platias and Rydell put it, 'When these modest capabilities are compared to the 7,000 [now 6,000] aggregate total of European theatre nuclear weapons it is apparent that the Greek and Turkish nuclear contribution to NATO is minimal. Furthermore, the modest Soviet deployment of short-range *Scud* and *FROG* missiles in Romania and Bulgaria could probably be removed without seriously jeopardising the required balance'.[25] Be that as it may, withdrawal will nevertheless mean further alienation with the West. Papandreou would have had to assess the implications of such a decision (in view of his overall moderation towards the West during the Spring of 1982), but his visit to Sofia and Belgrade and the unwillingness of the Yugoslavs to discuss the nuclear-free-zone issue, may very well have relieved him from his dilemma.[26]

If the world continues to move from detente to confrontation with a resurgence of Cold-war attitudes and policies, Greece will drift further away from NATO, and US influence will diminish. She will have no alternative but to adjust her defence posture in order to face what is seen as the challenge from across the Aegean. PASOK certainly embodies that position. If a nuclear confrontation between the super-powers seemed to be imminent Greece might opt for non-alignment, and so might Turkey, given her past history. Both countries would then forfeit American patronage and be forced to rely on alternative sources of armaments. Neither might in that case be able to assume preponderance. If, on the other hand, a return to cold-war politics encouraged local confrontations between the clients of each bloc while containing the nuclear confrontation, Greece might turn back to NATO for support. Whether non-alignment secures an exemption from global involvement or not, more Greeks may come to feel that the risk of being drawn into nuclear holocaust is too large a price to pay for the sake of any political or social system, no matter how desirable. Keeping out of the way of the dinosaurs could become a major policy trend of the 1980s. National security in such an instance will be separated from wider defence considerations.

Relations between the super-powers will to a large extent dictate Greece's security options in the 1980s. If they demand conformity in the name of their own defence priorities and deny any alternative modes of local security, Greece's loyalty to NATO is likely to become severely strained.[27] If, however, a margin is allowed for independent decision-making, that margin will be much affected by domestic factors. Autonomy and flexibility in the realm of foreign policy presuppose the will of the state to run its own affairs and its readiness to grasp opportunities whenever they appear on the international scene.

NOTES

Introduction

[1] E. Kofos, *Greece and the Eastern Crisis, 1875–1878* (Thessaloniki: Institute of Balkan Studies, 1975), pp. 185–256; and D. Dakin, *The Greek Struggle in Macedonia 1897–1913* (Thessaloniki: Institute of Balkan Studies, 1966), pp. 360–74.
[2] J. Koliopoulos, *Greece and the British Connection, 1935–41* (Oxford: OUP, 1977), pp. 263–93.
[3] C. M. Woodhouse, *The Story of Modern Greece* (London OUP, 1968), p. 239.
[4] In response to Soviet accusations that Greece was violating Article 14, Paragraph 2, of the 1947 Treaty concerning the demilitarization of the Dodecanese, a top secret telegram was sent from the American Secretary of State to the Embassy in Athens on 29 July 1948, encouraging disregard of Communist pressure:

Dept's opinion is that victorious ally who has been awarded territory as result Allied victory should not be placed in less favourable position than defeated enemy. Military clauses Italian Treaty after specifying destruction of fortifications and prohibitions for new constructions, state in several places that 'this prohibition does not include other types non-permanent fortifications and installations designed meet only requirements of internal character and local defence of frontier' (Articles 47b, 48b, 50 para 4, Italian Treaty). Dept feels therefore that Greece has equal right to use Dodecanese military installations to maintain internal order or defend frontiers. (Marshall)

US Foreign Relations Documents 1948, Volume IV, pp. 116–17.
[5] J. Campbell and P. Sherrard, *Modern Greece* (London: Ernest Benn, 1968), p. 185.

Chapter I

[1] H. E. Shear, 'Southern Flank of NATO' in *NATO's Fifteen Nations*, December–January 1979, Vol. 23, No. 6, pp. 7–8.
[2] *Ibid.*; see also Jesse W. Lewis, Jr., *The Strategic Balance in the Mediterranean* (Washington DC: American Enterprise Institute, 1976), pp. 10–11.
[3] *Ibid.*, pp. 2, 33–4.
[4] Foreign Affairs and National Defence Division, Congressional Research Service, Library of Congress, *United States Military Installations and Objectives in the Mediterranean* (Report), 27 March 1977 (Washington DC), pp. 30–32.
[5] *Ibid.*, pp. 32–5; also Lewis, *op. cit.* in note 2, pp. 23–4.
[6] M. Cremasco, 'NATO's Southern Flank in the East–West Balance', *Lo Spettatore Internazionale*, January–March 1979, pp. 13–23.
[7] N. Canakakis, *Greece and Turkey: Disputes over the Aegean Sea* unpublished paper, 1979, p. 93.
[8] European Security Working Group of Harvard Center for Science and International Affairs, 'Instability and Change on NATO's Southern Flank', *International Security*, Winter 1978, p. 151.
[9] James Brown, 'Challenges and Uncertainty, NATO's Southern Flank', *Air University Review*, May–June 1980, p. 4.
[10] For a full discussion of these issues, see Andrew Wilson, *The Aegean Dispute*, Adelphi Paper No. 155 (London: IISS, 1980).

Chapter II

[1] According to the Greek census of 1928 there were 82,000 Bulgarians (Slavophones) in Greek Macedonia and practically none in Western Thrace. See Lada, *The Exchange of Minorities in Bulgaria, Greece and Turkey* (New York: Macmillan, 1932), pp. 27–8.
[2] John Kordatos, an articulate Communist opponent of the policy, accused the KKE's leadership in 1927 of having aligned itself with 'Bulgarian Chauvinism' (*Rizospastis*, 25 February, 1927) and resigned from the Party.
[3] E. Kofos, *Nationalism and Communism in Macedonia*, (Thessaloniki: Institute for Balkan Studies, 1964), pp. 121–2.
[4] *Ibid.* p. 188; see also R. P. King and S. E. Palmer, *Yugoslav Communism and the Macedonian Question* (Connecticut: Archon Press, 1971).
[5] Kofos, *op. cit.* in note 3, pp. 174–95.
[6] N. Zachariades, *Ten Years of Struggle* (in Greek), publisher unknown, 1951, p. 126.
[7] S. G. Xydis, 'Coups and Countercoups in Greece 1967–73', *Political Science Quarterly*, Vol. 89, No. 3, Fall 1974, pp. 534–5.
[8] N. Stavrou, 'Greek–American Relations and their Impact on Balkan Co-operation', in T. Couloumbis and John Iatrides (eds), *Greek–American Relations* (New York: Pella Publishing Co., 1980), p. 158.
[9] *Frankfurter Allgemeine*, 31 May 1977, correspondence by V. Meier; *To Vima* (Greek daily), articles by M. Ploumides, 7 and 30 July and 8 October 1978.
[10] *Christian Science Monitor*, 20 June 1978, correspondence by Eric Bourne; *To Vima*, article by M. Ploumides, 28 March 1978.
[11] *Avgi* (Greek Daily), editorial by S. Chrysostimides, 23 January 1977. Concerning the April 1979 meeting between Karamanlis and Zhivkov, see Romanian optimistic coverage in *Lumea*, 11–17 May 1979, p.16. Also, P. Mladenov, 'Bulgaria's Foreign Policy Today' in *International Affairs* (Moscow), No. 1, 1979, pp. 8–15.
[12] S. Valdin, 'The Significance and Structural Problems of Greece's Commercial Relations with Countries of State-Controlled Commerce' (in Greek), *Synchrona Themata*, Vol. 14, March 1982, p. 33
[13] *To Vima*, M. Ploumides, 9 July 1978; *Eleftherotypia* (Greek daily), correspondence by S. Oeconomou, 30 June 1978.
[14] Stavrou, *op. cit.* in note 8, p. 167.
[15] Karamanlis voiced his fears over the possible repercussions of the Sino–Soviet conflict in the Balkans in his 16 January 1979 speech at the Greek Parliament. *To Vima*, 17 and 18 March (articles by Linardatos and Ploumides) and 28 March 1979 (article by Efstathiades on Tito and Karamanlis).
[16] For an appraisal of a recent resurgence of the Macedonian issue, coinciding with Papandreou's visit in May to Belgrade, see K. Iordanides, 'Yugoslavia Poses the Macedonian Issue to Greece', *Kathimerini*, 28 May 1982.
[17] J. A. S. Grenville, *The Major International Treaties*

[17] *1914–1973* (London: Methuen, 1974), p. 197.
[18] Bernard Lewis, *The Emergence of Modern Turkey* (London: OUP, 1968), pp. 297–302.
[19] The bibliography on the Cyprus issue is immense. For the best comprehensive account of the problem, see P. Kitromilides and T. Couloumbis, 'Ethnic Conflict in a Strategic Area: The Case of Cyprus' in the *Greek Review of Social Research*, No. 24 (Athens, 1975), pp. 271–91.
[20] The complicity of the Turkish Government was established by the 1960–61 trials of the Menderes Government. See Walter Weiker, *The Turkish Revolution 1960–61* (Washington DC: Brookings Institution, 1963), pp. 25–47. A number of prominent members of the Greek community were deported, and the unfavourable climate after 1955 precipitated a rapid exodus of ethnic Greeks from Istanbul. The community of 80,000 in 1950 has shrunk to 8,000, yet those who have to take up residence abroad remain Turkish citizens. Most of the Greek nationals (some 10,000) were expelled from Turkey in 1965 following a unilateral denunciation of the Agreement of Establishment Commerce and Navigation which had been part of the Venizelos–Ataturk Pact of 1930.
[21] Grivas died in January 1974.
[22] T. Ehrlich, *Cyprus 1958–1967* (Oxford: OUP, 1974), pp. 65–86.
[23] Quoted in L. Stern, *The Wrong Horse* (New York: Times Books, 1977), p. 117.
[24] On 6 July Makarios made public his accusation that Greek officers of the National Guard were linked with EOKA-B and demanded their removal from the island. The Junta answered on 15 July with the coup by the National Guard.
[25] Stern, *op. cit.* in note 23, p. 121.
[26] Nancy Crawshaw, *The Cyprus Revolt* (London: Allen and Unwin, 1978), p. 394.
[27] The chronology of intercommunal discussions was taken from Wilson (*op. cit.* in Ch. 1, note 10), pp. 31–5.
[28] For a comprehensive view of US policy towards Makarios, see Van Cofoudakis, 'American Foreign Policy and the Cyprus Problem', in Couloumbis and Iatriades, *op. cit.* in note 8, pp. 107–29.
[29] *The Guardian*, 27 October 1978.
[30] For full text of legislation, see *Greece*, No. 93, 18 August 1978 (London: Greek Press and Information Office).
[31] See commentary in *The Guardian*, 21, 22 May 1979 and *International Herald Tribune*, 12 June 1979.
[32] Information provided by Yannos Kranidiotis, 'The Negotiations for the Solution of the Cyprus Issue, 1974–81' in a collective volume on *Cyprus* (Athens: Kollaros, 1982), pp. 649–60.
[33] These questions will not be discussed at any length here because they are covered in detail in Wilson (*op. cit.* in Ch. 1, note 10).
[34] Turkey has extended her own territorial sea limit to twelve miles in the Black Sea.
[35] See joint Brussels Communiqué of 31 May 1975 to resolve problems peacefully 'by means of negotiations and as regards the continental shelf [through] the International Court'. In February 1976 Turkey rejected a Greek proposal for a non-recourse-to-force pact.
[36] *Op. cit.* in Ch. 1, note 10.
[37] See C. Rozakis, 'Two Footnotes in the Discussion on Greek Reintegration' (in Greek), *Ikonomia Kai Kinonia*, No. 15, December 1980, pp. 42–3.
[38] A mimeographed paper circulated by the Greek Ministry for Foreign Affairs in 1979.
[39] For an analysis of American influence in Greece during the Civil War period see Michael Mark Amen, 'American Institutional Penetration into Greek Military and Political Policy-making Structures: June 1947–October 1949', in *Journal of the Hellenic Diaspora*, Vol. V, No. 3, Fall 1978, pp. 89–113. 'One does not gain the impression that members of Greek authoritative society participated in an equal or significant footing with Americans in creating policies' (p. 112).
[40] Maurice Goldbloom, 'United States Policy in Post-War Greece', in R. Clogg and G. Yannopoulos, *Greece Under Military Rule* (London: Secker and Warburg, 1972), p. 231.
[41] T. Couloumbis, *Greek Political Reaction to American and NATO Influences* (New Haven: Yale University Press, 1966), pp. 33–89.
[42] *Ibid.*, p. 201.
[43] Thanos Veremis, 'Union of the Democratic Centre', in H. R. Penniman (ed.), *Greece at the Polls* (Washington DC: American Enterprise Insititute, 1981), pp. 87–8.
[44] Goldbloom, *op. cit.* in note 40, p. 236.
[45] *Ibid.*, p. 247.
[46] *Ibid.*, pp. 240–57; T. Couloumbis, J. A. Petropulos and H. Psomiades, *Foreign Interference in Greek Politics* (New York: Pella Publishing Co., 1976), pp. 129–39.
[47] This point of view was communicated to the author between 1967 and 1969 by officers who had served in the Greek contingent in Cyprus.
[48] See an appraisal by *Stern, op. cit.* in note 23, pp. 81–2.
[49] In the autumn of 1974 a middle-ranking officer who had served in Cyprus reiterated this position to the author: 'If Makarios had died, Clerides would have legally succeeded him and the Turkish invasion would have been averted'. Glafkos Clerides, the Speaker of the House and successor under the 1960 constitution to the President, was favoured by the Americans.
[50] The 'Post-mortem of the Intelligence Community of Cyprus', released on 1 October 1975, quoted in Couloumbis *et al.*, *op. cit.* in note 46, p. 140.
[51] On 13 August 1974 the State Department took a favourable position on the Turkish claims in the dispute. According to the public briefings of that day: 'We recognize that the position of the Turkish community on Cyprus requires considerable improvement and protection. We have supported a greater degree of autonomy for them.' Quoted in *Stern, op. cit.* in note 23, p. 132.
[52] The bilateral agreement of 1961 prohibited the use of American weapons against Cyprus or any other country without the consent of the President.
[53] E. Hadzipetros, 'Through a Glass Darkly', in *The Athenian*, May 1982, pp. 15–17.
[54] Concerning the negotiations, see *Kathimerini*, 16 April, 30 May, 5 and 12 June 1981; *To Vima*, 23 April, 3 May, 12 June 1981; *International Herald Tribune*, 6–7 June 1981; A. Velios, *Mesimvrini*, 1 July 1981.
[55] Marvine Howe, 'Greece Seeks to Repair Strained Ties to West', *International Herald Tribune*, 27 April 1982.
[56] *To Vima*, 28 May 1982; *Pulse*, No. 4625–22, 31 May 1982.

Chapter III
[1] A. Elephantis, 'PASOK and the Elections of 1977: The Rise of the Populist Movement', in H. R. Penniman (*op. cit.* in Chap. II, note 43), p. 112.
[2] PASOK's most important views on foreign policy issues are expressed in a Party manual containing speeches of Andreas Papandreou (in Greek), *PASOK in the International Scene* (Athens, 1978), pp. 5–48.
[3] See records of Parliamentary discussions – Session MH', 16 January 1979, pp. 1,675–83. Also PASOK's newspaper *Exormisi*, 4 March 1979, for the decision of the party's Central Committee concerning policy issues.
[4] *To Vima*, 26 April 1981.
[5] See speeches in Parliament by Karamanlis, 19 December 1977 and 19 January 1979.
[6] The abolition of the Monarchy in 1974 had also deprived the Centre Union of a potent political slogan.
[7] Nicos. C. Alivizatos, 'The Greek Army in the Late Forties: Towards an Institutional Autonomy', *Journal of the Hellenic Diaspora*, Vol. V, No. 3, Fall 1978, pp. 40–41.
[8] *Ibid.*, pp. 42–3.
[9] Thirty years after the civil war, the armed forces retain certain rights and activities which have nothing to do with the military profession, for example a radio and television station, a bank (General Bank) and a construction agency.
[10] G. Karayannis, *The Drama of Greece: Glories and Miseries, IDEA, 1940–1952 (To Dramatis Ellados: Epikai Athliotites, IDEA, 1940–1952)* (Athens: published by the author), p. 206.
[11] *Ibid.*
[12] N. Stavrou, *Allied Policy and Military Interventions. The Political Role of the Greek Military* (Athens: Papazissis, 1976), pp. 127–8. Stavrou rightly points out the responsibility of politicians who never took seriously accusations against right-wing military associations.
[13] *Ibid.*, p. 214.
[14] N. Pantelakis, *L'Armée dans la Société Grecque Contemporaine*', Thèse pour le doctorat du 3ème cycle de sociologie, Université René Descartes (Paris V) 1980, pp. 74–5.
[15] *To Vima*, 18 and 20 January 1976.
[16] A. Spanidis, *Kathimerini*, 16 March 1975 and 18 January 1976.
[17] *Ibid.*, 18 January 1976.
[18] P. Loucakos, 'The Control of Political Authority over the Armed Forces', *Synchrona Themata*, October 1980, pp. 37–8.
[19] *Ibid.*, pp. 38–9.
[20] This is the view of Loucakos, *op.cit.* in note 18.
[21] Spanidis, *op.cit.* in note 16, 18 January 1976.
[22] Loucakos, *op.cit.* in note 18, p. 40.
[23] L. and M. Papayannakis, 'A Comparative Study of South-European Economies' (in Greek), *Politis*, No. 9, February 1977, pp. 12–37. See also *Greece*, No. 100, 15 December 1978 (London: Greek Press and Information Office).
[24] Papers of M. Papayannakis and S. Papaspiliopoulos in the Conference on 'Development or Underdevelopment: Greece' (London School of Economics, 16–17 March 1979).
[25] Remittances have covered 42 per cent of the deficit. Tourism and foreign loans cover the rest.
[26] T. Yannitsis, 'Problems of Greek Development' (in Greek), *Iconomia kai Kinonia*, May 1979, pp. 26–45.
[27] L. Minard, 'Greece Goes Left', *Forbes Magazine*, 28 September 1981, p. 36.
[28] *Financial Times*, 6 July 1982.
[29] S. Papaspiliopoulos, 'Entry or not into the EEC. A False Dilemma' (in Greek) from *EEC, Greece, Mediterranean* (Athens: Nea Synora, 1978), p.93.

Chapter IV
[1] For details see *Greece*, No. 135, 2 April 1981. See also a critical article by J. K. Mazarakis-Anian, *To Vima*, 13 March 1981.
[2] *Pulse*, 9 March 1981.
[3] Among other Greek dailies, see *Mesimvrini*, 16 April 1981.
[4] *To Vima*, 23 December 1980. See also A. Velios, 'On a Razor's Edge', in *Mesimvrini*, 27 December 1980.
[5] Y. Roubatis, 'The United States and the Operational Responsibilities of the Greek Armed Forces, 1947–1987', in the *Journal of the Hellenic Diaspora*, Vol VI, No. 1, Spring 1979, pp. 46–7.
[6] 'The European Community and the Greek–Turkish Dispute', *Journal of Common Market Studies*, XIX, 1980, pp. 50–51.
[7] Stanley Hoffman, 'The Unhappy Choice', *New York Review of Books*, 20 November 1980.
[8] David Watt, 'Europe and America', *The Economist*, 11 October 1980.
[9] Interview with Gen. Bernard Rogers (SACEUR), 'Europe's Risky Drift towards Neutralism', *US News and World Report*, 15 June 1981, pp. 25–6.
[10] Tass News Agency, 29 December 1975.
[11] Marian K. Leighton, *Graeco–Turkish Friction: Changing Balance in the Eastern Mediterranean*, Conflict Studies No. 109 (London: Institute for the Study of Conflict, July 1979), p. 7.
[12] Brown, *op.cit.* in Ch. I, note 9, p. 6.
[13] *Kathimerini*, editorial of 26 September 1979.
[14] *The Athenian*, April 1981, p. 41.
[15] For a most precise account of Soviet–Turkish relations, see Duygu Bazoglu Sezer, *Turkey's Security Policies*, Adelphi Paper No. 164 (London: IISS, 1981), pp. 31–6.
[16] *Kathimerini*, editorial of 16 April 1981.
[17] Brown, *op.cit.* in Ch. I, note 9, pp. 13–14 (and relevant sources quoted).
[18] J. Snyder, 'Strengthening the NATO Alliance', *Naval War College Review*, March–April 1981, pp. 33–4.
[19] *Greece and Turkey: Some Military Implications Related to NATO and the Middle East* (Washington DC: Congressional Research Service, 28 February 1975), pp. 14–15.
[20] Although varying in degree and kind, the demand for more autonomy in the pursuit of national policy has been the common denominator in the public statements of all major political forces in Greece. The daily *Kathimerini*, abandoning its pre-Junta editorial policy of unqualified reliance on the West, now offers through its effective editorials words of caution to the US on American policy towards Greece.
[21] See A. Papandreou's interview with the *Financial*

Times, 24 February 1982.

[22] T. Couloumbis, *The Structures of Greek Foreign Policy* (unpublished Paper presented at King's College London, January 1981), p.18.

[23] The seven-to-ten ratio regulating US military aid to Greece and Turkey was questioned by American officials in the Winter of 1981/2.

[24] *To Vima*, 20 April 1978.

[25] A. G. Platias and R. J. Rydell, 'International Security Regimes: the Case of a Balkan Nuclear-Free Zone' in D. Carlton and C. Schaerf, *Arms Control in the 80s* (London: Macmillan, 1982), p. 289.

[26] *Kathimerini*, leader article, 28 May 1981.

[27] H. Macdonald, 'NATO's Dilemma: Defence, Security and Arms Control', *Millenium*, Journal of International Studies, Vol. 9, No. 2 , Autumn 1980.

2 Turkey's Security Policies
DUYGU BAZOG̈LU SEZER

INTRODUCTION

Since the end of the 1939–45 War, Turkey has based her security on defence ties with the United States and the collective security system of the Atlantic Alliance, but for many years now she has felt uneasy with her security policy. Turkish security can be reduced to the fact that Turkey is a small power which has to exist alongside a global power – the Soviet Union. She is in control of the strategic Turkish Straits and thereby in a geographical position to hold a great power 'by the throat', as Stalin put it.[1] Yet the ratio of military and economic power between them is unfavourable for Turkey – a classical relationship between a small power and a great power with mutual borders. Her proximity to the Soviet Union gives her a particular importance in an East–West context and her security cannot be examined apart from superpower rivalry or East–West confrontation. Her formal association with the United States automatically increases the risk of involvement. On the other hand, cancellation of that association would not automatically eliminate the risk for Turkey.

At the roots of Turkey's current uncertainty about the viability of her NATO-based security policy lie the deep changes in the super-power relationship and the reverberations of this altered relationship on the collective security systems. At the same time the Soviet Union's peaceful policy towards Turkey has significantly reduced the perception of threat. This has led to a state of detente – in itself partly a by-product of the 'balance of terror' maintained by the two super-powers – and a consequent appreciation that, since the Cold War is a thing of the past, some experimentation with fresh approaches towards security, by great powers as well as small, might produce an alternative to military confrontation. The impact of this change on Turkey has been two-fold: first, there has been a mutual reduction in the perception of the convergence of Turkish and Alliance security interests; and secondly, Greek-Turkish rivalry has re-surfaced and has come to be focused on the Cyprus conflict and the Aegean. The problem, therefore, has been how Turkey, as a small power, should approach security at a time when the perception of the threat from the Soviet Union and the credibility of US protection have both declined and when the socio-economic differences between Turkey and the majority of the Alliance members have merged as a perplexing barrier to close security co-operation.

The domestic situation in Turkey is very different from that of a quarter of a century ago, when the defence ties with the West were established. Needs, values and opinions have multiplied and diversified. Further, Turkish society is basically more self-confident (despite its obvious and considerable internal problems) and may be ready to reclaim some of its Middle-Eastern mould in contrast to the previously exclusive Western orientation. The socio-economic demands of a politically emancipated population that has enjoyed democracy almost consistently for three decades have turned development goals into the primary objective. This has led to defence having to compete with other requirements for its allocation of national resources.

Turkey's proximity to the Middle East – a region known for its oil, instability, armaments and super-power involvement – is the other major security problem. Regional conflicts and the rising tempo of internal tensions and division, particularly since the Peace Treaty between Israel and Egypt, challenge her uninvolved position in respect of Arabs and Israelis while sharper super-power rivalry tests her ability to maintain her freedom to stay out of questions or conflicts not of direct concern to her. The instability of the region and the changing fortunes of the super-powers constantly confront Turkey with new situations, new choices and new power alignments. While the military

43

coup in Turkey in September 1980 has underlined the intensity of internal tension within Turkey herself, Turkish domestic and foreign policies have certainly not gone untouched by the developments of the last few years in the Middle East. The recent Revolution in Iran, one of those rare spontaneous movements against authoritarianism in the developing world, has highlighted the unsettled nature of the region, and the way in which both Iran herself and the region will respond in the long run to this kind of challenge will have important implications for Turkey. Turkey will have to live with this sense of unpredictability, adjust to it or even become part of it.

This Paper will trace domestic developments and examine how the Turkish people have regarded security concerns and how security policies have evolved. It will look at the way Turkish security has been affected by the world around her and particularly at the way her relationship with the Western Alliance has changed. The links between security policy and foreign policy are analysed and, finally, the alternatives for the future are set out and discussed.

It is a personal paper. It does not necessarily reflect official views, although these are given the appropriate weight and prominence, particularly insofar as they have shaped policy in the past. It tries to avoid prescription and prediction, while at the same time making clear the context and constraints within which any future security policy for Turkey must be formulated.

1. DOMESTIC CHANGE

The Turkey of today is very different from the country that in the early post-war years opted for a security relationship with the US and NATO. Her economic potential is greater and her industrial base is stronger, and she has enjoyed democratic freedoms and institutions for most of the past thirty years. The circle of decision-makers has expanded beyond the small elite of the 1940s, then made up of party officials and bureaucrats. Newly emergent social groups vie with each other to have a say in the formulation of official policy. Many more people have come out of the universities. More people have travelled abroad and returned with new ideas, communication networks have increased, and television enters almost every home, bringing world events readily to people's attention. A generally quiescent and largely rural population of 20 million in 1950 had grown by 1978 to a population of over 43 million which was both more mobile and more urban. A new and less Eurocentric generation with new ideas has joined the ranks of the foreign-policy decision-makers. The dream of being in Europe which has persisted since the Congress of Vienna now looks irrelevant to the young who move to Istanbul, Ankara and Izmir from the provincial towns. They learn that their daily problems are more like those encountered by the youth of third-world countries than those of young Europeans. Domestic priorities have become more important at the moment when alternative ways have merged of looking at the world in general and security issues in particular. In short, Turkey's domestic political, economic and social structure is now more diverse as well as more developed.

Nevertheless there are very serious economic and social problems to be faced. The political process is not functioning effectively. Political and ideological polarization has intensified, and the use of terror for political purposes has reached dangerous levels. Although domestic transformation has brought many advances, it has at the same time created new demands, new power groups, new areas of dissent, and therefore new causes for tension.

This internal change has affected attitudes to foreign policy in many different ways. Bipartisan foreign policy has ended. The expansion of liberal democratic institutions has encouraged freedom of thought and speech and the left-wing parties which have emerged demand a review of foreign policy. Political developments in other parts of the world have been followed closely, creating a sense of solidarity between some of the population and other progressive forces engaged in a struggle for liberation. At the same time resurgent radical nationalism opposes the importation of foreign ideas and culture. Traditionalism opposes the continuation of ties with the West and has proposed a foreign policy based on religious affinities with Islam.

On the economic front, the need for exports to finance industry's growing demand for imports has spurred policies seeking outlets to new markets. Dependence on oil for growth and the desire to preserve a relatively high standard of living have made it necessary to forge better ties with oil-producing neighbours. Population growth and unemployment have fuelled the search for foreign employment opportunities.

With so many domestic and economic cross-currents pressing upon it, Turkish foreign policy has oscillated. There is little doubt that Turkey is entering a period of extreme difficulty and that this could have the effect of bringing about a fundamental re-appraisal of security policy. At the very least, radically different approaches to security will be considered.

Socio-economic Transformation

Turkey today is Atatürk's creation. Therefore, while change has been inevitable, the tradition of Atatürk (or Kemalism) as a Turkish ideology, has provided the broad framework within which forces of change have, at least until recently, had to operate. In fact, during the past ten to fifteen years Atatürk's dicta have with increasing frequency been invoked as the basis of legitimacy by groups with opposing views and visions for Turkey. The founding concepts, precepts and policies of modern Turkey have therefore performed two opposing functions simultaneously: they have defined the constants and the constraints on change while at the same time creating the momentum for it.

The twin goals set by Atatürk – independent self-preservation within the national boundaries, and modernization – put a fundamental imprint on the future course of Turkey's development. Externally they implied distant but peaceful relations with foreign powers. Internally, they were interpreted as a search for development along the lines of the 'contemporary civilization' of the West. Traditional value systems, modes of behaviour and their institutional and organizational manifestations were to be replaced by their modern counterparts through the application of western rationality, science and technology.

At the same time the religious-political-civil code of Islam that regulated all aspects of human life was no longer to be taken as the ultimate authority. The Caliphate was abolished. The *Seriat*, the religious law, was replaced by an adaptation of Swiss Civil Law and Italian Criminal Law and modern secular courts replaced religious courts. *Medreses*, the religious schools, were closed, and education was secularized under a unified national system. Religious leaders were stripped of their power, and the hierarchy was re-organized under the control of the state exercised through the Presidency for Religious Affairs. Women were emancipated, and a new dress code forbade traditional garb for women and the traditional headwear for men.[2] Commitment to republicanism, secularism, nationalism, populism, reformism and, later, statism, became the semi-official ideology. An authoritarian government, for which Atatürk's Republican People's Party (RPP) was the only contender during most of his rule, kept a vigilant watch (with the help of the military) to forestall any reaction against these far-reaching reforms.

Economic reforms were less sweeping. Relations between productive forces were left largely intact. The memory of capitulations and the Ottoman debt inhibited recourse to external borrowing and foreign enterprise was carefully scrutinized. One major move towards industrialization was the establishment of several state enterprises in the early 1930s.

Post-war internal and external developments helped to shape a new attitude to the world as well as affecting internal political and economic priorities. Aspirations for economic development coincided with the introduction of political liberalization in the immediate post-war period. Opposition to the RPP from within its own ranks, organised around the Democrat Party (DP), espoused liberal economic policies. The country opted for a place in the West and welcomed western foreign assistance. The intensified economic activity of the 1950s, subsidized in part by American assistance and operating within a liberalized political framework, had a profound impact on the political and socio-economic profile of the country.

45

The alternative to one-party government and the offer of economic freedom and rewards spurred record voter participation and accelerated business initiative. The rural masses aspired to relief from endemic poverty, business and commercial interest groups enjoyed new profits, and the new middle class expanded. Technical, managerial and professional skills increased, and the possessors of these modern skills and the new rich began to compete for political power.

What started as an ambitious development venture in the post-war period brought about considerable economic growth, particularly after planned development began in 1962.[3] The average annual rate of growth in the gross domestic product (GDP) was 5.5% in 1963-7, 6.7% in 1968-72, and 7.1% in 1973-7. Per capita income of about $100 in the 1950s rose to about $300 in the mid-1960s and $1,000 in the mid-1970s. Increasing industrialization attracted the rural population to the cities at the same time as the mechanization of agriculture released more people from the land; migration from the villages to the cities accounted for 42.6% of urbanization in the 1960s and 63% in the 1970s. The result has been that nearly 30% of İstanbul's population and 20% of Ankara's now live in slums and shanty towns.

Industrialization has turned labour into a power group, and efficient trade-unionism and the right to collective bargaining (granted in 1963) bolstered its position. A large proportion of the 900 trade unions whose 2 million members represented 13% of the work force in 1977 are affiliated to one of the two major national labour organizations, the Confederation of Trade Unions of Turkey (CTUT) and the Confederation of Revolutionary Trade Unions (CRTU), each of which is an active and effective political force. The former has a membership of about 1.5 million and supported the social democratic platform of the RPP although it shuns party affiliations on principle; the latter (with a membership of about half a million) is dedicated to Marxism. Powerful trade-unionism and the right to collective bargaining have significantly altered industrial relations in favour of labour and improved the status and buying power of the expanding working class. However, the frequency and duration of industrial disputes involving pay rises and fringe benefits have put Turkey among the first in Europe in terms of the number of days lost on strikes.

Economic growth has improved living standards in general but the development process has been painful. The development strategy was based on import substitution. Borrowing from external sources and inflationary measures were the major means of financing development. The export sector failed to meet expectations, and the basic assumption – that import-dependent industrialization would spur exports, which would in turn pay for imports – was slow to be fulfilled. Industry's share of GDP, 13.3% in 1963, had risen to 19.7% in 1977. Despite this structural change from agriculture towards industry, however, neither the State Economic Enterprises, which constitute the backbone of industry, with their unproductive resource allocations and uninspired management, nor private enterprise, which found supplying the large domestic market more lucrative than competing in external markets, could reach the necessary level of exports.

The momentum and costs of development could be maintained as long as there was no major shock in the international environment that would upset the pattern of import substitution and the means of financing it. Concessional aid began to dwindle in the 1970s, but the adverse effects of this trend were compensated for largely by the foreign currency remittances of about one million Turkish guest workers employed in Western Europe (mostly in West Germany) following Turkey's association with the EEC in 1964. Between 1973 and 1975 these remittances almost reached the level of annual export earnings, with both standing a little below $1.5 billion.

After 1975, however, Turkey began to feel the effects of developments in the world economy. The rise in the price of oil and petroleum products, the recession in the West and the rise in the price of capital and intermediary goods which figured regularly on her import list threatened the 7% minimum growth rate target. The number of Turkish workers in Europe decreased, and so did their remittances, which fell to under $1 billion in 1976. The bill for crude oil increased from $124 million in 1972 to $1.2 billion in 1977, and the overall import bill almost quadrupled in the same period, jumping from about $1.5 billion to $5.8 billion.

By 1978, the economy had reached a point where investment had to be slowed down. There was a mounting balance of payments deficit – over $3 billion in 1976, and over $4 billion in 1977 – and to make up for the deficit Turkey borrowed heavily from foreign commercial banks over short terms and at high interest rates and cashed her reserves. The total foreign debt reached $11 billion in 1978, with long-term debts totalling $6 billion and short-term debts $4.5 billion. It should be noted that Turkey's case is not unique among developing countries, a number of which have over-extended their debt-servicing capacity during the same period.

The means of generating the foreign currency needed for imports – external resource transfers and exports – seemed to have reached their limits by 1977-8 and imports of raw materials and equipment have had to be cut down. GNP increased by only 2.7% in 1978, and official figures quote the inflation rate at 36% and unemployment at 14% (2.2 million) for 1977. Unofficially, a 70% inflation rate was reported for 1978.

Given such a backlog of problems, it was inevitable that economic policy should have become one of the central themes of debate. The economic crisis has focused both the policy-makers' and the intellectuals' attention on the question of the relevance of the capitalist road to development for Turkey. Her recent experiences have demonstrated the interdependence between, on the one hand, domestic development, foreign trade and the international monetary system, and, on the other, the dangerous vulnerability of a developing economy to international economic and financial fluctuations. The Atatürk policy of maximum self-sufficiency and restraint towards foreign loans has been offered as a remedy.

Issues not directly economic have also widened the range of problems. Though its rate of growth has been gradually declining (to 2.4% in 1979) the Turkish population nevertheless doubled between 1950 and 1975 (from 20 million to 40 million) and is expected to double again within the next thirty years. In the early 1960s, when planned economic development became official policy, the high rate of population growth was recognized as one of the impediments to development, and modest moves for family planning were undertaken by the Ministry of Health. Over subsequent years, public disinterest and general complacency have replaced that concern, and the new Five-Year Plan for 1979-83 has left the question of controlling population growth largely to the restraining influence of social and economic factors such as industrialization and urbanization. The pressure of population growth on the economy does not appear to be an issue for any of the political parties. Another source of strain on the economy has been the increase in defence expenditures in the aftermath of the Cyprus crisis. The defence share of total government expenditures jumped from 20.5% in 1974, to 26.6% in 1976. It stabilized at around 22% in 1977-8.[4]

The Ecevit government tried two solutions: internally it attempted to establish closer state supervision of the economy, to curb spending, and to pass a major tax reform bill; and externally it tried to secure new loans and reschedule the debts. Except for an agreement with the IMF for a standby credit of $450 million in April 1978, only a fraction of which was released, little progress was recorded until the summer of 1979, because governments and creditor institutions had tended to insist on an International Monetary Fund (IMF) approved stabilization programme before they agreed to advance loans. On 30 May 1979, several months after the four Western leaders reached an understanding at the Guadeloupe Summit to assist Turkey, agreement was announced to extend $900 million in economic assistance within the framework of the Organization for Economic Co-operation and Development (OECD) consortium to aid Turkey. It was also understood that the World Bank was favourably inclined to provide a $150 million programme loan and a $300 million project loan in the year beginning 1 July. The European Community will consider a $100 million special action loan in 1980 and 1981 while a $120 & 150 million project fund could be disbursed relatively quickly under the Third Financial Protocol recently ratified by Turkey. Bilateral agreements between Turkey and the donors were finally reached in June 1979. The rescheduling of some of the huge foreign debts has also been achieved with creditor nations agreeing to reschedule $2.2 billion debts falling due in 1982 over a ten-year period.

An entirely new package, geared to liberal principles was implemented by the government of Mr Suleyman Demirel, after he came to power in November 1979. His measures counted on market forces, limited state intervention and new foreign loans and credits to be negotiated with the OECD countries and the IMF to remobilize productive capacity and to curb inflation.

The OECD countries (and among them the EEC members) have been Turkey's major trading partners. In 1977, 49.5% of her exports went to EEC countries and 42% of her imports came from them. The Association Agreement of 1963 was intended to lead Turkey to a 'common destiny with the Western World', as Prime Minister İnönü put it at the time.[5] With the Additional Protocol of 1970, and other accords signed later, the transitional period began which committed her to progressive trade liberalization with a view to a customs union in the mid-1990s. However, problems arose between Turkey and the EEC in the mid-1970s. Phased tariff reductions by Turkey and the 1974 enlargement of quotas for EEC goods have moved the terms of trade further against her in real terms and exacerbated her balance of payments problem, changing her import-export ratio from about 2:1 in 1973 to 3:1 in 1977. The goal of free movement of Turkish workers into the EEC countries has not been achieved, and EEC protectionism against Turkish textile products (the country's most competitive manufacturing industry) has also been a controversial issue. At the same time, the relative export advantages granted to Turkey under the Protocol have been eroded. The application of general trade preferences to a number of developing countries under the Lomé Agreement and the EEC's Global Mediterranean Policy have put Turkish associate status on a par with non-associate status, and the EEC's expansion to include Greece, Spain and Portugal has caused concern, since all three have exports similar to Turkey's.

Turkey herself had no clear idea of how to approach these new problems. A series of coalition governments made a firm stand very difficult, and diplomatic and political tension generated by the Cyprus crisis made things more difficult still. Neither the Government nor the key economic interest groups (such as private enterprise and labour) contemplated application for entry to the EEC until late 1979. While both the Justice Party (JP) and the Republican People's Party (RPP) seemed, in principle, to be in favour of political and economic integration with the EEC in the long run, opposition to integration was common to the parties on the extreme right – the National Salvation Party (NSP) and the National Action Party (NAP). These last joined the coalition government from 1975 to 1977 and, although numerically small, were influential; they favoured trade with the EEC, but they refused to advance towards integration on the grounds that this would turn Turkey into a colony of Western Europe and eradicate her national identity. Only the Marxists had a clearly-stated position: total opposition to the EEC. Otherwise confusion and evasiveness surrounded the positions of nearly all key interest groups, even concerning policy objectives for the transitional period. For a long time they directed their energies towards solving problems centring around the Protocol of 1970. In October 1978, Turkey asked the EEC to suspend for five years the implementation of the present stage of trade liberalization, hoping to continue the process after putting her economy in order.[6] The Demirel government reversed this decision and dialogue was resumed with the EEC at the January 1980 Association Council meeting. Statements by government officials gave the impression – to the consternation of several member countries – that Turkey intended to apply for full membership before the end of 1980.

Third-world and Socialist Bloc countries have assumed increased importance as potential markets for exports, and dependence on oil as the primary source of energy has made the Arab markets the major target – Turkey's own oil wells supply only between 10% and 20% of her needs.[7] The largest supplier of imported oil in the last few years has been Iraq, but the trend changed in 1978, when imports from Iraq fell to roughly one-third of what had been planned, largely owing to problems over payment. Under a new agreement with Libya signed during Prime Minister Ecevit's visit in January 1979, that country promised to become the major supplier for the next three years. However, there were acute shortfalls from all three major traditional sources – Iraq, Iran and Libya –

throughout 1979 which in turn necessitated imports from world markets. In 1978 the Soviet Union agreed in principle to provide crude oil in exchange for Turkish goods, but subsequently withdrew the barter offer in favour of cash sales. Pressed by the need to meet energy requirements, the Government has pushed forward the plans to build Turkey's first commercial nuclear reactor and signed an agreement with Sweden in December 1978 for its purchase. Agreement was also reached for a second reactor in June 1979, with the Soviet Union providing credits and technology.

Success in the drive to multiply and diversify foreign economic relations has been rather limited, except for the substantial economic co-operation established with the Soviet Union. The decline in the percentage of Turkish exports going to the OECD countries was a slow process – dropping from 82.9% to 70.4% between 1963 and 1977, accompanied by an important improvement in exports to the Free Exchange Agreement countries from 10.2% to 19.8% over the same period.

Over the short-term, too, the regional distribution of the export pattern showed some favourable trends. Exports to Arab countries increased by nearly 50% between 1972 and 1978 and those to the Council for Mutual Economic Aid (COMECON) countries nearly doubled. However, there are obstacles to this process. Besides traditional bureaucratic and political attitudes, hard core economic and commercial factors must also be reckoned with – notably Turkey's low level of domestic productivity and the limited competitiveness of her products by world standards. Moreover, the rush for foreign trade is not peculiar to Turkey, and, even when there may be an important political incentive to promote trade and credit relations with Turkey (which does not seem to be the case in general), prospective partners' approaches will still be dictated by considerations of self-interest. The chances of successfully entering COMECON markets, for example, must be weighed against the background of the priority that some COMECON countries assign to trade with the West (a major credit source for them) and with third-world countries. The oil-rich Arab world, for its part, has the entire world to choose from for investment and trade. And for Turkey to consolidate a third-world identity seems inconsistent so long as she remains a member of the OECD.

Democracy Under Strain

The Republican People's Party (RPP), founded by Atatürk, takes a left-of-centre position, and the Justice Party (JP) a right-of-centre one. The smaller National Salvation Party (NSP) represents the traditional Right and the Nationalist Action Party (NAP) the extreme Right. The Marxist left, torn by factionalism, has no parliamentary representation as a separate political party. At the last general elections in June 1977, Mr Ecevit's RPP mustered 42.4% of the popular vote. Mr Demirel's JP 38.3%, Mr Erbaken's NSP 8.6%, Mr Turkes' NAP 6.4%.[8] The Ecevit Government, formed in December 1977, when several JP party members switched support to the RPP, enjoyed a precarious majority until 14 October 1979, when a series of by-election defeats forced Mr Ecevit to resign.[9] Mr Demirel formed a Government in November 1979 based on his own JP supported by the small right-wing parties. On 12 September 1980 the military intervened.

Turkey has been a multi-party democracy for most of the period since the end of World War II. Despite military rule in 1960-61 and civilian rule under the shadow of the military in 1971-3, she has made considerable headway in establishing democratic institutions. Political evolution advanced steadily and domestic politics were relatively stable until the pressures of social change out-paced the ability of old and new political groups and institutions to adapt, respond or re-orient themselves. Political polarization and radicalization during the last ten years have come to threaten further peaceful evolution. Ideological polarization into Right and Left has spread through the universities, the youth of the country, teachers, the security forces, the bureaucracy and parts of organised labour. Ideological radicalism took more than 1,000 lives in 1978 with most of the assassinations carried out by the youth movements, but terror cannot be organised by the young people alone. The young certainly face serious problems – migration from the village or town to the big city, social adjustment, financial deprivation, unemployment, over-crowded universities and, finally, alienation. With terror posing a serious challenge to state authority and governmental legitimacy, Mr Ecevit declared martial law in December 1978, in the aftermath of communal armed clashes at Kahramanmaras (in south-eastern Turkey) between the adherents of the Sunni and Alevi religious sects, which caused the death of 100 people. The clash was not in fact a struggle over religious differences, though it looked like it on the surface, but (as the Minister of the Interior explained) an ideological struggle between the leftist Alevis and rightist Sunnis. This brought home the message that extremist factions are intent on exploiting religious differences. Also becoming a target in the ideological struggle is the Kurdish population (unofficially estimated at 6-8 million) living mostly in eastern Turkey. The Left is making headway among this socially and economically deprived section of the population.

In order to understand how Turkish democracy reached this point, it is necessary to look back to the 1960s, a decade which constitutes a milestone in Turkish political evolution. The experiences with modernization in the previous decades – exposure to political opposition, competitive politics and popular participation, social reforms, expanded national education, improved communications, the rush to the city and economic growth – had by then eroded most of the traditional loyalties. This changed the earlier crude stratification of society and crystallized class consciousness around economic interests. The efficient nation-wide party organizations of the 1950s educated the people in the merits of democracy, and relative emancipation from poverty and changes in the lifestyle of both the peasantry and the urban population as a result served to stimulate yet higher aspirations.

In the first half of the 1960s, therefore, Turkey seemed to be ready and willing to move to a pluralist democracy where any view and interest could be organized to compete for political and economic power. Political democracy required that all ideas should be allowed to find free expression, including those of the Left, while economic democracy required that all groups should share equitably in the allocation of national opportunities and resources, including the wealth created by economic growth. Social justice became a goal.

The political spectrum was refined and differentiated. The RPP introduced a left-of-centre philosophy in 1965, adopted social democracy and brought in Mr Ecevit to be its chairman. Its electoral strength has since increased markedly although it has fallen somewhat short of an outright majority. The JP stayed right-of-centre but improved the social content of its policies. With Mr Demirel as its leader, it won electoral victories in the 1960s but its popular support did not hold steady in the 1970s. Its rural base remained nearly intact but urban labour changed its allegiance and began to vote for the RPP. Despite differences of style and emphasis on specific issues, neither of the two major parties have proposed radical changes in foreign policy, although 'Third Worldism' is an attractive option for some in the RPP.

In 1965 a Marxist political party entered the Assembly – the Turkish parliament's lower house – for the first time, a most important event for Turkish political development. Since the criminal law bans Communism, this party – the Turkish Workers Party (TWP) – must call itself socialist. Its spectacular achievement of 1965, when it won 14 of the 450 seats in the Assembly, held out the prospect that the Turkish left might prosper within the rules of democratic competition. However, following a change in the election laws, the TWP's parliamentary strength fell to 2 seats in 1969, and after the military intervention of 1971 it was banned for acts of terrorism. Though legalized again in 1975, it has not recaptured its leadership potential. It did, however, initiate the great foreign policy debate of the mid-1960s, when the Cyprus crisis had first mobilized anti-American sentiment. For the first time in post-war history, ties with the US and NATO came under vigorous attack in public, neutralism and non-alignment were proposed instead, and memories of the Atatürk-Lenin period were revived.

Although the left failed in electoral terms, left-wing ideologies became popular both in the universities and more widely among the young. The TWP had promised to lead the movement, but its electoral failures and the divisions within its own ranks made it largely ineffectual in this role. No alternative leadership emerged and the left broke into splinter groups. Then some young people, and among them the Federation of the Revolutionary Youth, the youth affiliate of the TWP, assumed the role. Frustrated at the ballot box, some youth groups turned to terror. The violence and terror of the late 1960s brought about the military intervention of 1971, and the subsequent drive against the left further diminished its strength and broke up its unity. There are currently no less than seven Marxist-oriented parties, four of whom together obtained about one per cent of the total national vote at the last local elections, and 50 different factions among militant Marxist groups were identified in 1978, according to the Minister of the Interior.[10]

Turkey has not therefore experienced legitimate political activity of the Left for any length of time. However, the Left's initial electoral success and its appeal to the youth immediately made it seem a threat to the Turkish right. This mobilized the extreme Right into action, and in the mid-1960s it found a new leader in the person of Mr Alpaslan Turkes. He reorganized an older nationalist party into the NAP, which then led the struggle against 'Communism' (i.e. the left, no distinctions being made between the shades of socialism). Its youth affiliate was the Organization of the Hearths of Idealists, which implemented the fight. Terror became their weapon too. The militant right emerged from the quasi-military rule of 1971-3 cohesive and intact, in contrast to the left, and the NAP consolidated its strength and won 16 seats at the 1977 elections. While rejecting organic ties with the West, for fear that they would eliminate Turkish culture and identity, the NAP considers association with NATO a necessary component of Turkish foreign policy because of the organization's anti-Communist and anti-Soviet stand.

Another significant development has been the emergence of the National Salvation Party (NSP) in the latter part of the 1960s. This has campaigned for the revival of Islamic values and traditions. Because it views the penetration of Turkey by western values and influences as part of western imperialism, it is against close ties with the west, advocating instead co-operation with the community of Islam. Its present leader, Mr Erbakan, champions heavy industry as a means to self-sufficiency and therefore independence of the West. An Islamic party should not be viewed as a novel phenomenon in Turkey which contradicts the principle of secularism. Multi-party politics in the 1950s had freed the adherents of Islam from many of the official and unofficial restrictions imposed during the early years to protect the Atatürk reforms, and the NSP emerged when every shade of political aspiration could join in the democratic competition. Traditional votes made the NSP the third largest party at the elections of 1973, with 50 seats in the Assembly. In 1977, the number of seats fell to 24.

The role of religion in Turkey should not be exaggerated in the light of developments in Iran (although the recent events there are bound to affect Turkish domestic politics), for social transformation has pursued very different courses in Iran and Turkey. Atatürk's secularist reforms, with which the armed forces have traditionally been identified, were comprehensive and uncompromising, and economic growth and industrialization reinforced the secular foundations. Religious education has been kept firmly under state control, rather than being left to the responsibility of the community. Transition to democracy established a reasonable balance between secularism and the freedom to practice Islam, although the criminal law makes acts purporting to establish the State on religious foundations a crime. However, with over 90% of the population professing to be Moslem, it is impossible to claim that influences from neighbouring countries will not act as stimulants to raise new interest in Islam and new hopes for an Islamic state. The NSP can therefore be expected to be more vocal and active in the dissemination of its ideas and is likely to recruit more adherents; just as the young tend to be vulnerable to ideology, they are also open to religious propaganda. But because secularism is an essential part of Atatürk's reforms, and because feelings on the subject are very strong among those loyal to the Atatürk tradition, any movement aiming to wreck the secular foundation of the Turkish state will prove extremely divisive.

Turkey today has all the vulnerabilities of democracy in a transitional society. The two major political parties, the JP and RPP, have not been successful in meeting the conflicting demands and challenges of social change. Although the social thinking and the socio-economic priorities of the 1960s set the future course of development, the competition of ideas and policies between the two parties soon turned into a fierce conflict which was later caught up into the battle of ideologies. Because changes in social structure had eroded the traditional power bases of both parties, broken up the solidity of constituencies and created shifts in party allegiance, they could no longer count on the composition and strength of their traditional votes. Moreover, the revision of the electoral system in the 1960s further reduced the chances of election of any government by a decisive majority and allowed the rapid growth of small parties.

Unsure of their electoral following, the JP and RPP tacitly tolerated radicalism when it first appeared on the political scene in the late 1960s, and both of them drew strength from minor radical parties or social groups. However the failure of the TWP and the ban on Communism were not helpful, for they led to confusion both in the self-image of the RPP and in the image it conveyed to the JP. The Assembly was less effectively used as the arena for mutual political control and bargaining, and, as radicalism increased in the late 1960s and early 1970s, all political parties became more ideological. The centre was reduced to the small minority which had broken away from the RPP and JP. With the formation in April 1975 of the Nationalist Front Coalition Government, including the four parties of the Right, the process of polarization was nearly complete. The result was that politics in Turkey seemed to have turned into a struggle between 'fascism' and 'Communism'.

The changes in the electoral support of the two major parties and in the electoral system have also had important consequences for foreign policy. Together they have made coalition governments almost a foregone conclusion. The minor parties have acquired a potential or actual key role in the formation of any government, and this has endowed them with a power disproportionate to their parliamentary strength, as was demonstrated in the cases of the Ecevit-Erbakan coalition in 1973-74 and the four-party coalition under Mr Demirel in 1975-77. The JP and the RPP have to adjust their policies to suit these more extreme parties if they choose to form a coalition government with any one of them.

Role of The Military

The view that ascribes a modernizing role to the military in developing societies certainly applies to the influence of the Turkish military in the initial stages of Turkey's political development. Atatürk's reforms became an organic part of the social system largely with the backing of the military. However, it was also Atatürk, a soldier turned civilian, who initiated the depoliticization of the military. In the post-war period the introduction of democracy and American military assistance further strengthened the separation of the armed forces from politics, and, with increased professionalism in the military and the entrenchment of democratic institutions in the body politic, subordination of the military to civilian rule has become the established code of behaviour. Turkey today is not the Turkey of the 1920s in which the bureaucratic-military elite was the predominant power group. Though now better equipped with relatively modern weapons, the military is socially and politically less able or fitted to rule the country. The experiences of military rule in 1960-61 and military intervention in 1971 seemed to suggest that it could not govern an increasingly modern and complex society.

Yet, as the 1980 coup demonstrated, one cannot insulate a specific institution from the rest of society. The loyalty of the armed forces to the memory of Atatürk as the founder of the modern state and to his reforms has made them the guardian of those reforms, and this responsibility gives them latent power to intervene in politics when the basic principles of Kemalism are threatened. In such times of internal crisis the armed forces are therefore faced with an uncomfortable choice between preserving the sanctity of the Turkish reforms or accepting the primacy of civilian rule.

With Turkey caught up in one of the worst periods of social tension in its republican history, the rule of law was undermined and the Armed Forces faced a challenge. On the one hand, previous experiences had driven home the danger of intervention. On the other, the public was extremely tired of anarchy and demanded effective government.

On 12 September 1980 the military intervened, installing a six-man junta led by Army Chief of Staff General Kenan Evren. The military quickly reaffirmed Turkey's loyalty to

NATO, supported the economic reforms initiated by the Demirel government, promised constitutional reform and pledged a speedy return to civilian rule. Whether the intervention, and the political reform measures resulting from it, will lead to more long-term cohesion in Turkey remains unclear.

The armed forces are represented on the National Security Council, which, chaired by the President (or in his absence, by the Prime Minister), is the highest body that reviews and makes recommendations on internal and external security to the Government. It is here that the military can act legitimately to affect the formulation of defence policy. As long as civilian rule is functioning, there is widespread consensus that foreign and defence policies should be determined by the Government, with the military only providing professional military advice. This consensus and the principle of civilian supremacy, however, does not prevent people making references – resented by the military – to the possibly dominant influence of the armed forces in the choice of Turkey's foreign and security policy and to their pro-Western orientation, strengthened by their thirty-year defence co-operation with the US and, later, NATO.[11]

II. THE BACKGROUND TO SECURITY POLICY

The Turkish policy that sought a security arrangement with the US at the end of World War II culminated in membership of NATO in 1952 and has shaped Turkey's security policy ever since. What brought her into alliance with the West? Can one pinpoint some trends before the war that explain some of the strengths and weaknesses of her association with the West or throw light on her present rather uncertain commitment?[12]

Neutralism was the major feature of Turkish foreign policy in the formative years of the 1920s and 1930s. Though never systematically defined, it implied a commitment to correct diplomatic relations with European powers, non-involvement in the affairs of Europe, friendly relations with the Soviet Union and peaceful relations with other neighbours. At the root of this attitude lay the experience of the War of Independence between 1919 and 1922, which was formative for foreign policy. This was not simply a struggle against territorial occupation and dismemberment by Britain, France, Italy and Greece; politically and economically, it had an anti-imperialist thrust.[13] As a result, distance and reserve continued to dominate Turkish relations with the West for many years, while the anti-imperialist nature of Leninist foreign policy and Soviet support for the War of Independence contributed to the maintenance of warmer relations with the Soviet Union.

Domestic concerns also affected this choice. Once independence was sealed by the Treaty of Lausanne in 1923, a small, economically weak and militarily exhausted Turkey was bound to give priority to internal reconstruction, particularly if Atatürk's radical social reforms were to take root. This required a quietist foreign policy that excluded alliances and external commitments of any kind. Yet, to forestall isolation, diplomatic relations with all major powers were improved and particular attention was given to the need to build friendly relations with neighbours. By 1930 the settlement of several outstanding issues with Greece ushered in a period known in Turkey as the Ataturk-Venizelos period of friendship.

Relations with the Soviet Union occupied a special place. The Treaty of Mutual Friendship of March 1921 (the first treaty with a great power the Turkish nationalists entered into) was strengthened by a Treaty of Neutrality and Non-Aggression in 1925, and the assurance of Soviet friendship, though it lost some of its original glow in the late 1930s, was one of the main planks of Turkish foreign policy. The Montreux Convention, signed in 1936, came about largely because the Soviet Union supported Turkey's request for an international conference on the Straits. It reversed the demilitarized status of the Bosporus and Dardanelles, reinstituted Turkish control over them, and set the rules concerning transit and navigation by foreign vessels. Turkey also accepted Soviet technical and economic assistance in the 1930s, in marked contrast to her general reluctance to accept foreign assistance from European powers.[14] This special relationship was a unique

53

development, considering the history of suspicion and war between Russia and the Ottoman Empire. However, the USSR's contractual obligations and the generally friendly relations between the two countries reassured Turkey that there would be no reversion to the Czarist policy of expansion at her expense. Her major military antagonist of the past two centuries began to shed its traditional image.

Departures from Turkish neutralism occurred in the late 1930s and led to a cooling of Soviet relations. Not only had the success of modernization along Western lines strengthened the power of the political and economic elite who feared Communism and tended to favour a pro-western foreign policy, but the external environment looked more threatening because of the rise of Mussolini and Hitler. The Italian invasion of Ethiopia in 1935 was a dramatic warning to Turkey that the storm was gathering not far from her borders, and her self-imposed isolation from European affairs became difficult to sustain in the face of the rising interest of Mussolini in the Mediterranean and Hitler in the Balkans. Turkey concluded a Treaty of Alliance with Great Britain, which was ratified in October 1939 after the disclosure of the German-Soviet Non-Aggression Treaty of August of that year. Soviet foreign policy seemed concerned to accommodate Germany, and Turkish-Soviet relations went through their coldest stage in twenty years (though Turkey in fact managed to remain neutral until the closing days of World War II).[15]

Turkey's fear of German aggression was counter-balanced by misgivings about Soviet intentions, and when Soviet victories over Germany established the USSR as the unchallenged power in Eastern Europe. Turkish suspicion turned to fear. The core issue, evident even in 1939, was the Soviet wish to have *droit de regard* over the status, use and defence of the Turkish Straits, which would in effect turn them into joint Turkish-Soviet territorial waters. In March 1945 the Soviet Union notified Turkey of her intention not to extend the Treaty of Neutrality and Non-Aggression, due to expire in November of that year, on the ground that it needed revision in the light of the changes brought about by the war, and in June proposed that Turkey grant her bases on the Straits and cede two north-eastern provinces. At Potsdam and Yalta, Stalin coaxed the Western Allies to agree – they were not unwilling[16] – to a change in the status of the Straits through a revision of the Montreux Convention, and throughout 1946 the Soviet Union pressed Turkey to agree to joint control and defence of the Straits.

These demands wrecked the mutual confidence that had grown up between the two countries. They replaced the non-aggressive and inward-looking image of the youthful Soviet Union with that of an aggressive and expansionist great power.[17] Soviet demands were resisted but Turkey felt insecure.

Timing was of great importance for this shift in Turkish perceptions. What weighed heavily in Turkey's calculations was the emerging picture of a very different Europe, where a totally new configuration of power was in the making. The Soviet Union, no more the isolated, rejected outcast of world politics, dedicated to building socialism in one country, was unchallenged domestically and strong internationally, having come out of the war as one of the two strongest powers in the world and the strongest in Europe. When it could no longer depend on its own military power for security the Ottoman Empire's security policy had relied on the existence of a balance of power in Europe. The security concept of the new Turkey did not differ fundamentally from that of the later Ottomans. Security was not thought of merely as a matter of preparing to repel incursions across her borders but also as linked to the balance of power in Europe. The later Ottomans had sought security by leaning towards one or other of the European countries. The new Turkey continued to view the balance in Europe as essential for security but deliberately pursued a strikingly different foreign policy. She declined military association and overt choice in favour of one European power. But World War II had demonstrated the inadequacy of relying on the great power balance to provide security for small states, and although the proposed UN system held out the promise of a new international order, based on equality and outlawing aggression, the great powers' right of veto in the Security Council weakened this in Turkish eyes.[18]

Therefore, Turkey looked again at the balance in Europe. As that balance was in the initial stages of construction under the aegis of the US, she turned to America, the only power with the capability to counter the emerging predominant power in Europe, the Soviet Union.

Ideological considerations certainly played a role in Turkey's choice, but it is hard to say how big a role. Turkey's leaders did have an aversion to Communism, but Turkish diplomatic history suggests that the response would have been essentially the same had the threat come from a non-Communist Russia. The cycles that Soviet – Turkish relations had gone through since 1939 complicated the Turkish decision makers' diagnosis of the real intentions and objectives of the Soviet Union concerning Turkey. On the other hand, for the long-term choice, one should look for the answer in the domestic structure and the socio-economic basis of power. The lure of co-operation with a capitalist giant and the desire to be accepted by the community of Europe must have influenced the decision of a generation of officials and interest groups trained in, and moulded by, western concepts of modernization.

The past, then, offers some insights into Turkish foreign and security policies, and these were particularly relevant when those policies entered a transitional stage with the phasing out of the Cold War. Turkish neutralism was short-lived, in contrast to (say) the 150-year old tradition of Sweden and it was never a constitutional neutralism, like that of Switzerland. Nevertheless, when problems appear in Turkey's relations with the Western Alliance, and domestic groups propose a neutralist foreign policy, the period of the 1920s and early 1930s seems not unattractive as a model. Furthermore the memories of Turkey's War of Independence against several major European powers not only arouse sympathy for wars of liberation in Asia and Africa but also provide a rationale for a third-world identity and raises questions about the perpetual validity of that adversary image of the Soviet Union which has become a near cliché in Western thinking. As one western commentator has said, 'It is an often-asserted half-truth that Russia is Turkey's ancestral enemy. So it is. But the Turkish Republic won its independence in alliance with the Soviet Union, and until the Forties suffered no interference from it in spite of a policy of neutrality'.[19] Yet if these are the attractions of the past, the Soviet behaviour of the 1940s tended to offset them.

Europe today is stable because there is an approximate balance of military power. Balance of power has serious shortcomings as a mechanism of peace; its spectacular failures in recent history are sufficient proof. It requires constant alertness to keep it stable, it encourages the arms race, it subordinates the national will and tends to freeze a country as a constant adversary in the eyes of the other side. Still it is this balance that has preserved the peace in Europe, and all states, large and small, have benefited from it. However, had the Soviet Union not pushed Turkey into the western fold with her demands in 1945-6, the same balance might have been maintained without Turkey's participation, and she might then have enjoyed the benefits of peace without having to choose between the two poles. Since nuclear deterrence protects all the small powers of Europe, it is possible to contemplate enjoying the fruits of the European balance without any actual commitment to maintaining it except in a negative sense, but a Turkish move to neutralism might have the effect *now* of altering the rather delicate political and military balance in Europe.

All recent Turkish governments have reaffirmed their belief in the need to contribute to the maintenance of that balance. Nevertheless, the present stability of European security might seem to provide room for smaller powers to opt out of the military blocs built and run by the major powers and to fall back on their individual security efforts. The examples of Sweden and Yugoslavia, which have deliberately stayed out of the European balance-of-power system and based their security policy on national efforts, tends to complement the Turkish precedent of the 1920s and 1930s and hold out a prospective alternative under contemporary conditions. Moreover, the legacy of Turkey's War of Independence, over half a century ago, continues to assign supreme value to the concepts of complete sovereignty and equality in relation to the rest of the world. Turks find it difficult, particularly in time of peace, to reconcile the restrictions on sovereignty that Alliance ties require with the ideological basis of the new Turkish State at its birth.

III. THE SECURITY ENVIRONMENT

In the narrow sense Turkey's security environment is influenced by three factors: geographical location, the uneven distribution of political-military power and history. In the broader sense, however, it is the salient issues and the rhythm of world and regional politics that spotlight and even overaccentuate her security sensitivity and therefore her security needs. The general bipolar structure, its strategic priorities in political and military terms, the pivotal position of Europe and the critical importance of the Middle East tend to create political, military and ideological behaviour patterns in the super-powers, as well as in local actors in the neighbourhood around Turkey which then are inclined to intersect around her.

Geography has given Turkey command of Asia Minor and the Straits, which together form the link between the Balkans and the Middle East. It has also given her a geopolitical and strategic significance which is due, above all, to her common borders with the Soviet Union. The immense discrepancy in the power position of each and in their respective strategic foreign policy objectives has rendered Turkey's geopolitical significance a touchy subject for security. Proximity to the Middle East is the other dimension of her security sensitivity. She is a potential stepping stone for any world power who may contemplate reaching the area of the Persian Gulf. She could also be used as a shield and hence her importance is enhanced for East and West, both of whom suspect the other of intentions to gain control of the Gulf area. Her value to outsiders not only puts her in the middle of the super-power contest but complicates her relations with her Arab neighbours and friends who have the freedom of political association with either of the super-powers, while enjoying physical disassociation from both.

The Soviet Union
Historically, all Turkey's immediate neighbours, with the exception of the Soviet Union and Iran, were at one time part of the Ottoman Empire, and this still gives rise to issues such as territorial claims. Yet, of all these neighbours, it is the Soviet Union that occupies the predominant position. In north-east Turkey there is 610 km of common border, and the two countries also face each other across the Black Sea.

The Straits remain at the heart of Turkish Soviet relations. According to the Montreux Convention, they are open to the transit and navigation of warships in time of peace, subject to certain restrictions on the size, type and number in transit at any time, and to advance notification of intent to transit. In time of war, the Straits would obviously be closed in the event of Turkey's belligerency but a non-belligerent Turkey can also close them if she feels threatened.

The Soviet Union has traditionally sought to create neutral or friendly neighbours, yet she has shaped her security policy in the post-war period within the broader framework of competition and confrontation with the United States. Turkish security interacts with Soviet security at both levels but this interaction is rarely an independent phenomenon. It has been – and will be – influenced by Soviet relations with other centres of power. The Soviet pressures and demands on Turkey in the 1940s can be construed as part of the USSR's need for greater security on her southern borders. Soviet naval weakness in the Black Sea left part of these borders exposed, not to a threat from Turkey but to one from non-Black Sea powers – such as the United States – operating in the Mediterranean. Soviet insistence on a change in the regime of the Straits, in order to close them to warships of non-Black Sea powers, was a manifestation of that concern. But what may have appeared as legitimate from the standpoint of Soviet security seemed to threaten Turkish security.

How the Soviet Union would like its neighbours to behave was set out by Mr Khrushchev in a note to the Turkish Prime Minister Gen. Gürsel in 1960: 'You are well aware of our attitude to military blocs, and also our views on participation in them on the part of our neighbours, and I would not be frank if I did not state this now, too. Of course, I shall say this frankly – it is our deep conviction that the most sincere relations between our two neighbour countries would develop if Turkey embarked upon the road of neutrality.' Neutrality in the Soviet view, it was mad clear, did not mean armed neutrality. 'This neutralism would only benefit the country. Turkey would receive an opportunity to use her resources, not for war preparations, on which huge funds have so far been squandered, but for raising the level of the country's national economy. Military expenditures are a bottomless pit and not every country can endure the burden of them and develop its economy at the same time.'[20]

In terms of their direct impact on the security environment of Turkey, the Soviet Union's interest and involvement in the Middle East, the Horn of Africa and the Mediterranean stand out. Though at least in part intended to counter American power and influence, the regional manifestations of the Soviet Union's global policy have direct implications for Turkey, which sits between the USSR and the region in which she is interested. The Straits and Turkish airspace are astride the Soviet routes to the Middle East and the Mediterranean, and Soviet power projection is affected so long as Turkey has full control over them. If Soviet aircraft could overfly Turkey at will, this could greatly reduce the time needed to deploy forces by air to the Gulf, to Lebanon or to Syria.[21]

The growth of Soviet naval power in the Mediterranean since the 1960s is one major element that has changed the military balance to the south of Turkey. The Soviet Fifth Eskadra has not only broken the American naval monopoly in the Mediterranean but has triggered a debate among Western strategists about the future ability of the US Sixth Fleet to project power ashore and to keep open the sea lanes, particularly in the Eastern Mediterranean. With the withdrawal of one of two carrier task forces for tasks in the Indian Ocean, this debate can only become sharper.

This is another manifestation of the way the Soviet Union interprets her security needs. She sees herself now as a Mediterranean power. Admiral Gorshkov was quoted by Tass in 1968 as follows: 'The Soviet Union as a Black Sea power and, consequently, a Mediterranean power, is exercising its indisputable right to have a presence in this region'. Accordingly, he said, the contemporary Soviet Navy has the same mission as that of the old Russian Navy in the Mediterranean, namely to provide 'the foremost line of defence of the country' against threats from the southwest.[22] On the basis of this reasoning, Turkey falls within the forward defence zone of the Soviet Union. Because she also forms part of the forward defences of the West, her position is peculiarly exposed and she is driven to seek security ties with others.

The rights of the Soviet Union as a Mediterranean power brings with it prerogatives because, again in the words of Admiral Gorshkov, 'The location of her forces in these waters is based not only on geographical conditions, but also the age-old need for the Russian Navy to stay there'.[23] The bulk of the Soviet Mediterranean Fleet comes from the Black Sea Fleet, except for the submarines. How the Soviet Union could practically exercise her rights to be a Mediterranean power without compromising Turkish rights is therefore not clear if, for example, a non-belligerent Turkey, feeling threatened, wished to close the Straits.

The passage of the aircraft carrier *Kiev* through the Straits in 1976, after being built in a Black Sea shipyard, was a vivid example of the interplay of the Soviet Union's global strategy with Turkish rights and security. The *Kiev* has been described by the Soviet Union as an anti-submarine cruiser, though she is usually viewed as an aircraft carrier in the west.[24] Aircraft carriers are not listed among the capital ships that Black Sea powers are permitted to pass through the Straits according to the provisions of the Montreux Convention and its Annex II. Turkey accepted the official Soviet description, but there was a general feeling in the West that the *Kiev's* passage was a violation of the provisions of the Convention. The incident emphasized the Soviet Union's dependence on the Straits and the limits on Turkey's ability to influence the strategic environment and events despite the Montreux Convention. If the Gorshkov quotation is any guide, Turkey must be prepared to face new interpretations of the Convention as Soviet naval technology progresses and naval capability expands.

Turkey's significance for the Soviet Union (as for the West) is not confined to the Turkish control of the Straits. Turkey is a large and potentially influential country. A Soviet radio commentator made this point: 'There is no doubt that Turkey will be able to play a considerably more positive role in international relations, particularly in the region where it is situated. First, it should not be forgotten that Turkey of today is a country with a population of 40,000,000. There are rich natural resources in Turkey to ensure her rapid economic development. Finally, from the point of view of the position of her territory, Turkey cannot, of course remain indifferent to events in Europe, particularly in the Balkans and east Mediterranean region, and to the Middle East question'.[25]

Besides the Straits, North-western Turkey is also a particularly important area for security. Called Turkish Thrace, it is Turkey's only foothold in Europe and has frontiers of 269 km with Bulgaria and 212 km with Greece. In contrast to its small size (3% of the country's land area), Turkish Thrace is one of the most densely populated and developed areas of Turkey, and, with the Straits behind it and lacking depth and natural barriers, it is clearly very vulnerable. Because of the primary psychological importance of the Straits and İstanbul and because of its industrial potential, a threat directed at this region will always be taken very seriously. While good relations with Bulgaria within the larger framework of detente have removed the sense of imminent danger, this sense of vulnerability will continue to ensure that top priority will be given to the security of this region. It is Bulgaria as a Warsaw Pact member rather than as a neighbour that weighs on Turkish security priorities and plans.

Turkey and Greece
The exacerbation of antagonism in Greek-Turkish relations has, since 1963, been the salient security issue in Turkish eyes. Disagreements over Cyprus, and more recently over sovereign rights in the Aegean are at the basis of the hostility. Whatever the arguments, history dominates perceptions and conditions behaviour, and this history is a long one of bitter disputes, enmities and wars between two peoples with different cultural creeds and values. For the Greeks, the struggle has been about liberation from alien rule and the recovery of historic lands. For the Turks, it was, until 1919-22, a story of defeats and retreats. The Cyprus conflict of 1963-4 rekindled for Turkey the suspicion of a revival of Greek irredentism and the memory of great-power support that stood behind the major Greek-Turkish confrontations of the past.

Greek-Turkish relations were normalized by the Treaty of Lausanne in 1923, which was signed by Turkey, Greece and the Western powers after the Greek-Turkish War of 1919-22. This established a balance between Greece and Turkey by defining the boundaries of territorial sovereignty in such a way that neither could obtain military preponderance in the Aegean. The Dodecanese Islands in the south-eastern Aegean were given to Italy, which in turn lost them to Greece after the Second World War as a result of the Paris Treaty of 1947. Both these Treaties stipulated the demilitarization and defortification of the islands along Turkey's coastline.

There are four disputed issues: control over airspace in the Aegean, delimitation of the continental shelf, the limits of territorial waters, and Cyprus.[26]

Control of Air Space
Within the spirit of co-operation that emerged with Greek and Turkish admission into NATO in 1952, control of Aegean airspace was left to the technical responsibility of Greece by bilateral agreement. Turkey argues that this technical responsibility was used as though it entitled Greece to establish sovereignty over the Aegean airspace. Following the Turkish military intervention in Cyprus in 1974, Turkey declared a 'security zone' west of the Flight Information Region (FIR) line agreed in May 1952. This roughly divided the Aegean airspace into two. The response of Greece was to declare a 'danger zone' which amounted to the closing of the Aegean airspace to all non-Greek civil and military traffic. In February 1980, Turkey withdrew her claim to control all air traffic over the Eastern Aegean and Greece responded by revoking the civil aviation notice of 1974 which declared the Aegean unsafe for all air traffic but her own. Direct air links could resume.

Continental Shelf
The jump in oil prices in 1974 was a major impetus to this dispute. Greece began to search for oil in 1963 and started to drill near the island of Thasos, in the northern Aegean in 1973. A Greek note of February 1974 protested against Turkey's granting oil exploration licence areas

in the Aegean to the Turkish Petroleum Company. In effect, Greece maintained that such oil exploration ventures in the Aegean violated the continental shelf of Greek islands. The Greek position is based on legal grounds, specifically the provisions of the 1958 Geneva Convention on the Continental Shelf which provide islands with continental shelf areas. If applied to the Aegean, this view would deny Turkey almost all continental shelf rights and turn the Aegean into a *de facto* Greek lake, by virtue of the existence of some 3,050 Greek islands scattered through the Aegean and the proximity of a number of them to the Turkish mainland. Turkey, on the other hand, maintains that the Aegean has special characteristics which require a special solution. Turkey is not a party to the 1958 Geneva Convention and disagrees with its provisions in view of recent developments that are taking place in the UN Conference on the Law of the Sea (UNCLOS). She proposes to seek a political solution to the question of the delimitation of the continental shelf based on the principals of equity and equality. Greece took the issue to the International Court of Justice in August 1976, but in December 1978 this ruled that it had no competence in the matter. There have been negotiations on this issue also, but without tangible results. Turkey has suggested the joint exploration and exploitation of the resources of the Aegean seabed, which would amount to the establishment of an international oil consortium, but Greece has so far not accepted the suggestion.

Territorial Waters
The Treaty of Lausanne set the limit of territorial waters at 3 nautical miles. Greece unilaterally extended her territorial waters to 6 miles in 1936. Turkey followed in 1964. The trend of UNCLOS is to allow a limit of 12 miles, which, if implemented in the Aegean, would solve by proxy the continental shelf issue in favour of Greece and reduce the international navigable waters by more than half. Turkey considers that a Greek declaration of a 12-mile limit in the Aegean would be a *casus belli*, since such a declaration, however much it might be in line with the draft international convention prepared by UNCLOS, would intolerably restrict Turkey's communications to and from the Mediterranean, with serious consequences for her defence, and economic and commercial viability. Greece, however, states that she has no intention of adopting the 12-mile limit for the moment. A related issue concerns the militarization and fortification by Greece of her islands off the Turkish coast, which, Turkey argues, violates the pertinent Treaties and she feels that the consequence of the changes in the past few years have been to upset the balance established at Lausanne to the disadvantage of Turkey. The Turkish 'Army of the Aegean' also seems to frighten Greece.

Cyprus
Turkey's interest in the status of Cyprus is, in essence, a response to the situation in the Aegean. An extension of Greek sovereignty to Cyprus through *Enosis* would substantially enlarge the maritime area under Greek control. Moreover, the size of Cyprus and its proximity to the Turkish mainland make it particularly important for Turkish security. The island lies at the entrance of the Gulf of Iskenderun, the innermost corner of the north-eastern Mediterranean, and is large enough for any hostile power to deploy sufficient military force for sustained air, naval, or amphibious operations against Turkey. It is close enough to allow an enemy to launch a substantial surprise attack, in marked contrast to problems that would be faced in an air raid taking off from mainland Greece.

Turkey's Southern Borders
Turkey shares common borders with Syria (877kms) and Iraq (331kms). The unfavourable memories of Ottoman domination and the excesses of Turkish foreign policy in the 1950s have diminished. Since the 1960s a degree of mutual confidence prevails between the three countries, and neither Iraq nor Syria poses a threat to Turkey. The only major potential source of discord between Syria and Turkey is the former's dissatisfaction over Hatay (Alexandretta), a Turkish province on the Mediterranean. When relations were strained in the past (as in 1957, when they were on the brink of war) Syria has often launched a campaign demanding the return of Hatay, but the possibility of the question being revived is small, so long as Syria does not have other complaints against Turkey.

The major source of security concern for

Turkey is a more general regional instability – increasing tension among the local contenders and between the super-powers, rather than the threat of direct military aggression. The change of regime in Iran and the Peace Treaty between Israel and Egypt have caused all regional states to search for new bargaining positions, whether by consolidating old alignments or creating new constellations of power.

Until the early 1960s Turkey could not avoid siding with pro-Western Arab States in inter-Arab disputes. Her membership of the Baghdad Pact and her anti-Communist and anti-Soviet stand during the Cold War infuriated the proponents of Arab nationalism, socialism and anti-colonialism. Indeed she actively interfered in inter-Arab disagreements. But in the 1960s she began to take a neutral stand in inter-Arab disagreements, and this, combined with her pro-Arab position in the Arab–Israeli conflict since 1967, has removed the major sources of conflict with the Arab world.

At a time when the region as a whole is undergoing rather rapid political, social and military change, Turkey is trying hard to avoid any commitment with regard to the Israeli-Egyptian Peace Treaty, although she is in favour of a comprehensive settlement and has called for Israeli withdrawal from the occupied territories and the recognition of the legitimate rights of the Palestinians (including the right of statehood) as a basis for a just and permanent peace. Furthermore, diplomatic recognition of the PLO, which she had already agreed to in principle in 1975-6, was consummated in August 1979, shortly after the seizure of the Egyptian Embassy in Ankara by four terrorists, members of the PLO's Syrian-based affiliate *Al-Saika*.

Turkey was reported to have denied a US request in early spring 1979 for landing rights for military helicopters to help with the evacuation of US citizens in Iran. Iranian army units were reported to have crossed the Turkish border in the summer of 1979 in order to encircle Kurdish forces in Iranian towns close to the border, but the Turkish Government denied this, except in the case of the entry of 88 Iranian soldiers, who were duly returned. There were also reports that Turkish security forces discovered large arms caches in eastern Turkey, one of which contained 400 Soviet-made anti-tank rockets, apparently smuggled from Syria by Turkish radical groups engaged in Kurdish separatist activities.[27] References to American plans to use Turkey as a staging post in a Middle Eastern contingency were also most disconcerting. *Fortune* magazine wrote that the spearhead of any US Middle East intervention force would include the 82nd Airborne Division and that the planning exercises indicated that the entire division could be moved to Turkey in 24 hours.[28] In an interview with a Turkish daily, Ronald Spiers, the American Ambassador to Ankara, described an American intervention in the Middle East as unlikely,[29] but Turkish concerns have not been eased. Examination of American policy statements and studies indicate that the US has certainly not discarded the option of using force to protect Western interests in the Middle East.

Turkey's preoccupation with an American airlift and staging posts is acute. While the possibility of Soviet military moves aimed at the Gulf would also be threatening to Turkey, this seems less likely than a contingency in which the US might use force overtly, while Soviet involvement might be exercised through a proxy. In this event Turkey could find herself in a dangerous predicament if the US wanted to use, for example, Incirlik air base – a scenario reminiscent of the US intervention in Lebanon in 1958, but more dangerous. Such an eventuality would not only destroy the Arab-Turkish rapprochement carefully built up during the past decade but would make Turkey a partner in an extremely risky military operation which is not within NATO.

A new element for Turkish security is the on/off union between Syria and Iraq. The Syrian-Iraqi rapprochement in 1978 reduced the degree to which Iraq relies on the Mosul-Iskenderun pipeline, since Iraq could then pump her oil to Mediterranean ports via the new pipeline that runs through Syria. The pipelines have become vital to Iraq as a result of the war with Iran. Though not directed against Turkey, a political and military union of the two countries, however unlikely that now appears, would introduce a new security factor. In the event of military integration, the combined strength of Syrian and Iraqi armed forces would be equivalent to those of Turkey,and both countries' combined annual defence expenditure would be roughly twice Turkey's. Moreover the

Soviet Union has a fifteen-year Treaty of Friendship and Co-operation with Iraq (signed in 1972 and amended in 1979), and one with Syria was signed in 1980. The Soviet Union may well respond to any calls for support from Syria and Iraq (whether linked or separate) in order to demonstrate her support for the progressive faction in the Arab world, although both super-powers seem likely to move with caution.

Short of general war, developments in the Middle East threaten Turkey in two ways. First, by raising the spectre of political and economic pressure from local neighbours and, secondly, because the super-powers are likely to demand support for their positions. If she has to make a choice, it is more likely to follow the line taken by Syria, Iraq, Libya and the Soviet Union, not only because the three of the four are neighbours, and because Turkey depends on oil supplies from Iraq and Libya, but also because she has become sympathetic to the cause of the Palestinians. The Soviet Union, too, has shown that she would like to see Turkey support a comprehensive settlement. The US asked for support against Iran. The prospects of Turkey insulating herself from the political and military cross-currents in the Middle East look dim. Furthermore, there are domestic forces which would like Turkey to have influence in the region. Yet Turkey must have learned from the lessons of the 1950s that to play an active role in Arab disputes creates problems for her own security. On the whole, abstention would seem preferable to involvement though such a policy would not exclude giving diplomatic support for a comprehensive settlement.

The Effects of Recent Developments in Iran

The revolution in Iran is important for Turkey for political and social reasons and for internal security. The Turkish-Iranian border has traditionally been free of incidents, and the Revolution was greeted with favour, but an Islamic state with a Kurdish minority clamouring for autonomy has rather serious security implications for Turkey, because she too has a Kurdish minority. Whether or not the new regime survives, the Revolution has set a dynamic example for all those desiring emancipation from central authority (even if Iran seems unlikely to escape from authoritarianism), for this remains a common feature of radical and traditional Arab regimes alike. It has also enhanced the status of Islam as a socio-political system.

Turkey is left as the only country in the northern Middle East with a contractual defence arrangement with the West, and this is an uncomfortably isolated position. If Iran pursues an independent foreign policy (as she seems likely to do), her example will strongly attract Turkey, especially if Iran manages at the same time to keep a distance from the Soviet Union, and calls for non-alignment are likely to receive a new impetus in Turkey. The formal dissolution of CENTO in March 1979 was not in itself a blow, since it had lost most of its security value long before, but the dissolution, coming as it did at a time of acute uncertainty and against a background of drastic change, including the coup in Afghanistan in the Spring of 1978, sharpened the sense that Turkey is vulnerable and exposed. It is impossible to speculate about future Iranian-Turkish co-operation, because the internal picture in Iran is so unsettled, but civil war in Iran and the disintegration of the central authority leading to outside intervention is an eventuality which would touch directly on Turkish security, for that instability may not be confined within Iran.

A fundamentalist Islamic state next to Turkey's borders is clearly a challenge. It will not wreck the foundations of the secular state in Turkey, but it will encourage pro-Islamic political forces into more overt and uninhibited activities, and this in turn will add a new dimension to internal polarization. The impact on foreign policy may be more pronounced. The Revolution in Iran has already tended to channel the search for alternative foreign policies towards the idea of Islamic co-operation. The National Salvation Party (NSP) has been pointing in this direction for over a decade and has now become more outspoken on the question. The Marxist and Maoist Left is still nearly unanimously convinced that a rupture of ties with the West will be in Turkey's interests, and might settle for a temporary coalition with pro-Islamic forces to promote this. The Maoist Left in particular is also a staunch advocate of the idea of security co-operation with Islamic countries in order to thwart the growth of Soviet influence in the region and as part of the anti-imperialist struggle in general.

It is possible that the Kurdish moves for autonomy in Iran have already provided a new source of strength for the Kurds in Turkey. The issue of the Kurdish minority in Turkey has always been a sensitive one, and there has been a semi-official silence on the question of its loyalty to the central government. The Kurds were provoked to revolt in the time of Atatürk, but the designs for Kurdish independence go back into Ottoman history, when the great powers did not refrain from using such ethnic groups for their own purposes. In the last few years there have been quite frequent reports of a drive by several leftist groups to arouse the Kurds to press for demands ranging from autonomy to independence. It is possible that, at a time when Turkey already faces a host of internal and external problems, the Kurds may have become a useful tool for both internal and external forces seeking to put pressure on her.

When the Middle East is in turmoil and the stakes for outside powers are so high, Turkey is bound to feel insecure, fearing pressure for concessions, blackmail or aggression against her. Nevertheless, it is still her internal unity that is most acutely and immediately threatened.

IV. PAST REMEDIES: ALLIANCES AND WESTERN INTEGRATION

The Truman Doctrine of 1947 marked the beginning of the American policy of 'long-term, patient but firm and vigilant containment of Russian expansionist tendencies'.[30] It was this doctrine that first established a defence relationship between Turkey and the United States which was eventually to lead to Turkey's accession to NATO in February 1952.

In the specific cases of Turkey and Greece, containment policy aimed at preventing the Soviet Union from gaining control of Europe's flank in the Eastern Mediterranean. While Turkey's admission to NATO was essentially a continuation of this policy, it must also be seen in the context of new international developments. The most important of these was the Korean War, which was viewed in the West as the opening round of a new, aggressive phase in Soviet policy for which Europe could be the next possible target.[31] It also showed that the policy of containment was inadequate without the willingness and capability to fight a limited war.[32] The North Korean invasion of South Korea in 1950 precipitated western military integration. NATO's strategic doctrine was revised in 1950 to incorporate the concept of a 'forward strategy' to be implemented by means of a large conventional build-up in Europe,[33] and the NATO Council meeting at Lisbon in February 1952 set a goal of 96 ground-force divisions (excluding reserves) to be achieved by 1954.

Apprehension about over-extending the Alliance's area of responsibility into the Eastern Mediterranean and the Middle East had been among the reasons for NATO's previous reluctance to admit Turkey, as had social, cultural and economic differences. When the policy of containment was reformulated, in the light of the Korean experience, so as to draw a clear line around the Sino-Soviet periphery and support that frontier with strategic air power,[34] the implications of Turkish accession changed. Turkish bases became important, and Turkey helped to complete the frontier from Norway to the eastern end of the Mediterranean. Her consent to participate in a Middle Eastern Command promised to extend the frontier still further in order to keep the Soviet Union out of the Middle East. The large Turkish army became an asset at a time when strategic thinking assigned a significant deterrent value to local ground forces.[35] And as NATO strategy and defence plans evolved to suit new needs and new circumstances, Turkey's role also changed. NATO began to incorporate tactical and theatre nuclear weapons into its strategy between 1954 and 1957. Evidence appearing in the autumn of 1957 that the Soviet Union was advancing towards an ICBM capability increased the United States' sense of vulnerability and led her to deploy *Jupiter* and *Thor* IRBM in Europe as an interim measure, and after the NATO Council meeting in December 1957 Turkey consented to the stationing of the *Jupiters* on her soil. With the deployment of the *Polaris* SLBM, these IRBM became obsolete and were withdrawn from Turkey in 1963 but not before the Cuban missile crisis had allowed Krushchev to tie the removal of the Soviet missiles from Cuba to the removal of the *Jupiters* from Turkey.[36]

Turkey then appeared very vulnerable both to a Soviet pre-emptive nuclear attack and to a retaliatory strike. During the Cuban crisis, as during the U-2 incident of 1960, the concept of 'hostage Europe' was viewed in Turkey as 'hostage Turkey'.

The advent of a policy of mutual assured destruction in the late 1960s and the attainment of strategic parity by the Soviet Union changed the rules of super-power interaction and opened the way for a dialogue; containment became much less relevant. Also in the 1960s, NATO adopted the strategy of flexible response, and the Soviet Union began to acquire global reach. She outflanked Turkey and established her influence in the Middle East and a presence in the Mediterranean. Together, these forward moves enhanced Turkey's value for western security. The control of the Turkish Straits and Turkish airspace have become more critical for the defence of western interests in the Mediterranean and the Middle East, and they are generally seen as Turkey's major tasks in NATO defence.

The question of Turkey's strategic significance and her contribution to western security became a subject of renewed public controversy with the imposition of an arms embargo by the US Congress as a result of Turkey's intervention in Cyprus. This was effective between 5 February 1975 and 4 September 1978. Congressional advocates of the embargo tended to accept the view that technological developments had eroded Turkey's value to NATO. The Ford and Carter Administrations' spokesmen took the opposite view. At a hearing before the Senate Foreign Relations Committee on 5 September 1976, Deputy Defence Secretary Robert Ellsworth summarized Turkey's significance as: allowing NATO to control the Straits, forming a buffer between the USSR and the Middle East, diverting Warsaw Pact forces from the central region, and denying the Soviet Union overflight privileges. The availability of bases and facilities that played an important role in the US strategic position in the Middle East and eastern Mediterranean were also stressed, as was the availability of electronic intelligence facilities that allowed the US to collect unique and important data on Soviet scientific, technological and military activities, and to monitor Soviet compliance with SALT I and the pending SALT II agreement. He also noted the political significance of American-Turkish ties as a symbol of US interest in the Middle East.[37] Professor Albert Wohlstetter, in a statement on 15 April 1978 before the House International Relations committee, testified in a similar manner and specifically rejected the argument that new weapons technologies have made the Turkish armed forces, facilities and geographical position obsolete: 'It simply romanticizes technology to suggest that ICBMs or any other sophisticated technology erase the strategic importance of Turkey or Greece'.[38]

The current assessment seems to be that Turkey remains vital to the security of NATO's southern flank and that, while she is not directly vital to the defence of the central sector, her contribution will be important indirectly, because 'if the southern flank is not secure, other NATO forces, particularly those in central Europe will be greatly weakened' and because 'the defence of the Center cannot be separated from the defence of either flank'.[39]

Admission to NATO fixed Turkey's place in the West. The initiative for increasing ties with the US and later for membership of NATO had come during the last years of the RPP Administration. The landslide victory of the Democrat Party in 1950 therefore only strengthened the new direction of Turkey's foreign and defence policies. Prime Minister Menderes was an articulate supporter of the idea of solidarity with the 'free world'. Except for some opposition to legal and procedural matters by the major opposition party (by then the RPP), bipartisan foreign policy was the rule until the 1960s.

The security link with Europe was buttressed by others. Membership or ties of association with a number of western European institutions, ultimately aimed at European unity or integration of one type or another, broadened the relationship into the political, social and economic spheres. Having been a recipient of Marshall Plan assistance, Turkey became a member of the OEEC; in 1949 she became a member of the European Council, and in 1964 an associate member of the EEC. Within a decade Turkey became, for all political and strategic purposes, a member of the West. Although socially and economically she lagged far behind, there was domestic consensus which looked forward to full association with the West until the mid 1960s.

Military Integration and Defence Co-operation
Turkey's land, air and sea area comes under the Commander-in-Chief, Allied Forces Southern Europe (CINCSOUTH) whose Headquarters are in Naples. Two NATO subcommands, LANDSOUTHEAST and SIXATAF used to operate at Izmir, Turkey but their headquarters were turned over to Turkish command on 1 July 1978. The land commander is now directly responsible to CINCSOUTH and the air commander to CINCSOUTH's principle air subordinate, COMAIRSOUTH.

Turkey earmarked the equivalent of 15 divisions for assignment to NATO at the time of her entry. Three-quarters of her ground forces of about 470,000 men, now organized in to some 23 divisional equivalents, are therefore formally earmarked for NATO.[40] Her air forces, which now include 13 fighter attack squadrons and about 50,000 men, are also earmarked for assignment to SACEUR. Her navy comes under the 'other forces earmarked for NATO' category. Of the three land armies, the First Army is responsible for the defence of the Straits and Turkish Thrace, the Third Army for eastern Turkey along the Soviet border, and the Second Army for the south along the Syrian and Iraqi borders.[41] The Fourth Army, outside NATO and basically a new command established in 1975 in case of a dangerous escalation of tensions with Greece, is known as 'The Army of the Aegean'; the assignment of Turkish forces to NATO has been unaffected by its creation.

Despite the NATO links, defence co-operation has proceeded more or less as a bilateral relationship between Turkey and the United States, almost to the exclusion, at least until recently, of co-operation with Western Europe. In practice, co-operation meant American access to Turkish territory for facilities and bases, and the improvement of the defence capability of the Turkish armed forces with American help. Between 1946 and 1974, Turkey received $3.7 billion in military assistance[42], the form of assistance changing over time from grants to credits and cash sales. In 1964 West Germany became the second major source of military help, providing about DM 35 million of assistance annually in the 1960s, rising to an annual DM 70 million in the 1970s, and by 1979 a total of DM 800 million had been received from West Germany. In 1980, the German defence budget earmarked a further DM 600 million for the modernization of the Turkish armed forces to be spent up to 1984.

Expansion of the Turkish military infrastructure was also carried out with NATO infrastructure funds, and, as with other Mediterranean members of NATO, the value of Alliance infrastructure projects in Turkey ($150 million up to 1971) has exceeded Turkey's contribution to the programme.[43] There are 14 NADGE (NATO Air Defence Ground Environment) early-warning sites spread throughout the country. Briefings on the sensitive and sophisticated Airborne Early-Warning and Control System (AWACS), given to Turkish officials by American officials in Ankara in 1978, suggest that there are plans to further enhance the early-warning system.[44]

The American presence and activities were regulated by the so-called 'bilateral agreements'. Based in principle on Article 3 of the NATO Treaty and the NATO Status of Forces Agreement of 1951, they became the subject of intensive public debate in Turkey in the mid-1960s, because they lacked a coherent, systematic structure, and it was therefore impossible for Turkey to possess comprehensive knowledge of, and exercise control over, American activities.[45] Under public pressure, the Turkish government renegotiated these Agreements with the United States and a Joint US-Turkish Defence Co-operation Agreement was signed on 3 July 1969. This formed the basis of defence co-operation until 1975, when the Cyprus crisis of the previous year and the ensuing arms embargo had severely strained US-Turkish relations. On 25 July 1975 the Turkish Government declared that the 1969 Agreement had lost its legal validity in view of the American action since 5 February 1974, on which date the sale and transfer of arms to Turkey had been forbidden, thereby unilaterally violating the principle of defence co-operation on which the Agreement was built. Turkey asked the United States to suspend operations at all major installations except the Incirlik air base, where American aircraft also have NATO missions. A new Agreement was signed on 16 March 1976 to regulate the status of the facilities and ensure the flow of military assistance for the following four years, but the arms embargo overrode this in the light of the deadlock over a Cyprus settlement. The US Congress reversed its embargo decision (already partially lifted in October 1975) on 4 August 1978, and arms transfers were resumed in September 1978 on a conditional basis. In October 1978 the operations of many of the major US facilities were re-started on a temporary (one-year) basis. A new defence agreement was signed on 30 March 1980. Under it, a total of 12 installations remain US-controlled. These include the major air base at Incirlik, two intelligence-gathering radar installations on the Black Sea and a seismic station near Ankara, together with logistic and navigational facilities.

Several of these American facilities and bases in Turkey are of primary importance.[46] Installations at Sinop on the Black Sea coast and Karamursel on the south-east shore of the Sea of Marmara are involved with electronic intelligence activities. Sinop is a radar monitoring and communications facility, collecting data on the Soviet air and naval activities in the Black Sea and on missile testing activities both in the Black Sea and inside the Soviet Union. The radar installations track Soviet missile launches from various testing sites and monitor other Soviet military activities. Belbasi, near Ankara, is a seismographic detection base monitoring Soviet nuclear tests. The Incirlik air base houses US aircraft deployed in rotation from Torrejón in Spain and Aviano in Italy; this, the most forward deployment of land-based American aircraft in the Eastern Mediterranean, provides a capability for launching a tactical nuclear strike against the Soviet Union. Iskenderun and Yumurtalik are the most important supply, fuel and storage centres for American military forces in the region.

Turkey's relationship with the Alliance was tested by the Cyprus conflict, first in 1964, and again in 1974. The persistence of intercommunal armed clashes in Cyprus after December 1963 and the failure of both diplomatic attempts and the UN Force in Cyprus (UNFICYP) to resolve the situation led Turkey to contemplate military intervention several times in 1964. Article 4 of the Treaty of Guarantee, signed when the Republic of Cyprus was established, permits unilateral action to restore the *status quo* if collective action by the guarantor powers – Britain, Greece and Turkey – fails. In June 1964 the United States warned Turkey against military action. This warning (popularly known as the 'Johnson Letter') forestalled Turkish intervention, but it also shook Turkey out of the comfortable feeling of security she had found in NATO, for President Johnson reminded her that 'a military intervention in Cyprus by Turkey could lead to a direct involvement by the Soviet Union. I hope that you will understand that your NATO allies have not had a chance to consider whether they have an obligation to protect Turkey against the Soviet Union if Turkey takes a step which results in Soviet intervention without the full consent and understanding of its NATO allies'.[47]

Prime Minister Inönü replied that 'there exists between us wide divergence of views as to the nature and basic principles of the North Atlantic Alliance. I must confess that this has been to us the source of great sorrow and grave concern. Any aggression against a member of NATO will naturally call from the aggressor an effort of justification. If NATO members should start discussing the right and wrong of the situation of their fellow-member victim of a Soviet aggression, whether this aggression was provoked or not and if the decision on whether they have an obligation to assist this member should be made to depend on the issue of such a discussion, the very foundations of the Alliance would be shaken and it would lose its meaning'.[48]

The Cyprus conflict of 1964 marked the turning point in Turkey's foreign policy. This was not simply because of the frustrations she felt when prevented from pursuing a national policy over Cyprus, nor because Greece, an ally, also appeared to pose a threat. More important was the sudden realization that subtle changes were taking place in the interaction between the United States and the Soviet Union that were bound to affect the security relationship between the United States and Turkey. The Johnson Letter explicitly told Turkey that neither the security afforded by the NATO Alliance under American leadership nor the Soviet threat were unconditional and irreversible propositions. The leader of NATO's most powerful member had explained that he differentiated between the types of Soviet threat and reserved

65

to himself the right to define when and under what conditions the Soviet Union could be a threat to the security of Turkey. This American re-examination and refinement of the Soviet threat forced a fundamental change in the Turkish view of the security afforded by NATO. No longer would it seem to provide firm, all-embracing and nearly automatic collective security. Prime Minister İnönü realized that the Cold War was over beyond doubt, and the major theme of his foreign-policy statements in subsequent years was constant caution against involvement in the issues between the superpowers. This was a complete reversal for a statesman who was one of the first to come out on the side of the United States during the Cuban missile crisis only two years before. The security formula of the cold-war years (exclusive reliance on the US and unswerving hostility to the USSR) was no longer realistic and could be dangerous for Turkey.

For the next ten years Turkey tried to make readjustments. References to the Soviet policy of peaceful co-existence increased, particularly in unofficial circles. The Atlantic Alliance continued to be the basis of her security policy but it was felt to be essential to enhance Turkey's individual security by dissociating herself somewhat from the global policies of the US, by limiting security commitments to NATO and by softening the rigid evaluation of the threat from the Soviet Union. It became a deliberate Turkish objective not to provoke the Soviet Union. Risks in security co-operation came to be weighed against gains. Cancellation of American reconnaissance flights from Turkey over the Soviet Union in 1965, the negotiation with the US of the Defence Co-operation Agreement of 1969 and the refusal to allow the use of bases in Turkey for missions during the June 1967 and October 1973 Middle East Wars serve as examples of this new policy direction.

The dilemma posed by Cyprus and Greece, which had plagued Turkey's Alliance relations since 1964, reached a new climax in the summer of 1974. A coup on 15 July by Greek officers of the National Guard and the National Organization of Cypriot Fighters (EOKA-B) overthrew Archbishop Makarios' Government and installed an ex-EOKA terrorist, Nicos Sampson, as President of Cyprus. Turkey feared *enosis,* since the coup appeared to have been encouraged by the military government in Greece. She failed to persuade Britain to undertake joint intervention and therefore launched a unilateral offensive on 20 July, occupying a substantial part of northern Cyprus. Security Council Resolution 353 called for a cease-fire, the withdrawal of foreign troops and the initiation of negotiations. Two Geneva Conferences were unable to settle either the form that the internal constitutional and the administrative structure should take or the territorial arrangements between the Greek- and Turkish-Cypriot communities. Following these failures, a second offensive, launched on 14–17 August in order to consolidate the Turkish foothold, left Turkey occupying about 40% of Cyprus, and this further hardened the positions of the adversaries. In September 1974 Prime Minister Ecevit resigned partly as a result of disagreements within his coalition over Turkish attitudes toward a settlement in Cyprus, and the question of Turkish interests and presence became further bound up with Turkish domestic politics; Prime Minister Demirel's four-party coalition government, in which Mr Erbakan and Mr Turkes opposed concessions, was unable to put forward acceptable proposals for a settlement. The imposition of an arms embargo against Turkey by the US Congress, on the grounds that her use of US-supplied weapons during the intervention was a violation of the US Foreign Assistance Act of 1961 and the Foreign Military Sales Act, complicated the chances for settlement. On the one hand, the embargo created a strong Turkish desire to resist foreign pressure; on the other, it fostered Greek hopes that Turkey would have to give way to that pressure.

The effects of the Cyprus conflict, the arms embargo and the Greek-Turkish hostilities brought American-Turkish relations almost to breaking point. Turkey argued that the Cyprus conflict and defence co-operation were separate issues and that curtailing the flow of equipment and spare parts was a hostile act, and moreover, one that undermined her overall defence capability. NATO military officials, including the Supreme Allied Commander, Europe (SACEUR), General Haig, pointed out on various occasions that the Turkish Armed Forces had lost about half their effectiveness, particularly in the Air Force, and Admiral Shear, then

NATO's Commander of the Southern Forces of NATO (CINCSOUTH), agreed that they were suffering in terms of military readiness. On the other hand, against the background of the arms race with Greece, she now engaged in an ambitious military procurement programme, which strained her economy. Turkey's traditional reliance on one source of supply, together with the need to maintain technological continuity, the rudimentary nature of her indigenous arms industry and weakness in the heavy-industrial base, created difficulties, as did the scarcity of foreign exchange and her political isolation.

The cumulative impact of the arms embargo on Turkish security was profound. Having once realized how vulnerable her defence capability was to external manipulation, Turkey would never again trust her security to allies in quite the same way.

Turkish Military Budgets

Turkey's budgetary allocations for defence increased from $995 million for fiscal year 1974 to $2.8 billion for 1976, but by 1978 the budget had declined somewhat to $2.2 billion.[49] The ten-year project for the reorganization and modernization of the armed forces (REMO), initiated in 1973, involved a total appropriation of some $1.5 billion in 1973, and this, too, received increasing allotments from 1975 to 1978 to meet purchases abroad and investments at home.[50] However, inflation, successive devaluations of the Turkish lira by a total of 50% over the period, and limited foreign currency reserves all diminished the effectiveness of this expansion of the defence budget. The value of defence funds for 1978, for instance, passed by the Turkish Parliament during the last week of February 1978, fell from $2.2 billion to $1.7 billion in March 1978, when the Turkish lira was devalued by about 30%.

Turkish Weapons Acquisition

It is not easy to ascertain facts about Turkish arms acquisitions between 1975 and 1978 because Turkey maintains official secrecy on the subject and because such politically charged issues as the embargo and the Greek-Turkish arms race are liable to produce different figures from all sides. Two developments favoured Turkey: first, the US Government was not strict in enforcing sanctions on supplies by the European members of NATO; and, secondly, the US Congress partially lifted the embargo in October 1975, allowing military assistance credits of $125 million for 1976 and $175 million for 1977 and 1978, and releasing spares and weapons already in the pipeline. When Congressional action appeared imminent in the autumn of 1974, Turkey purchased 18 F-104S *Starfighters* from Italy, and another 18 in February 1975 – one day before the embargo went into effect. In June 1975 it was reported that Britain was agreeable to a Turkish request to buy weapons worth about £100 million, including 36 *Jaguar* strike aircraft and *Rapier* anti-aircraft missiles. In 1976 negotiations were under way to buy McDonnell Douglas aircraft, more Italian-built *Starfighters* and West German *Leopard* tanks, as well as helicopters and unspecified training aircraft,[51] while in 1977 agreement was reached for the purchase of 32 F-4E and 8 RF-4E *Phantoms,* and in 1978 240 *Sparrow* air-to-air missiles were ordered. The F-16 fighter, of which the Turkish Air Force reportedly required some 200, and 56 Agusta-Bell AB-205 helicopters were considered for purchase in 1976.[52] In January 1976 requests for 60 *Alpha-Jet* trainers, *Roland* II surface-to-air missile systems, and *Milan* or *Mamba* anti-tank missiles (to replace the *Cobra* 2000s built under licence in Turkey) were also reported to have been discussed with a German Defence Ministry team visiting Turkey,[53] along with the building of 4 *Harpoon*-equipped Lurssen fast patrol boats and factories to build *Leopard* tanks and vehicles for the *Roland* system. The possible supply of F-104G *Starfighters,* the transfer of French-made *Alouette* II helicopters by Germany and German efforts to persuade Messerschmitt-Bölkow-Blohm (MBB) to set up extensive facilities in Turkey for overhauling air force equipment were mentioned in press reports during 1978.[54] Whether Turkey has yet taken delivery of all the items mentioned in the various reports is uncertain, but she has clearly made a determined effort to keep herself armed.

The Turkish arms industry has received much encouragement since 1974. An embryo national defence industry had been started around 1925, when the Turkish Air Authority was established to help raise funds to supplement the defence budget. In the late 1930s a plant in Kayseri began to manufacture the GO-145 training aircraft under licence, and two plants in İstanbul put out the 'National Development', a training aircraft of domestic design.[55] Modern ammunition factories were also built at Kirikkale. Between 1939 and 1945 more than half the national budget was allocated to defence, and industry was geared to the war economy to sustain an army of over half a million men. By 1945 some potential existed for further growth, but economic development assumed a higher priority, and US military assistance removed the incentive to develop defence industries further. The need for a domestic industry was felt again with the Cyprus crisis of 1964. The army and navy have considerable rebuilding and maintenance capacity, but limited production facilities. The air force also has significant capacity for overhaul. Armoured vehicles, electronic equipment and shipbuilding are the major areas of production.

The organization of the defence industry has left little room for private enterprise. The industry is owned and operated partly by the armed forces and partly by the Machinery and Chemicals Industries (MCI), a state enterprise established in 1950 based on the General Directorate of Military Factories, which had been responsible for arms production between 1921 and 1950. Nearly half the commercial production of MCI is channelled to civilian purposes, since Turkish military orders and foreign orders do not take up its whole capacity; its exports amount to about $60 million annually. The Armed Forces Industries turn out landing craft, patrol boats and submarines – most of them under licence from Germany – as well as howitzers and mortars, bombs, anti-personnel mines and anti-tank mines and missiles. Aselsan Military Electronic Industries was established in 1975 for the design and production of electronic equipment for military and civilian use. TUSAS, the Turkish Aircraft Industry, blueprints for which had been laid down in 1972 within the framework of the REMO Plan, was officially established in October 1974. Preliminary contacts were established with several foreign aircraft firms, among them Aeritalia, but no serious headway has yet been made. Turkey's limited heavy industrial base and foreign-currency shortage remain formidable barriers.

The General Staff is reported to have estimated that Turkey is 90% self-sufficient in light arms, 30% in heavier weapons and 15% in sophisticated equipment.[56] A recent public display by the Armed Forces, however, gave little evidence to support the last two figures. In briefings with NATO officials in Ankara in September 1979, Defence Minister Neset Akmandor was reported to have explained that Turkey had achieved her target with respect to the maintenance and overhauling of fast patrol boats, submarines and surface ships and had some capacity to rebuild tanks and overhaul aircraft.[57] The Minister stressed that Turkey must enter the arms export market in order to raise the foreign exchange necessary to buy sophisticated weapons. German technical assistance has been the single most important external source in the development of some of these capabilities.

The arms embargo, which affected major weapons most adversely by the withholding of spare parts, tended to highlight the extent of Turkey's dependence on US good-will for the preservation of her defence capability, and a desire arose to reduce this degree of dependence. The development of a heavy arms industry emerged as a goal, and the interdependence of heavy industry and self-sufficiency in weapons directed attention to further investment in heavy industrial projects. Mr Erbakan, in control of the Ministry of Industry and Technology between 1975 and 1977, was the driving force. The Fourth Five-Year Plan, adopted in 1978, defined the development of a heavy armament industry as a major goal and emphasized that TUSAS would be strengthened. Research and development facilities were to be expanded as was shipbuilding capacity.

Obviously expanding and modernizing Turkey's conventional forces would have the effect of raising the nuclear threshold, and this highlights what has been a major dilemma for Turkey ever since NATO's official adoption of the strategy of flexible response. Some have argued that such a strategy would tend to make Turkey less secure, because it might encourage limited moves by the Soviet Union against NATO's less-strongly defended flanks in the expectation that the Alliance would not be likely to use nuclear weapons in this eventuality. It was also argued that a limited Soviet aggression of this kind against Turkey might fail to activate NATO. It has been suggested, too, that Turkey could be a target for Soviet nuclear pre-emption because the American bases on her territory might tempt the USSR to initiate a limited nuclear exchange.[58]

Although the debate on doctrine has somewhat abated, apprehension over Turkey's inability to modernize her conventional capability to meet the requirements of the new strategy has remained. This concern must be seen in the wider context of the continuing assessment among Western strategists that NATO has become relatively more vulnerable on the flanks. Reports to the effect that if the Soviet Union demanded direct lines of access to the Middle East and gave Turkey an ultimatum, the Alliance might urge Turkey to accommodate[59] may approximate to reality, and they certainly aggravate Turkish anxiety. It is understandable that NATO has continued to look inwards, 'hypnotized by the Central Region', as Sir Peter Hill-Norton has put it, where 'lies the route to the heartland of NATO'. What is not understandable is that, again in his words, 'It is very hard indeed to persuade even the Council and the Military Committee to give any serious weight, much less due weight, to the Flanks. Does history not show that an aggressor will always seek chinks in the defender's armour?'[60]

Co-operation with the Alliance

NATO strategy for the defence of Turkey relies almost exclusively on the Turkish armed forces. Evasiveness in official circles on the subject of reinforcements leads one to assume that Turkey cannot count on them, and in any case facilities for their speedy and orderly reception are limited. The Allied Command Europe (ACE) Mobile Force is more symbolic in peacetime as a sign of political will to come to the assistance of a threatened NATO member than as a defence force in time of conflict, when it would be too small to make much difference. Turkey's geographical isolation has already made for logistic problems. If NATO assistance is in doubt, it follows that Turkey must try to develop her conventional defence capability in peacetime so as to be able to face any opponent alone in war.

That Turkey had an underdeveloped economy which was unable to equip forces to NATO standards was acknowledged from the very beginning of Turkey's association with NATO, even though Turkey has regularly ranked among the first five of NATO members in terms of the proportion of GNP devoted to defence (her GNP is one of the lowest). Of course Turkey has not been the only NATO country dependent on US military assistance – American support for Europe was an essential aspect of the Atlantic Alliance – but the developed European members have emerged as economic and industrial powers, while Turkey has merely reached a take-off stage and stayed there.

Nor has Turkey been in a position to benefit from co-operative developments in European weapons procurement, partly because no comparable evolution has taken place in her economic and industrial development. Although industry has reached a level where it can undertake substantial defence production, the need for capital and for technology transfer has been a major obstacle. Defence production has not made a significant contribution to the national economy, and defence co-operation with other NATO members in the meantime has continued to be confined to financial assistance in the form of credits – an archaic system considering the costs of advance technology requirements. The pace of technological change is such as to make credit arrangements politically unattractive both for the donor and the recipient countries. Turkey is formally a member of the Eurogroup and the Independent European Programme Group (IEPG) but in practice her membership has not resulted in concrete schemes for co-operation, apart from West German co-operation in the development of the shipbuilding industry. Elaborate ideas developed to promote a two-way street between the US and European NATO. Turkey was not considered in this context.

Like the developed members of NATO in Europe, Turkey feels the need to co-operate in the procurement of defence equipment, but her traditional position as an American protégé and the wide gap in the level of development between Turkey and the other European members have prevented the emergence of a dialogue on how unequal allies should co-operate for security in a period of detente. At an informal meeting of the Eurogroup in Brussels in May

1978, Turkey offered her airfields, formerly used by the US, for a pilot training scheme, but the idea was rejected and training was to be conducted in the US.[61] Turkey proposed co-production more or less consistently throughout 1978 but the United States was reportedly sceptical of Turkey's ability to produce sophisticated or heavy weaponry and suggested that she should co-operate with the Eurogroup.[62]

In the absence of a domestic defence industry, and if she is to come anywhere close to NATO standards, Turkey must go on buying from foreign markets on a scale that is bound to upset domestic priorities. In a country where the per capita income is barely $1,000, the margin between a high and low standard of living is not wide enough to allow diversion of resources to defence without causing major sacrifices. Turkey's inflated defence budgets from 1975 and 1978 took their toll on the national economy and demonstrated very clearly how easily a developing economy can be affected by over-spending on arms. The size of the armed forces becomes a target in any public discussion on improving Turkey's defence capability for suggestions about trading quantity in manpower for quality in equipment.

Turkey's position as the least developed ally also makes her participation in long-term NATO equipment and force planning a problematical proposition. Turkey is, according to Eurogroup descriptions a Category A member country, which is one with no or virtually no, industrial bases and thus not in a position to produce or co-produce a wide range of sophisticated equipment. Such a country needs external aid to finance its defence effort. When the defence effort is dependent on several important external factors, as in the case of Turkey, long-term national planning can be a highly uncertain exercise.

Turkey and Detente
Because the arms embargo came at a time of super-power detente, it could have implied either that the US believed that the USSR would not act against Turkey or that it would not matter if she did. The embargo could have been interpreted as a signal to the Soviet Union of a reduction of the American commitment to Turkey's defence.

Detente, despite its positive contribution to peaceful relations between the members of the two military blocs, has created some real problems for Alliance cohesion and, until recently, Turkey's interpretation of detente was more reserved than that of some other members of NATO. She did not see it as the basis of security nor as synonymous with security. She accepted it as a new phase whose potentialities and limits were still in the making but whose durability would be tested by super-power behaviour. Her initial reserve and watchfulness about super-power detente and its effects on Europe derived from the logical conclusion that it would inevitably touch on military alliances and on her own security policy. Certain major questions emerged from statements of government officials on detente in the mid-1970s. Would it lead to the final elimination of the bipolar system? What would emerge as the dominant features and rules of conduct of the new system? Would these possible changes imply equal security for Turkey, and, if not, would Turkey suddenly find herself in a security vacuum? Anxiety over the unknown led Turkey to stress on the one hand that defence must not be neglected and, on the other, that the detente process must include the smaller powers. If detente in the first part of the 1970s was not a solid basis for peace, but at most a calculated hope that required calculated moves, the preservation of a strong defence seemed to be one essential pre-condition. The Conference on Security and Co-operation in Europe (CSCE) and arms-control negotiations were followed closely. The negotiations on Mutual and Balanced Force Reductions (MBFR) in Central Europe were particularly relevant for Turkey, since there were fears that the withdrawal of Soviet troops from the 'Guidelines area' in Central Europe could result in the redeployment of more troops to the area of the USSR lying north-east of Turkey.

Despite inital caution, it is now admitted that detente has allowed room for national interests to exert greater pressure on foreign policy. Nonetheless, despite the widely held view that the smaller allied countries, motivated by self-interest and enjoying the security provided by the central balance, have benefited from detente, this has not been true for Turkey. Neither political nor trade relations between Turkey and the Soviet Union have improved to the extent that they have for the other countries of Europe since normalization began in the 1960s.

The three-year arms embargo helped to elevate the security and peace aspects of detente to a more prominent position in Turkish security thinking in the second half of the 1970s. It transformed detente into a major supplement to the security sought through military defence arrangements. The need to reaffirm trust in detente and to pursue a peaceful posture in her exposed position has been reinforced as the problems with the US cut deeper into the latter's credibility and as the sense of isolation from Western Europe increased.

Any attempts to explain Turkey's difficulties with the Alliance solely by reference to the Cyprus conflict would therefore be an oversimplification – although the course of the Cyprus conflict can be explained partly by reference to detente. In the 1960s, the Cyprus conflict was seen as a potential East-West issue, and it seemed better to freeze the situation in Cyprus rather than resolve it. It therefore persisted into the 1970s. But whereas Turkey could obediently yield in the 1960s, before detente, she did not yield in the 1970s when she felt less threatened by the Soviet Union. That neither the US Sixth Fleet nor the Soviet *Eskadra* would move against her are likely to have figured in the Turkish calculations when the decision was taken to intervene in Cyprus in 1974. Furthermore, Turkey could now afford to maintain a sizeable military force outside her borders only under conditions of detente. The Cyprus issue remains unresolved, but not because Turkey has turned into an expansionist country or because there are voices in Turkey who advocate a strong military presence on the island. All Turkish governments have assigned a temporary role and limited objectives to the force. The issue remains because a federal internal structure that would guarantee the security of the Turkish community has not been forthcoming.

The Central Treaty Organization

Once she had joined the West, through membership of the Atlantic Alliance, Turkey became an active proponent also of the idea of a Middle East security arrangement and saw herself as the natural link between NATO and the Middle East. In the face of Arab opposition and domestic cleavages of opinion in Britain, the British idea of a Middle Eastern Command had been dropped. The concept of the 'northern tier', expounded by Secretary of State Dulles following his tour of the Middle East in 1953, seemed a more practical idea around which to organize an alliance, largely because of Arab refusal to join any Western-sponsored defence arrangement. Arab suspicions of the West in general (and of Britain in particular), together with inter-Arab rivalries for leadership, exposed the idea of a regional defence organization sponsored by the West to attack by Arab nationalists. For most Arabs – as for President Nasser – the possibility of Soviet influence penetrating the Middle East was not seen as a threat. Partly out of a feeling of obligation to the United States and Britain for supporting her admission into NATO and partly because she was enamoured of her role as a staunch ally of the West, Turkey was active in promoting the Baghdad Pact, signed in 1955 between Turkey, Pakistan, Iran, Iraq and Britain. The US had observer status until 1958, when she became an associate member of the Pact's successor, the Central Treaty Organization (CENTO), which was formed after Iraq's withdrawal from the Baghdad Pact. CENTO however, disintegrated in 1979 upon the formal withdrawal of Pakistan, Iran and later Turkey.

The final dissolution of CENTO was no surprise. Its defence value had been eroded within a few years of its establishment. Set up at a time when the Cold War was still alive in Europe, it was doomed from the outset by the divisive influence it had on the development of regional politics. But other factors, too, contributed to its loss of credibility as a regional defence organization. The absence of a full American role in the initial stages of its development accounted for much of the flagging enthusiasm, and in 1959 all the regional members tried to compensate for this weakness by signing separate bilateral agreements with the United States. Pakistan subsequently came openly to spurn CENTO, as a result of the independent foreign policy she evolved in the 1960s, and Iran's attitude also changed as her financial and military potential changed drastically in the 1970s, giving her the power to assume a new and much more independent political role in the

71

region. For Iran the security of the Gulf became an overriding concern, and, as the security concerns of the individual CENTO members diverged, they collectively came to lack the incentive to plan seriously for joint defence.

Although the relations between Turkey and Pakistan remained substantially unchanged, Turkish – Iranian relations cooled in the 1970s when Iran's new wealth and military investments reduced the dominant position which Turkey had previously enjoyed – partly because of her linking role between NATO and CENTO and partly because of her steady economic and social progress in the early post-war period. Turkey now approached Iran for economic assistance and trade co-operation, and an Economic and Technical Co-operation Agreement was signed in June 1975 which envisaged Iranian credits to, and investments in, Turkey totalling $1.2 billion. However these arrangements, together with suggestions for establishing joint arms industries, were left on paper. Divergence in the two countries' political regimes and what many in Turkey saw as Iran's hegemonial aspirations stood in the way.

CENTO never had a permanent command structure, nor forces assigned to it. There was a Permanent Military Deputies Group, composed of representatives of the five national Chiefs of Staff, and a small permanent military staff under an American general who acted as CENTO Chief of Staff. Exercises were held annually, the most important of which were *Midlink* naval exercises in the Persian Gulf or in the Indian Ocean. Certain NATO operational procedures were reportedly adopted by CENTO forces to improve the co-ordination of naval operations.

CENTO's major achievements were limited to co-operation in improving telecommunication systems and building modern railways, highways and ports in the border regions between Iran, Turkey and Pakistan. Economic co-operation between the three never reached significant proportions, however. The Organization for Regional Co-operation for Development was established in 1964 as an unofficial economic subsidiary of CENTO, but it failed to spur trade or to achieve any move towards the limited initial object of a customs union.

CENTO's dormant state nonetheless failed to dispel the Soviet Union's concerns. Soviet commentators were particularly sensitive at the time of the CENTO Council meeting in April 1978, when the conflict in the Horn of Africa was alleged to be being used by the regional CENTO leaders to close ranks and to 'unite CENTO with NATO'.[63] Iran's heavy military purchases were also interpreted by the Soviet Union as part of a scheme to extend CENTO despite the fact that the organization had clearly already lost its vitality.[64]

Even if CENTO had remained in existence, it could never have offered Turkey a security alternative. It is doubtful whether any of the local members ever took it seriously as a defence organization.

V. NEW APPROACHES TO SECURITY

Beginning in the mid-1960s, Turkey adjusted and, in a way, expanded her conception of security. She maintained defence ties with NATO and the US as the military component of security but she also began to incorporate an active diplomatic component. Concluding that hostile relations, particularly with the Soviet Union, exacerbated mutual security concerns and delayed the development of mutual confidence, she reorientated her exclusively pro-Western foreign policy towards one which was more 'multi-faceted', which meant above all the improvement of relations with neighbours and a more active interest in and an independent attitude towards world politics.

The new process was naturally counted on to produce positive results for her position in Cyprus – a calculation which has not materialized – and to reduce her regional isolation. She is at least much less isolated than before. Whether she initially sought to play one super-power against the other and thus reap benefits from both sides is a question that only the decision-makers who initiated the process can answer. Economic considerations were also clearly in the Turkish mind as early as 1960.

Her rapprochement with the Soviet Union at a time of acute problems with the Western Alliance has developed gradually into a source of political strength and has created during the last few years the realization that this kind of political leverage can be used to enhance her own security. Turkey made her initial moves towards the Soviet Union in 1964 when East-West relations at the super-power level had entered the post-Cuban crisis stage. The 'hot line' between Washington and Moscow and the Partial Test Ban Treaty of 1963 had underlined the convergence of interests between the super-powers in managing their strategic relationship. The Sino-Soviet rift emerged to make the security of the USSR's eastern borders a new cause of Soviet concern. Divisions in the socialist camp intensified also in Europe and new intra-alliance problems appeared in NATO. The pace of building detente picked up throughout the decade. Though the Vietnam War threatened to halt the process, the Non-Proliferation Treaty (NPT) was signed in 1968. An apprehensive Western Europe, engaged in its own detente, built bridges with the Soviet Union and refused to be dragged into the Vietnam war. France withdrew from the military structure of NATO to be master of her own defence. De Gaulle reached out to the Soviet Union – and was hailed as a hero during his visit to Turkey in 1969. Bonn engaged in *Ostpolitik*. European publics resisted increases in defence spending and condemned the American role in Vietnam. Romania defied directives from the Soviet Union and condemned the invasion of Czechoslovakia. Tourism and trade began to flourish between the East and West Europeans.

In the early 1970s, the super-powers agreed on major economic and trade contacts and on the technological development of the Soviet Union with Western assistance. Peaceful co-existence, proffered by the Soviet Union in the mid-1950s, seemed to have been assimilated into Western policy. The United States not only withdrew from Vietnam but revised her threat perception of China dramatically. President Nixon pronounced that defence must first be an individual and then a regional responsibility. SALT I and the Basic Principles of Mutual Relations between the two super-powers – the official mutual recognition of strategic parity – seemed to indicate a mutual super-power willingness to settle for the *status quo* rather than change, and a determination to prevent the outbreak of nuclear war, thus marking the apex of the detente process. The Conference on Security and Co-operation in Europe (CSCE) further reinforced the political *status quo*.

The underdeveloped world of the 1950s emerged as the Third World and began to demand the adjustment of the inequalities of the world economic system. The East–West conflict, already somewhat modified under the constraints of the balance of terror, became subject to new, though inchoate, constraints as the non-aligned countries and the Third World claimed independent places for themselves. The vision of Third Worldism sought to resolve the problem of underdevelopment while non-alignment promised security through moral dissuasion.

A country like Turkey which was part of the larger East–West configuration and which had particularly felt the pressure of the cold war years – partly as a result of her own misperceived fears – could not be immune to these developments and to the opportunities they presented.

The Soviet Union

Soviet–Turkish relations remained frozen until the 1960s. The USSR had sought 'normalization but Turkey had abstained. In a note of 30 May 1953, the Soviet Union withdrew the territorial claims of 1945 and 'considered possible the provision of security of the USSR from the side of the Straits on conditions acceptable alike to the USSR and to Turkey'.[65] The cumbersome language concerning the Straits did not fully satisfy the Turkish Government at the time.

The first major break was expected with the exchange of visits between Prime Minister Menderes and Premier Khrushchev, scheduled for July 1960. The need to tap new resources for economic assistance was one reason behind the move; an assessment that American–Soviet relations could be entering a new phase was the other. The first signs of an American–Soviet dialogue – Premier Khrushchev's visit to the US in 1959 and the proposed Paris Summit Conference in May 1960 – had aroused misgivings that an improvement in US–Soviet relations could weaken Turkey's ties with the US. During his trip to the CENTO countries in December 1959, President Eisenhower, confronted with an apprehensive Turkey, tried to calm her fears of declining US commitment. But her intuitive concerns seemed to be confirmed in 1964 when it became clear that the 'Soviet threat' was definitely under review in Washington.

Normalization of relations between Turkey and the Soviet Union moved forward steadily after the clash with the US over Cyprus in the summer of 1964. Normalization relied on three main instruments: high-level official visits; explicit agreement on the basic principle of international law on state independence and sovereignty and on the principle of peaceful co-existence between two different social systems; and Soviet economic assistance. The Soviet Union agreed to respect Turkey's commitment to NATO, and the number of global issues on which there was agreement increased with time. Both called for an early end to the war in Vietnam, for Israel's withdrawal from the occupied territories, for the strengthening of detente, and for the convening of a World Disarmament Conference.

On the Cyprus question Turkey found the USSR a major source of support – at least until 1974. Originally a strong supporter of President Makarios and the Communist Party, AKEL, the Soviet Union adopted a more pro-Turkish attitude as normalization of relations proceeded. Soviet antagonism to the military regime in Greece further tilted the scales and the USSR seemed to concur with Turkey on the issues of a federal structure for Cyprus, the recognition of 'two communities' and opposition to *enosis*. The Turkish military intervention in 1974 and the fall of the military regime in Athens, however, changed Turkey's favoured position. Fearing NATO control of the island, the Soviet Union joined UN calls for the dismantling of foreign (i.e. British) bases on Cyprus and the withdrawal of foreign troops from the island, and she proposed an international conference for a settlement.

Economic relations dominated the normalization process for a long time. In March 1967, the Soviet Union agreed to help finance six major industrial projects: an iron and steel complex at Iskenderun, an aluminium factory at Seydisehir, a petroleum refinery near Izmir, a sulphuric acid factory at Bandirma, the Seyit Omer transmission line and a fibre-sheet factory at Artvin. The joint construction of the Arpacayi dam on the Soviet-Turkish border was completed in 1978. Loan agreements from 1967 to 1975 totalled around $700 million. The volume of trade increased from $50 million in 1973 to $80 million in 1977 and $105 million in 1978,[66] and in June 1978 agreement was reached to further expand the volume of trade, largely on barter terms, including the purchase of electricity and petroleum. A protocol of June 1979 announced agreement on Soviet technology and further credits for twenty projects amounting to $4 billion.

Do Soviet credits and technical assistance to Turkey fit the general pattern of Soviet assistance to developing countries described by some western observers as 'showpiece projects'? If the starting point is a comparison of the relative economic power of the Soviet Union and the West, they clearly do. The local significance of these projects appears much more than 'show-piece', however, when the intermediate stage of Turkey's industrial and technological development is taken into account. Furthermore, in some cases – as with the aluminium factory – Soviet technology was all that was available as Turkey had failed to find a supplier in the West.

Soviet credits to Turkey are among the largest made available to any developing country,[67] which underscores the significance of Turkey in Soviet estimations in general. Restoration of confidence was necessary so that Turkey would cease to threaten Soviet security. Premier Krushchev, in a 1960 Note, set out what the Soviet Union expected from improved relations and outlined the improvement process. Neutralism was to be the ultimate goal, but any step in that direction, including a return to the friendly relations of the Atatürk–Lenin period, an independent Turkish foreign policy while staying loyal to her contractual ties with the West, and a step-by-step restoration of confidence between the two, were to be encouraged.

Restoration of confidence necessarily began with better economic relations. Analysing Turkey's moves towards rapprochement, a Soviet commentator explained: 'Political tendencies are greatly influenced by economic factors, whose effect intensifies as various propaganda-induced prejudices disappear'.[68] The potential role of the 'firm material foundation' of economic and trade co-operation in building confidence was obvious, a point stressed by Soviet commentators and officials repeatedly since the initiation of the normalization process. Economic assistance was also linked with the favourable imagery of the Atatürk–Lenin period (during which the Soviet Union had helped to establish the first state enterprises) and with the political desire that 'the precepts of Kemal Atatürk must be implemented', as Mr Kosygin put it in 1967.[69]

If Turkish neutralism was the ultimate objective, the improvement of bilateral relations was expected to yield short-term benefits for the Soviet Union, hinted at in unofficial commentaries. They would lessen the possibility that Turkey might be used as a strategic base against the USSR, shake the image of the 'Soviet threat' propagated by NATO, undermine NATO's claim to be an alliance that strengthens a country's security, turn the Middle East into a nuclear-free zone, and eliminate foreign bases. They would also reduce the 'threat to the peace in the Mediterranean', make US fleet visits to Turkish ports unnecessary, reduce Turkey's dependence on the West and demonstrate that she could manage without US and NATO aid.[70]

Several of the short-term objectives have been achieved. Turkey is no longer a possible launching base for strategic weapons – an element of the utmost importance for Soviet security and a prerequisite for Soviet confidence in Turkey. The American presence has been reduced considerably – from 27,000 in 1965 to about 6,000 by 1979. Although changes in military technology, American policy on overseas bases and the course of American–Turkish relations have been largely responsible for this outcome, Turkey's desire to reassure the Soviet Union of her non-offensive intentions has been a consistent element in her approach to major security-related issues and choices since the mid-1960s. The Declaration of the Principles of Good Neighbourliness, signed in April 1972 in Ankara, and the Political Document on the Principles of Good Neighbourly and Friendly Co-operation, drafted in 1975 and signed in June 1978 in Moscow, have come to stand as proof that the level of mutual confidence achieved so far allows for political as well as economic contacts. There have also been several exchange visits of high-ranking officers between the two countries.

Nearly fifteen years of official contacts, technical assistance and the absence of intimidation led Prime Minister Ecevit to declare, on 15 May 1978 in London, that the Soviet Union was not a threat to Turkey. Elaborating his statement later, he explained that the Soviet Union had not shown any aggressive behaviour towards Turkey for years, which therefore resulted in the emergence of mutual confidence between the two countries.[71]

Does the official attitude reflect public sentiment? There are no public opinion surveys available, but a major feature of public discussion on security is the subdued way in which reference is made to the Soviet Union. In the absence of threatening behaviour by the Soviet Union, the way people feel can only be discerned indirectly from views expressed on Turkey's security ties with the West. The right-of-centre parties, of which the NAP and NSP are the most explicit and vocal, continue to view the Soviet Union as threatening. The Marxist Left in general does not associate the Soviet Union with the question of Turkish security and the only clearly audible voices of dissent from the left are those of the Maoist faction[72] and, more recently, the Socialist Revolution Party. The RPP's stand, which is not entirely explicit, can be inferred from its line in favouring the preservation of a NATO-based security policy, although some apprehension exists within the present leadership. However, it is difficult to talk of uniform views within the RPP for it has several factions open to input from the universities, the press and labour. With a few exceptions, the general foreign-policy statements of RPP officials and parliamentarians do not discuss security. The JP is more unequivocal in reaffirming the need for Turkey's security link with the US and NATO.

The press reflects the range of opinion prevalent in political circles. Of the daily newspapers with the largest circulations, *Tercüman* has a prounounced anti-Soviet attitude, *Hürriyet* has a less easily identifiable position, and *Milliyet*, the symbol of prestige, reflects the position of the RPP with its pluralism of views. *Cumhuriyet*, although having a smaller circulation, is an established and serious newspaper with leftist views. The two major labour organizations hold divergent views of the Soviet Union – that of the Confederation of Trade Unions of Turkey, representing Western-type trade unionism has tended to be less benevolent towards the Soviet Union than that of the Confederation of Revolutionary Trade Unions, which holds to a Marxist political philosophy and has pro-Moscow leanings.

For the common man, who follows the news of Soviet technical assistance and the exchange of high-level visits from the media, neither the Soviet Union nor security in general seems to be a salient issue. No Turk can point to Soviet aggressive behaviour directly against Turkey on account of bilateral issues for over three decades. The man in the street is more concerned with American-Turkish relations, the Aegean and Cyprus.

Fifteen years of a steady policy of improving relations have helped to tone down the significance of the Soviet Union for Turkish security. Needless to say this evolution has not taken place independently. As Left-wing ideologies gained more adherents (as a result of greater ideological freedom) and economic problems within the capitalist framework piled up, the image of the Soviet Union as a peaceful socialist neighbour has tended to prevail while the West has come to be seen as neo-colonialist and militaristic.

Yet, under the present conditions of world and regional politics, the question of security in this highly sensitive area of the world is not defined exclusively by the boundaries of bilateral relations. Nor is it a question of intention or design on the part of the Soviet Union to compromise Turkish sovereignty or territorial integrity. The present system of super-power rivalry penetrates Turkey's security situation in many different ways. Unrestricted access to Turkey, the Straits and Turkish air space would afford advantages to one side at the expense of the other. In other words, Turkey *is* a third party in this rivalry, not by choice but by the fact of geography. Adjacency to Turkey both gives the Soviet Union a natural advantage and conditions her to think of Turkey as part of her defensive perimeter. A politically neutral or friendly Turkey can relieve Soviet vulnerability from the south to a considerable extent, even if it cannot totally eliminate concern. Nor can it reduce her need to move out of her borders within the framework of the global rivalry and her global role. The Montreux Convention accommodates both the Soviet and Turkish needs in time of peace but it does not permit the use of Turkish airspace by military aircraft, nor does it assure passage of the Straits in war.

Soviet military preponderance is also crucial not so much because the Soviet Union is expected to unleash all her power against Turkey but because overwhelming force can be put to political and psychological use. Power, which cannot be made politically effective in distant areas unless it is made visible, can be seen all the time in the Black Sea, in the Crimea, in the Caucasus and in the Eastern Mediterranean. When power is so close, it is difficult to feel secure.

The paradox is that while Soviet military power is so superior and so close, the Turkish military capability does not appear to be perceived as legitimate in Soviet eyes. Premier Kosygin reminded Turkish officials that 'the future of peoples is not in armaments' and unofficial Soviet commentaries scorn Turkey's military spending.[73] In her difficult geographical location and with her need for resources for development, Turkey would be among the first to welcome a security that could be brought about by general disarmament. Yet it must be acknowledged that a unilateral decision by Turkey to base her security on disarmament is unlikely to lead to the cancellation of any of the Soviet Union's military plans and programmes. They are set and pursued independently of Turkey and relate to the position of the Soviet Union as a world power in the existing international system – in the shaping and preservation of which Turkey has hardly any role to play.

The Soviet Union, for her part, may still be concerned about the possibility that Turkey could be used for offensive purposes, due to her defence ties with the US and NATO – hence the continuing Soviet sensitivity over the American bases and installations. An official and popular consensus has prevailed since the mid-1960s in Turkey that she should not allow any military deployment on Turkish soil that will directly or indirectly threaten Soviet security and in turn provoke Soviet threats. In essence, the Turkish position seems to rely on the US–NATO association for purposes of defence only, while at the same time moving Turkey out of the sphere of super-power interaction. This position must be as much a source of security for the Soviet Union as it is for Turkey, and it follows that Turkey is unwilling to assume any strategic-military roles that are not related to her own defence. Such a position should not conflict with NATO responsibilities, at least in principle, since 'defence' is the *raison d'etre* of membership. Yet it has created and will create problems at the operational level, particularly in Turkish relations with the US. The recent public debate concerning flights over Turkey by American U-2 reconnaissance aircraft in connection with the verification of Soviet compliance with SALT II Agreements have highlighted the difficulties and mistrust. The issue of these flights is a very sensitive one for Turkish public opinion because the memory of the U-2 incident of 1960 is still fresh (the aircraft piloted by Gary Powers took off from Turkey). Turkey is not a party to the SALT agreements and would have had no control over the U-2 flights, but she could be implicated, perhaps dangerously, if problems had arisen between the US and the Soviet Union as a result of them.

The improvement in Soviet–Turkish relations has implications that are not directly related to geopolitical concerns. Since Atatürk's struggle for independence was diagnosed by Lenin as a national bourgeois, rather than a socialist, revolution, Turkey has been concerned about the possibility of ideological propaganda and infiltration. This sensitivity was prevalent in the 1960s, when the first cultural agreement between the two countries came before the National Assembly for ratification, causing a heated debate. But as leftist ideology became part of the legitimate political system, anti-Communism ceased to be the near-official dogma that it had once been. In 1977 Prime Minister Demirel said that 'as long as the Soviet Union does not violate our territorial integrity, does not interfere in our internal affairs and respects our independence, it is to the advantage of our country to improve good neighbourly relations with the Soviet Union. We have made this very clear. We are anti-Communist. When you attempt to interfere in our internal affairs, there will be disaster. We repeat: we are against the export of ideology'.[74] However, such statements have become rare.

Extreme nationalism in Turkey is also disclaimed. Although the Turkic people comprise the largest non-Russian ethnic group in the USSR, and therefore have a special significance in the political demography of the Soviet Union, Turkey can hardly appear as a pole of attraction to them. Yet, just as Turkey's Kurdish population is vulnerable to external influences and propaganda, so the Soviet Union must be aware that as a multi-national state she, too, is vulnerable, even though references by 'bourgeois ideologists' to the possible influence of nationalism on the Soviet people are generally branded as 'bourgeois falsification' by Soviet sources.[75]

History provides an unhappy memory. Pan-Turkism, the aspiration to unite all Turks in one State, made a brief and tragic appearance at the end of the First World War, when Enver Pasha, leader of the Young Turks, tried to take advantage of the internal disruption in revolutionary Russia to reach out to the Turkic people in Central Asia. With the establishment of the secular state of Turkey, Pan-Turkism and Pan-Islamism, branded by Atatürk as dangerous and unrealistic, became officially dead as well as politically and socially repellent. On the other hand, it is impossible not to note the interest inside Turkey in Turkic peoples in other countries, whether purely on an academic cultural level or as part of a revival of nationalism. More recently, the US arms embargo also tended to encourage nationalist sentiment among those who saw it as a major foreign-policy defeat for Turkey at the hands of the Greek lobby in the US Congress. Ethno-cultural societies and publications exist to promote understanding of Turks in other lands. Some of them show evidence of a genuine intellectual and academic interest, particularly in Turcology, but others perpetuate the image of the 'enslaved Turks' in Russia (the NAP and the traditional pro-Islamic groups tend to use this kind of language), even though official policy has succeeded in dissociating Turkey from the Soviet Turkic people.

The Soviet Union, however, may still be uncomfortable with a nationalistic Turkey. There have been unofficial responses to Turkish polemical writings such as 'Red Imperialism', calling them the manifestation of Pan-Turkism harbouring the idea of 'the liberation of Turkistan'.[76] More recently Mr Türkes was reportedly the subject of official protest by the Soviet Embassy in Ankara. The Soviet Union is also particularly irritated by any ideas of pacts between Islamic countries. For instance, when moves seemed to be under way in 1966 for 'fraternal co-operation of Moslem countries', as King Faisal put it, Soviet commentaries saw the effort as another attempt by Western imperialism to confront her with a new military pact.[77] When all the countries lying along her borders in the south have the common bond of Islam, the USSR views the possibility of co-operation among them with alarm.

The improvement in Soviet-Turkish relations undoubtedly discourages the unbridled expression of extreme nationalistic ideas with reference to the Turkic people in the USSR; at the same time it allows increased contacts between the Soviet Turkic and Turkish people which can act as a safety valve. Further, the regional pull must also be discerned by the Soviet Union. A regional orientation that promises to erode Turkey's defence ties with the West should receive her blessings so long as it does not replace those ties with any form of Islam-based defence co-operation. This would probably be greeted with disfavour even if it had an anti-Western complexion.

The Middle East
Turkey's determined efforts to be accepted as a friend of the Arab world since the 1960s are, more than anything else, a coming to terms with herself. She has had to acknowledge the existence of common cultural and religious values inherited from the past and to accept the social and political realities of the Middle East.

It was not easy for Turkey to be accepted as a friend by Middle Eastern states. The last stages of Ottoman rule of nearly four centuries were filled with bitter memories, and territorial questions and disputes over property remained even after the liquidation of the Ottoman empire. The question of sovereignty over oil-rich Mosul in Iraq was settled only in 1925 when the League Council ceded it to Great Britain, the mandatory power. The Hatay question was not settled until 1939 – in favour of Turkey but to the dissatisfaction of Syria. Turkey's all-out attack on Islam and Atatürk's westernization policies caused Turks and Arabs to drift further apart. Arab nationalism, socialism and anti-westernism developed strongly after the war, at the same time as Turkey was seized by fear of the Soviet Union and Communism. The national pre-occupations and central concerns of Turkey and the Arab states were far apart, and specific points of difference soon emerged. For the Arabs the conflict with Israel assumed the highest priority, while for Turkey defence arrangements with the West seemed all-important. Though Turkey had originally opposed the partition of Palestine, she subsequently became the first Muslim country to recognize Israel in 1949. As already noted, she further antagonized the radical Arabs when she joined the Baghdad Pact in 1955, and, because she sided with conservative Arab forces in the 1950s, radical regimes like Egypt and Syria became the most virulent critics of Turkey. The isolation in which Turkey found herself in 1964 over the Cyprus question hurt most when she was snubbed by all the Arab countries except Saudi Arabia.

Public opinion began to insist on establishing friendly ties with the Arab States. This meant improving inter-state relations, a change of stand on the Arab-Israeli conflict and distancing Turkish foreign policy in the Middle East from that of the US. It also meant playing down Turkey's secularism. The economic element also became very important after petroleum became dearer in the 1970s.

In the spring of 1967 Turkey declared that the American bases could not be used in any conflict involving the Middle Eastern countries – to dispel Arab fears and memories of 1958, when the Incirlik Air Base was used to launch the American intervention in Lebanon. The Arab-Israeli War of June 1967 encouraged Turkey to take an openly pro-Arab stand for the first time, and support for the Arabs became more unequivocal in subsequent years as she voted in favour of UN resolutions calling for Israel's withdrawal from the occupied territories, including Jerusalem, and for the recognition of the legitimate rights of the Palestinians. Bilateral relations with the PLO were established in 1975 and, at the 7th Islamic Conference, held in Istanbul in 1976, Turkey invited the PLO to open a Bureau in Ankara. Full diplomatic recognition was granted in August 1979. Nevertheless, Turkey will not sever her diplomatic ties with Israel, and she insists that the PLO undertake not to support domestic terrorism in Turkey.

King Faisal's proposal in the mid-1960s that Turkey should join in an Islamic Pact was initially rejected on the grounds that Turkey was a secular state. However, after considerable public discussion and hesitation, it was decided that official secularism did not rule out religious ties and Turkey participated in the First Islamic Conference in Rabat in 1969 and in its subsequent meetings.

Following the oil embargo in 1973, economic relations became the focus of attention. The objectives were to secure oil, if possible on easy payment terms, to attract some of the new petrodollars for investment in Turkey, and to increase exports to oil-producing Arab countries. Turkey's share of trade with the Middle East increased from about 9 % in the mid 1960s to 13 % by 1979.

Syria, Iraq and Libya hold special significance for Turkey. The first two are neighbours, and Libya has traditionally been a friend. Relations with Saudi Arabia have also been close although it is the conservative faction in Turkey which tends to lean towards Riyadh. Libya's transfer of five F-5 aircraft and spare parts to Turkey during the war in Cyprus was received with gratitude. A 1,000-km pipeline between Mosul in Iraq and Iskenderun was put into operation in .1977. Yet, although there is mutual advantage in Turkish-Iraqi cooperation, it has not become very concrete. When Iraq has been faced with Kurdish insurgency, Turkey has refused to give sanctuary, but greater co-operation may come about in the future if there is a resurgence of Kurdish separatism. Libya, with large oil revenues, is both underdeveloped and underpopulated. Turkey could supply her with labour and technical advice and support, and indeed about 5,000 of the estimated 50,000 Turks employed in Arab countries are in Libya. In January 1979 Prime Minister Ecevit visited Libya, demonstrating solidarity and seeking to extend mutual co-operation. A series of new agreements envisage joint capital investments, co-production schemes and credit arrangements – though it must be noted that previous agreements were largely left on paper. The training of Libyan officers was also foreseen, and it appeared as if Turkey and Libya might begin to develop a quasi-defence partnership as well as economic ties. If this partnership was to be extended to include Iraq, there were those who believed that Turkey could free herself from her ties with the West and find security by cooperating with these radical Arab countries. In contrast, Saudi Arabia and Kuwait attract the attention of the religiously conservative elements in Turkey. Certainly the Islamic dimension is becoming more significant for some political groups and it seems highly probable that the political complexion of Arab regimes will come to matter less than the realization that these countries share with Turkey the Middle Eastern past and, possibly, the future.

These developments simply indicate trends and possibilities. Religious and cultural affinities have not yet provided a steady basis for co-operation, despite Turkey's efforts to focus Arab attention on regional investment and trade. Turkey has also discovered that she has to stress the political factor instead of merely concentrating on economic ties. Her relations with the Middle East do not as yet show many tangible results although Saudi credits worth $250 million were negotiated in 1979. However, it is the reassertion of her image as belonging to the Middle East and the dominant position that the region has come to occupy in people's minds that are significant for the future. External powers are seen to have caused the turmoil in the region, and this has bred a desire in Turkey to join forces with the Arab countries in a spirit of regional protectionism and common destiny.

The Balkans

What started as an attempt by Turkey to break the ice with the Balkan countries in the 1960s has been incorporated into CSCE in the 1970s. The difficult problems have concerned relations between Turkey and the Balkan countries, a legacy of the break-up of the Ottoman Empire. Specific problems have arisen from Turkish minorities, their cultural freedom and property compensation. Following the settlement of the question of population exchange with Greece, Turkey tried to initiate a Balkan Union, which evolved in 1934 into the Balkan Entente between Greece, Romania, Turkey and Yugoslavia. Bulgaria with territorial claims on Greece and unofficially on Turkey, stayed out. The political and ideological map of the Balkans born out of World War II and the Cold War froze Turkey's relations with the Balkan countries. Hostility, intertwined with Cold War attitudes and perceptions, was particularly strong in the case of Bulgarian-Turkish relations. About 150,000 people emigrated to Turkey in the early 1950s.

The general thaw in East – West relations and the Cyprus crisis of 1964 made a dent in this attitude. Romania's acts of independence within the Socialist bloc also attracted Turkey's interest. Exchanges of official visits in the 1960s and a series of bilateral technical co-operation agreements reached in the 1970s helped to establish normal diplomatic relations with nearly all Balkan countries while, ironically, Greek-Turkish relations deteriorated. Since the signing of the Helsinki Document, however, contacts have increased further and relations have improved.

While Bulgaria is of special importance for Turkish security, because of her proximity, relations with Romania are warmer. A Bulgarian-Turkish Declaration on Good Neighbourliness and a Romanian-Turkish Joint Solemn Declaration were signed in the aftermath of the Helsinki Conference in the summer of 1975. It became more evident during Prime Minister Ecevit's visit to Romania in November 1978 that Turkey regards Romania's example in foreign policy as a credible precedent and one which might be worth following. She might, like Romania, refrain from promoting bloc politics.[78]

Yugoslavia acquired a new significance with the change of government in Turkey in 1977. President Tito had paid an official visit in 1976, and Mr Ecevit, for his first official visit abroad as Prime Minister, went to Yugoslavia, implicitly underlining his intention to approach the non-aligned world at a time when the arms embargo continued to strain US-Turkish relations. The visit elicted declarations of goodwill from both sides but Yugoslavia remained adamant on the question of the withdrawal of Turkish troops from Cyprus, a view shared by all the non-aligned countries at their Belgrade Conference in the autumn of 1978 and at the Havana Conference in September 1979.

Turkey's Balkan initiatives are likely to follow the present pattern of bilateral relations cemented with technical co-operation schemes such as improving highway links, regulating transit traffic and undertaking modest joint investments in industry and tourism. Turkey hopes to improve trade with the COMECON countries, and some see the COMECON markets as a real option for the diversification of Turkey's foreign trade. Exports to these countries have risen from 7.7% of the total in 1973 to 14.2% in 1978.[79]

Meanwhile, Balkan relations in general have gone ahead without Turkey. To some extent, Greece and Turkey have been competing for positions of advantage in the Balkans. Each approached Balkan members of the Warsaw Pact in an effort to isolate the other, but Turkey has lagged behind Greece in this respect. History shows that the situation in the Balkans affects Turkish security directly, even though she is slightly further removed from the area than Greece; it also shows that security arrangements among the regional powers – such as the Balkan Entente and the Little Entente – are not guarantees against great power expansionism. Their initial appeal may not last long either; the Balkan Pact of 1954 between Yugoslavia, Greece and Turkey was simply allowed to fall into oblivion. Regional co-operation can work to Turkish advantage in many other ways, however. The elimination of Greek-Turkish disagreements is necessary not purely for the sake of bilateral peace between them but to remove one major hindrance to regional co-operation. If Greece and the Balkans draw closer while Turkey remains isolated, this has long-term political and psychological implications for Turkey and for the region as a whole.

Although the Turkish public has come to look with favour on closer links with the Middle East it has not shown the same interest in the Balkans, despite an official policy that stresses that Turkey is also a Balkan country. The legacy of caution against an open expression of affinity with the socialist Balkan countries may be partly responsible for this apparent apathy. Certainly Turkish tourists have visited Romania, Turkish politicians have made contacts with their Bulgarian counterparts, Turkish entrepreneurs have established ties with co-operatives in Bulgaria and scholars have exchanged views at international conferences on Ottoman-Balkan history. Meanwhile the ban on Communism has come under review in Turkey. If large sections of the public continue to lack interest in the Balkans, the aloofness of the Balkan countries towards Turkey, in contrast to Arab acts of interest must also be in part responsible. When mutual interest is absent, then any proposals for Balkan arrangements that might include Turkey will meet with scepticism.

VI. FUTURE PROSPECTS

This overview of the past and present trends in Turkish security policy and thinking should support the view that there are indeed very intimate linkages and interdependencies between national policy, internal developments and the international system. This will hold good for the future but there are several competing conceptions of what that future should be.

Of all the alternatives, the idea of development has attracted the most attention. Yet different models of development imply different alternatives for foreign and security policy. Those who propose development along the present mixed-economy model tend to see Turkey's ties with the West as a necessary element for Turkish security; those who propose a centrally-planned economy for development on the socialist model suggest that Turkey should move out of the Western security system; those who stress fundamentalist values propose a security structure based on Islamic concepts of social and defence organizations. Finally, for those whose point of departure is Turkey's systemic under-development 'Third-worldism' offers the only road to security by first guaranteeing economic security. There are, of course, many subdivisions, combinations and domestic alliances that blur the outlines of these four basic alternatives. Particularly at a time when no direct threats are present, therefore, it is not surprising that individual and group preferences, predispositions, and ideologies should shape the diverse views of what is likely to constitute security in the years ahead.

It is only a limited exercise to propose simple military formulae for security when development priorities, models and ideologies exert powerful and conflicting influences on the setting of priorities for foreign and security policies and when the multi-dimensional nature of security has become manifest. Resource security, for example, may prove to be more compelling in the very near future than military security. This domestic focus is both welcome and essential, since external security cannot be achieved without a stable internal environment and a degree of consensus. Domestic social and political institutions must be strong and must be able not simply to adapt to change but to institute and implement it. The economic and industrial structure must be able to sustain a mentally and physically fit population. Unfortunately, despite the absence of obvious military threats, the very precariousness of Turkey's domestic situation exposes her to precisely the kind of internal and external pressures which may dangerously undermine her ability to stand on her own feet and to formulate a coherent security policy. This internal instability is currently the major source of Turkey's insecurity. East-West detente is both an opportunity for, and a precondition of, the diversion of effort to the reconstruction of the domestic ingredients of security.

Ultimately, security will lie in a new world order in which destruction no longer threatens. Until then most smaller states will continue to seek the semblance of military power as a sign of their will to resist external threats, even if that power, acting on its own, may lack decisive defensive value, and even if it absorbs some of the resources needed for human development. Turkey, like some other states, faces the twin questions of how much she can afford to devote to defence in view of the constraints of development needs, and how credible her limited defence effort will be in the eyes of the Soviet Union and of the Western Alliance. The USSR's global enterprise, highlighted by her airlift of military supplies to the

Horn of Africa partly through Turkish airspace, and her concept of security, which includes Turkey within at least her maritime defensive perimeter, continue to create a situation in which Turkey's sovereign rights intersect with both the Soviet Union's perceived security needs and her desire to operate outside her own borders. Turkey's security objective cannot be to halt, complicate or deter Soviet global or regional objectives by posing as an obstacle to them; her objective is, essentially, to ensure that her sovereignty will not be compromised. If one precondition of Turkish security in this situation is a peaceful foreign policy towards the Soviet Union, a determination to maintain Turkey's sovereign rights is the other. The problem is that it is difficult to ascertain how the Soviet Union perceives this determination to defend Turkish sovereignty when that determination is largely based on intention rather than on capability. NATO can therefore continue to be an additional element of Turkey's security – an additional means of rendering her will to defend herself more convincing than it might be if she stood alone. This of course places an additional constraint on Turkish defence policy, because the Western Alliance will expect Turkey to make a contribution to the common defence commensurate with her means. That contribution may be more than Turkey feels she can or should afford. It is, in a sense, an additional cost, which must be weighed against the greater sense of security which membership of NATO would seem to provide.

The incompatibility of this proposition – that Turkey should continue to incorporate the NATO association – with the presence of very serious problems in Turkey's relationship with the Alliance becomes the next critical question that needs an answer. And on this point one has doubts, for the problems are substantive and systemic. As outlined here, they relate to: the credibility of collective security in conditions of nuclear stalemate and detente (detente may have been weakened but the balance of terror survives); the dis-jointed state of NATO's Southern Flank (Greek return will not correct the inherent weaknesses); the unhappy management of defence co-operation; budgetary constraints on weapons modernization; risks inherent in co-operation with a super-power; the political and geographical limits of Alliance and Alliance commitment; and growing distance from Western Europe. Some of these are not exclusively Turkish problems. They arise as a result of the radical transformation of the original security concepts and calculations on which the Alliance and, more importantly, military integration were built. If the Greek-Turkish disagreements threaten the Alliance's solidarity, many other issues, such as the controversy over the deployment of enhanced radiation weapons, the modernization of tactical nuclear forces and recent events in Iran and in Afghanistan, underline some of the other difficulties of maintaining a single Alliance voice. If the US arms embargo against Turkey can be construed as a sign of declining American commitment to Turkish defence, or even as a forewarning that the commitment might be ended, super-power arms control negotiations, such as SALT, also have implications which may be just as serious for the American commitment to the defence of Europe as a whole, as Europeans have been quick to point out. Furthermore, when the issue of resource scarcity becomes more critical, the military concept of co-ordinated security that underlines NATO military integration may come under strain, and unilateralism and bilateralism may become the norm. In short, if the Turkish case is now in question, the whole concept of Alliance viability, as well as the concept of American protection of Western Europe, are also in question in the longer term. The Turkish case is only one example of the impact of changing conditions on Alliance credibility and cohesion. The Turkish case is more complicated than others, and local difficulties greater because Turkey's dependence on the United States covers the whole spectrum from economic to military matters, while the rest of Western Europe's dependence is largely confined to the military guarantee. What makes the Turkish case unique and points to the basic contradiction that is at the source of several of the major problems is the fact that Turkey is in reality a developing country yet is also closely associated with the industrialized West. On the other hand, the very uncertainty of the American commitment has forced Europeans to take a fresh look at detente and to wonder whether new approaches to security can be found. The detente that collective security has helped to bring about in Europe has tended to emphasize economic and political and even regional co-operation as alternative ways to ensure security. Greece, for example, has displayed remarkable skill in adapting to this evolutionary stage. Turkey, unclear as to what she expects from her future relationship with the EEC, will probably continue to be left out of this new approach to security.

Alternative Roads to Security

Are there other security alternatives for Turkey? Could she adopt the French formula? Would a bilateral arrangement with the US be more profitable? Or is neutralism an avenue to explore?

Though there are two similarities between the French and Turkish positions (doubts about American commitment and a general desire to be independent) there are few others. The most obvious symbol of France's desire to pursue an independent policy is the French nuclear force. Its rationale is the desire to be in a position to control the course of a confrontation in Europe and to have the ability to threaten to escalate the conflict. This threat, it is hoped, would prevent the super-powers from terminating a conflict in Europe at a stage, or under conditions, that might be against French interests. Turkey obviously cannot think in these terms, nor can she realistically think in terms of conventional independence in the short run. Moreover, she lacks the advantage of distance from the Soviet Union that France enjoys in conventional terms.

A more comprehensive US-Turkish bilateral defence agreement might seem to strengthen the American commitment but at the roots of the tension between Turkey and the US has been the Turkish public's revolt against the unequal nature of the relationship. A multilateral arrangement provides some restraint against domination, even though Turkey's position in NATO is in fact heavily geared to a bilateral relationship with the US. What concerns Turkey – as it concerns others – is that American policy is apparently subject to rather wild fluctuations, and it is uncomfortable for anyone to feel that their security is in the hands of an unpredictable super-power: recent developments in US – China and US – Taiwan relations are cases in point. On the other hand, Western Europe without the US would be neither able nor willing to enter into a defence association with Turkey. These constraints leave the present multilateral framework as the most workable arrangement for Turkey.

Non-alignment is ideal for small countries in principle, particularly if they wish to keep clear of East – West confrontation and prefer to view the world in more pluralistic terms. Yet the question of how much security non-alignment gives depends on the internal and external conditions of the individual country. To provide a basis for security, neutralism must, above all, draw strength from within and moral support from neighbours and friends. A closely-knit social and political fabric, effective and consistent leadership, and convincing diplomacy – features observable in Sweden and Yugoslavia – mould and uphold a national consensus not to be drawn into conflicts which do not concern them and not to yield to pressure from outside, prerequisites that Atatürk tried to build with meticulous care. The regional environment is extremely important, for it can act as a moral check against violation, and neutralism then becomes a significant element in a regional balance – as in Scandinavia. If Turkey could build internal cohesion, maintain unswerving leadership and establish an industrial-military capability of her own that could convince the two super-powers of her ability to keep an equal distance from both while defending her own interests, neutralism or non-alignment might be a realistic alternative. But without these assets, Turkish determination might crumple in the face of internal or external pressure. In the 1920s and 1930s both the world and the regional context were congenial to the preservation of Turkish neutralism. Both have changed. In the world of today, Turkey would find it hard to hold her course, not so much when super-power relations are stable but when the super-powers are competing in surrounding or adjacent areas.

A non-aggression pact with the Soviet Union has been suggested to bolster a policy of neutralism. The Helsinki Final Act assiduously repeated the principle of respect for the inviolability of borders and ruled out acts of aggression but any non-aggression pact would only add a new documentary pledge. An internationally guaranteed neutralism, on the pattern of Austrian neutralism, might be a more convincing arrangement if Turkey were to become internally cohesive enough to opt for neutralism. Of course, the historical conditions of Austrian neutralism were different, yet its clearly defined structure and the consensus between the super-powers that it is untouchable make it an attractive option for Turkey. Here again the internal factor is extremely important. Turks would have to re-educate themselves not to capitalize on Turkey's geographical position either for foreign policy or for domestic purposes, and to eschew the temptation to use that position to extract concessions.

The recent adoption of a formula for the reintegration of Greece into NATO (which involved Turkish concession) and the settlement of the technical issues of air traffic arrangements are signs that the political will to settle all outstanding matters of concern may now be present in a way that it has not been in recent years. It is too early to be more positive than that.

Any improvement in Greek-Turkish relations will certainly make it easier to resolve the question of Cyprus and the Turkish military presence on the island. The world regards Cyprus as an independent state, yet Greece and Turkey constitute a frame of reference for the political moves of the two ethnic communities on the island. The sooner Turkey and Greece can settle their other differences, therefore, the more receptive the Turkish and Greek communities will be to the idea of a negotiated settlement, and this should open the way to a withdrawal of the Turkish force from the island. International lobbying by both Greece and Turkey has not helped the situation. If it continues, Turkey, who lacks an international political and ethnic constituency, can only respond by retaining her force on the island. She may also try to build her own constituency in another direction – the Middle East.

Turkey's turn towards the Middle East is likely to continue with increasing pace and intensity. The need for oil supplies and development funds are only two of the impulses that are encouraging her to establish cordial ties with Arab and Islamic countries. The larger political objective is to make it clear that Turkey is part of the region and that her own security is intimately connected with regional security; closer contacts and exchanges should follow. To succeed in this rather sweeping re-orientation, Turkey must convince other regional powers, as well as the US, that her foreign policy is independent of the United States on matters pertaining to the Middle East and that she is in no sense to be seen as an agent of the West in the region.

Her return to the Middle East does not revolve around the issues of the Israeli – Egyptian Peace Treaty or Islamic fundamentalism. Her diplomatic commitment to the cause of the Palestinians is more than verbal; it is the expression of a political and moral conviction sustained for more than a decade, and it does not hinge on the question of maintaining or severing diplomatic ties either with Egypt or Israel. As noted above, Turkey consented to the establishment of a Bureau by the PLO in 1976. But the most tangible evidence that Turkey intends to distance herself from American policies in the Middle East has been demonstrated by her unwillingness to allow the use of her territory by the United States for military purposes. And she will certainly not encourage any new alliances or new formal security arrangements based on either super-power in the region.

Although the Islamic connection can enhance co-operation, it cannot initiate it, nor can Islam alone sustain co-operation which is not functional and mutually advantageous to the participants. Therefore, while the potential of Islam for fostering co-operation will be utilized by Turkey, its limits will have to be recognized. The recent 'revival of Islam' has a strong anti-Western impulse, and this reinforces the current Turkish disenchantment with Westernization, but it is too simplistic to suggest that Turkey's turn towards the Middle East is solely, or even mainly, a result of anti-Western sentiment. It would be mutually self-defeating for both Turkey and Europe – and the West in general – to isolate Turkey or to drift apart irrevocably. On the other hand, the visa requirements recently imposed on Turkish citizens by several Western European countries may be a new sign of Western European intention to slowly exclude Turkey from its circle, a possibility that the Turkish defence community and the pro-EEC forces have been wary of for some time. What is needed is an even-handed foreign policy which can capitalize on Turkey's unique position as a country in both Europe and the Middle East. It need not result in a question of identity or loyalty. In any case there can hardly be clear-cut, binding defence links between Turkey and the Middle East in the near future, for there are hardly any common perceptions of the threat beyond a general feeling that all are vulnerable to external influences and resentful of manipulation. CENTO is dead and cannot be resurrected in the near future.

CONCLUSIONS

It was never the intention of this Paper to prescribe a security policy for Turkey nor does it attempt to predict which direction Turkey will take. Whatever choice is made – or even if no choice is made, and things continue more or less as they do now (a much less than wholehearted commitment to the West) – the internal and external political factors seem unlikely to change much from those set out here. What is certainly true in Turkey's case is that there are extremely intractable problems of domestic political stability to be solved, and that solutions are needed for her systemic economic difficulties *before* security policy can be redefined. Turkey must discover where she is going. Only then can she give expression to a clear and logical security policy which derives from a confident foreign policy and a sense of knowing where Turkey fits into the overall scheme of things.

Events have occurred with bewildering rapidity since the latter part of 1979. Surprises and miscalculations are rarely absent in world affairs, which makes projecting the future a risky task. But not often do events have so swift and intense an impact on the international climate, directly or indirectly, as the recent series of dramatic developments. The Soviet intervention and continued presence in Afghanistan, the suspension of the process of ratifying the SALT II Treaty in the American Congress as part of the broader American response, and mounting tensions over the inability of diplomacy to resolve the issue of American diplomats held hostage by Iranian students – these and other developments (some older in origin, such as China's 'opening to the West', the pressures of oil dependence) signal a new and possibly a dangerous era in world politics in the '80s.

Not surprisingly, Turkish perceptions of national and world security do not remain static when actions and reactions in world politics echo with threats to peace. The detente process, never more than an illusion at best to the sceptics, has suffered seriously, though one hopes that it has not been totally and irreversibly destroyed. The spirit and the policy of detente between the super-powers was one of the major premises of this study of the Turkish security situation in the closing years of the 1970s. When the super-powers seem to have suspended mutual dialogue and co-operation publicly, and when the situation in South-West Asia and the Middle East is even more dangerously unstable than it was in 1979, it is no wonder that Turkish perceptions of insecurity have markedly increased.

The changes in the international climate roughly coincided with increasing strain in Turkey, which led to the military coup in September 1980. The Demirel government, which had come to power as a result of by-election victories won in October 1979, had already steered Turkey towards a firmer commitment with the West and the Atlantic Alliance. The NATO Council decision of December 1979 to modernize theatre nuclear weapons in Europe was upheld in principle, but Turkey would not accept them on her soil if asked. In early 1980 the Government let it be known that it would apply for full membership of the EEC before the end of the year. In March 1980 it withdrew the Turkish NOTAM 714 of 4 August 1974, as a gesture of goodwill towards Greece at a time when reports of the plan prepared by General Rogers concerning command and control arrangements over the Aegean first appeared in the press. Turkey withdrew from her previous position – that settlement of bilateral issues must precede Greek reintegration to the military structure – so that Greek return is now agreed, but there remains much hard negotiation ahead between the two countries. The Turkish-American Defence Co-operation Agreement was signed in April 1980, after arduous negotiations lasting over two years, reportedly with the explicit understanding that air bases in Turkey would not be used for non-NATO purposes.

It is highly likely that the Soviet action in Afghanistan exerted considerable, though not exclusive, weight on the shift of official policy towards a position of greater commitment with the West. But it should also be noted that, while the Soviet Union's public image has been seriously damaged as a result of her intervention in Afghanistan, (except naturally among the pro-Moscow political forces), neither official statements nor the public mood perceive an immediate and direct threat to Turkey from the Soviet Union. According to many, efforts to preserve what is left of detente must not be abandoned either by the Soviet Union, which dealt a blow to it by her actions in Afghanistan, or by the United States, which seems to have lost confidence in the merits of detente for American interests and whose recent frustrations with the Soviet Union and Iran seem to have strengthened the position of conservatives in the government and bureaucracy.

Turkey refrained from taking a hostile position towards Iran over the dispute with the US about the hostage issue, while denouncing the act of taking and keeping hostages as contrary to international law. She has also avoided taking sides in the Iranian-Iraqi dispute. These attitudes reflect Turkey's overall approach to several salient questions in her immediate neighbourhood: moderation and non-interference when neighbouring countries are faced with tremendous turbulence and internal and external challenges or, like Iraq and Syria, are at loggerheads.

In general therefore, it appears that – despite the rapid and extensive changes in the security environment in which Turkey must operate – the fundamental constraints affecting Turkish security policy remain largely unchanged. It seems reasonable to predict that, with the fundamental constraints largely unchanged, the policy will not change much either. Uncomfortable though it may sometimes be, Turkey will continue to seek security through ties with NATO and the United States.

NOTES

[1] From the excerpts of the Minutes of the Potsdam (Berlin) Conference. See Ferenc A. Vali, *The Turkish Straits and NATO* (Stanford: Hoover Institution Press, 1972), p. 238.

[2] For a lucid overview of Kemalist reforms, see Bernard Lewis, *The Emergence of Modern Turkey* (London: OUP, 1961), Part II.

[3] Unless otherwise stated, the figures and percentages quoted in this section have been obtained from the following sources: T. C. Maliye Bakanligi (Ministry of Finance of the Republic of Turkey), *1978 Yillik Ekonomik Rapor (The Annual Economic Report, 1978)* (Ankara: 1978); OECD, *Turkey* (Paris: 1978); State Planning Organization, *Developments in the Economy of Turkey, 1963-1978* (Ankara: 1978); T. C. Basbakanlik Devlet Planlama Teskilati, (State Planning Organization, The Prime Ministry of the Republic of Turkey), *Dördüncü Beş Yillik Kalkinma Plani, 1979-1983 (The Fourth Five-Year Development Plan, 1979-1983)* (Ankara: 1979); Turkish Industrialists' and Businessmen's Association, *The Turkish Economy: Prospects for Growth Within Stability: 1978* (Istanbul: 1978).

[4] *The Military Balance 1977-1978*, p. 82, and *The Military Balance 1978-1979*, p. 89 (London: IISS, 1977, 1978). The percentages may vary slightly when computed directly in Turkish Lira. For Lira figures see note 57.

[5] Türk Sanayicileri ve İşadamlari Derneği, (Turkish Industrialists' and Businessmen's Association), *Avrupa Ekonomik Toplulugu Üzerine Görüsler-Yaklaşimlar (Views and Approaches Concerning the European Economic Community)* (Istanbul: 1976), p. 6.

[6] For the highlights of the Turkish requests in Autumn 1978 and the EEC response in Spring 1979 see Avrupa Toplulgu Komisyonu Enformasyon Temsilciligi (Information Representative of the European Community Commission in Ankara), *Avrupa (Europe)*, no. 42 (June 1979), pp. 21-3 and no. 45 (October 1979), pp. 19-22.

[7] Petrol Ofisi Genel Müdürlügü (General Directorate of Petroleum Office), *İstatistik Bulteni, 1970-1977 (Statistical Bulletin, 1970-1977)* (Ankara: undated), p. 6

[8] *Resmi Gazete (The Offical Gazette)*, 19 June 1977, in Olgun, Cidar, 'Foreign Policy Issues in 1977 General Elections and Subsequent Government Programs', *Foreign Policy* (Ankara), vol. VII, no. 1-2, (July 1978) p. 9. 9.

[9] According to the press reports, the RPP polled only about 28% of the votes while the JP's votes went up to 47%. There was no major change in the position of the smaller parties.

[10] Aydin Yalçin, 'New Trends in Communism in Europe: The Case in Turkey', *Foreign Policy* (Ankara), vol. VII, No. 1-2 (July, 1978), p. 29.

[11] Retired Admiral Sezai Orkunt feels that allusions to the military's ultimate supremacy over civilian authority are unjustified and unwanted. Sezai Orkunt, *Türkiye-ABD Askeri İlişkileri (Turkish-US Military Relations)*, (Istanbul: Milliyet Yayinlari, 1978), p. 380.

[12] One of the more recent contributions to the documentary literature on the history of Turkish foreign policy is the five-volume series *Türkiye Dis Politikasinda 50 Yil (50 Years of Turkish Foreign Policy)* (Ankara: General Directorate of Research and Policy Planning of the Ministry of Foreign Affairs, 1973). Six more volumes are planned.

[13] For a first-hand account of the foreign policy developments and objectives of this period, see: Mustafa Kemal Atatürk, *A Speech Delivered by Ghazi Mustafa Kemal, President of the Turkish Republic, October 1927* (Leipzig: K. F. Koehler, 1929), and Yusuf Hikmet Bayhur, *Türkiye Devletinin Dis Siyasasi (Foreign Policy of the State of Turkey)* (Ankara: Türk Tarih Kurumu Yayini, 1973. First printing, 1942).

[14] The friendship of this period was recalled by Soviet writers and by Turkish intellectuals and foreign policy analysts after normalization began in mid-1960s. See V. Nikitin, 'Good Neighbourly and Equal Cooperation', *International Affairs* (Moscow), no. 7 (July 1970).

[15] The many works on Turkish policy during the war include Annette Baker Fox, *The Power of Small States: Diplomacy in World War II* (Chicago: University of Chicago Press, 1959); Türkkaya Ataov, *Turkish Foreign Policy: 1939—1945* (Ankara: Ankara University Faculty of Political Science, 1965), and Edward Weisband, *Turkish Foreign Policy, 1943—1945: (Small State Diplomacy and Great Powers Politics)* (Princeton; Princeton UP, 1973).

[16] For a picture of the evolution of the British and American positions, the records of the Yalta and Potsdam Conferences provide the best source. See also US Department of State, *The Problem of the Turkish Straits* (Washington DC: USGPO, 1947), pp. 36—60, and Harry N. Howard, *Turkey, the Straits and US Policy*, (Baltimore: John Hopkins UP, 1974), chapter VII.

[17] See, for example, Feridun Cemal Erkin, *Les Relations Turco-Sovietiques et La Question Des Détroits* (Ankara: Basnur Matbaasi, 1968).

[18] Faculty of Political Science, University of Ankara, *Turkey and the United Nations* (New York: Manhattan Publishing for the Carnegie Endowment for International Peace, 1961), pp. 132–45.

[19] Edward Cochran, 'Turkey Prepares for Shock Waves', *Guardian*, 5 August 1975.

[20] Quoted in Ferenc A. Vali, *op. cit.* in note 1, p. 303.

[21] From Professor Wohlstetter's testimony on 15 April 1978 before the Foreign Relations Committee of the House of Representatives, US Congress. Reprinted in *NATO, Turkey and US Interests*, (Washington DC: American Foreign Policy Institute, 1978).

[22] Sergei G. Gorshkov, *Red Star Rising at Sea*, translated by Theodore A. Neely, Jr. from a series of articles originally published in *Morskoi Sbornik* (Printed in the US, copyright 1974 by the US Naval Institute), pp. 20, 21.

[23] *Ibid.*

[24] Barry Buzan, 'The Status and Future of the Montreux Convention', *Survival*, November/December 1976, p. 243; also H. Gary Knight, 'The Kiev and the Turkish Straits', *AJIL*, January, 1977, p. 128.

[25] British Broadcasting Corporation, *Summary of World Broadcasts* (hereafter referred to as SWB, SU/5716/A4/1, 18 January 1978.

[26] For a discussion of the issues, see also: 'The Dispute Between Greece and Turkey Concerning The Continental Shelf in the Aegean', *American Journal of International Law*, vol: 71, no. 1 (January 1977), pp. 31-59, and Peter

87

Foster, 'Greece and Turkey: The Aegean Conflict', *Swiss Review of World Affairs* (March 1976), pp. 10–12. See also Andrew Wilson, *The Aegean Dispute,* Adelphi Paper No. 155 (London IISS, 1980) for a full discussion of these issues.
[27] *Milliyet,* 26 July 1979, 31 August 1979.
[28] *Newsweek,* 25 June 1979, p. 25.
[29] *Tercüman,* 14 July 1979.
[30] George F. Kennan, 'The Sources of Soviet Power', *Foreign Affairs,* XXV (July 1947), The Bobs-Merrill Reprint Series in the Social Sciences, p. 152.
[31] Thomas W. Wolfe, *Soviet Power and Europe, 1945-1970* (Baltimore: John Hopkins Press, 1970), p. 26.
[32] Spanier, *op. cit.,* p. 119.
[33] Harold van B. Cleveland, *The Atlantic Idea and Its European Rivals* (New York: McGraw-Hill, 1966), p. 38.
[34] Spanier, *op. cit.,* pp. 112–13.
[35] Robert E. Osgood, NATO: *The Entangling Alliance* (Chicago: University of Chicago Press, 1962), pp. 79–81.
[36] The circumstances of the missiles' removal were resented in Turkey primarily because the US rode roughshod over Turkey, removing them without prior consultation with Turkey in the interests of accommodation with the USSR. For an account of their place in the Cuban crisis, see Donald L. Hafner, 'Bureaucratic Politics and "Those Frigging Missiles": JFK, Cuba and US Missiles in Turkey', *Orbis,* vol. 21, no: 2 (summer, 1977), pp. 307–32.
[37] US Congress, Senate, *US Turkish Defence Cooperation Agreement.* Hearing Before the Committee on Foreign Relations, 94th Congress. 15 September 1976 (Washington DC: USGPO, 1976).
[38] *Op. cit.,* in note 21, p. 359.
[39] John M. Collins and John Steven Chwat, *Greece and Turkey: Some Military Implications Related to NATO and the Middle East.* Report prepared for the Special Subcommittee on Investigations of the Committee on Foreign Affairs by the Congressional Research Service, Library of Congress, 28 February, (Washington: USGPO, 1975), p. 18; *op. cit.* in note 21.
[40] Assembly of Western European Union, *Security in the Mediterranean,* 24th Ordinary Session, Document 776, 31 May 1978, p. 18. For the composition and strength of the Turkish forces, see: *The Military Balance, 1978-1979* (London: IISS, 1978), p. 28.
[41] For a general comparison of Turkish forces with Soviet and Warsaw Pact forces, see: William A. Knowlton, 'Security in the Mediterranean', *The Atlantic Community Quarterly,* vol. 15, no. 3 (Fall 1977), pp. 356–7; Admiral Harold E. Shear. 'The Southern Flank of NATO', *NATO's Fifteen Nations,* December 1978–January 1979, pp. 19-20.
[42] 'Controversy Over the Cutoff of Military Aid to Turkey', *Congressional Digest,* April, 1975, p. 104.
[43] Western European Union, *op. cit.,* in note 40, p. 14.
[44] Jack Anderson, 'Turkey: Neighbourly With the Soviet', *Washington Post,* 18 June 1978, in *Current News,* Main Edition, 19 June 1978.
[45] The major causes of Turkish uneasiness with the bilateral agreements are dealt with extensively in George Harris, *The Troubled Alliance: Turkish-American Problems in Historical Perspective, 1945-1971* (Stanford: Stanford U.P., 1975), pp. 54–9.
[46] Foreign Affairs and National Defence Division, Congressional Research Service, Library of Congress, *United States Military Installations and Objectives in the Mediterranean,*

Report Prepared for the Sub-committee on Europe and the Middle East of the Committee on International Relations, 95th Congress, 27 March, 1977 (Washington: USGPO, 1977), pp. 37–41.
[47] For the text of President Johnson's letter, see *op. cit.,* in note 1, pp. 309–13.
[48] For text of Prime Minister İnönü's reply, *ibid.,* pp. 313–24.
[49] Figures from the relevant editions *The Military Balance.* Official Turkish figures in Turkish Lira are as follows: for 1974, defence budget T.L. 13,4 billion, total budget T.L. 82, 4 billion; for 1975, defence budget T.L. 20,8 billion, total budget T.L. 107, 7 billion; for 1976, defence budget T.L. 33,5 billion, total budget T.L. 155,6 billion; for 1977, defence budget T.L. 42,5 billion, total budget T.L. 229,7 billion; for 1978, defence budget T.L. 52,8 billion, total budget T.L. 276,1 billion, in: T.C. Maliye Bakanliği, *1979 Mali Yili Bütçe Gerekçesi* (The Ministry of Finance of the Republic of Turkey, *The Budget Justification For Financial Year 1979)* (Ankara, 1978) p. 23.
[50] Appropriations for the REMO project increased from 1,6 billion Turkish Lira for 1973 and 1974 to 6 billion for 1976, and 8,6 billion for 1977, but fell to 8 billion lira for 1978 *(Resmı Gazete) (Official Gazette),* 1 March 1973, p. 65; 1 June 1974, p. 62; 1 March 1976, p. 92; 1 March 1977, p. 227; 1 March 1978, p. 228).
[51] *Financial Times,* 17 January 1976.
[52] *Air International,* February, 1977.
[53] *Flight International,* 24 January 1976.
[54] *International Defense Review,* May 1978.
[55] U. Albrecht, *et. al., Silahlanma ve Azgelismislik* (translated into Turkish by U. Kivanc and M. Budak, Istanbul, 1978), p. 287.
[56] David Tonge, 'Armed Forces Reassess Status in NATO', *Financial Times,* 23 November 1977.
[57] *Cumhuriyet,* 13 September 1979.
[58] For the highlights of the criticisms, see: Ferenc A. Vali, *Bridge Across The Bosporus: The Foreign Policy of Turkey* (Baltimore: Johns Hopkins UP, 1971), pp. 120–1. The debate was more pervasive in the press, though budget debates in the National Assembly occasioned a critical appraisal by a few parliamentarians, (see: *Millet Meclisi Tutanak Dergisi (The National Assembly Journal of Minutes),* vol. 26, 24 February 1968, pp. 337–43, 357–63; vol. 33, 17 February 1969, pp. 387–432; vol. 5, 24 May 1970, pp. 390–7 p. 544). For an incisive analysis of the implications of the NATO strategy for Turkey, see Mehmet Gönlübol, 'NATO and Turkey', in Kemal Karpat, *Turkey's Foreign Policy in Transition, 1950—1974,* (Leiden: Brill, 1975). For a systematic analysis of the new strategy by a high-ranking Foreign Ministry official, see Şükrü Elekdağ, 'Nükleer Cağda Strateji ve NATO Stratejisindeki Gelismeler'. (Strategy in the Nuclear Age and Developments in NATO Strategy') in *Türkiye ve NATO (Turkey and NATO),* (Turkish Atlantic Treaty Association, publication no. 1), pp. 93-111.
[59] *Op. cit.,* in note 56.
[60] Sir Peter Hill-Norton, *No Soft Options, The Politico-Military Realities of NATO* (London: Hurst, 1978), p. 151.
[61] 'Turkey Refuses to Reaffirm Faith in NATO', *Daily Telegraph,* 17 May 1978. For an official view of the role of Eurogroup, see Neset Akmandor 'Turkish and European Security – The Role of Eurogroup', *NATO Review,* vol. 27,

[62] "U.S. – Turkish Pact to Stress Economic Aid', *Baltimore Sun*, 18 October 1978, p. 6.

[63] SWB SU/5794/A4/1, 21 April 1978; SU/5795/A4/1, 22 April 1978; SU/5799/A4/1, 27 April 1978.

[64] SWB SU/5773/A4/5, 28 March 1978.

[65] *Op. cit.*, in note 58, p. 174.

[66] Turkish Industrialists' and Businessmen's Association, *The Turkish Economy, 1979* (Istanbul, 1979), p. 213.

[67] F. Stephen Larrabee, *Balkan Security* Adelphi Paper No. 135 (London: IISS, 1977), p. 23.

[68] G. Nikolayev, 'Soviet-Turkish Relations', *International Affairs* (Moscow), No. 11 (November 1968), p. 37.

[69] I. Shatalov, 'Ankara: New Climate', *International Affairs (Moscow)*, No. 3 (March 1967), p. 75.

[70] *Op. cit.*, in note 68, p. 39.

[71] *Milliyet*, 15 September 1978, from *Die Welt*.

[72] For Soviet commentaries on the anti-Sovietism of the Maoists and of Chinese Foreign Minister Huang Hua during his visit to Turkey in June 1978, SWB, SU/5733/A4/5, 7 February 1978, SU/5842/C1/1, 19 June 1978.

[73] SWB SU/5846/C/2, 23 June 1978; SU/5738/A4/3, 13 February 1978; SU/5782/A4/1, 7 April 1978; SU/5765/A4/1, 16 March 1978.

[74] T.C. Başbakanlik, Halkla İlişkiler ve Enformasyon Dairesi Başkanliği, *Diş Siyaset Belgeleri (Documents on Foreign Policy*, Published by the Office of Public Relations and Information), The Prime Ministry of Turkey, Vol. 1 (Ankara: Başbakanlik Basimevi, 1976), p. 193.

[75] E. Bagramov, 'The Soviet Nationalities Policy and Bourgeois Falsifications', *International Affairs* (Moscow), no. 6 (June 1978). For a comprehensive study that brings out the divergence between Soviet and Western perceptions of the nature of Soviet nationalities policy, see I. Zenushkina, *Soviet Nationalities Policy and Bourgeois Historians* (Moscow: Progess Publishers, 1975).

[76] 'What Colour is Pan-Turkism?', *International Affairs* (Moscow), no. 8 (August 1968), p. 97.

[77] 'Behind the Screen of the Islamic Pact', *International Affairs* (Moscow), no. 4 (April 1966); 'Inside and Outside the Islamic Pact', *Ibid.*, no. 8 (August 1966).

[78] 'Romanian-Turkish Relations', *Lumea* (Bucharest), no. 37(17-23 November, 1978), p. 7.

[79] Turkish Industrialists and Businessmen's Association, *The Turkish Economy, 1979*, (Istanbul: 1979), pp. 213, 219.

3 The Aegean Dispute
ANDREW WILSON

INTRODUCTION

The Aegean sea has been an area of military and political confrontation since the abduction of Helen of Troy. For long periods conflicts in the area have tended to reflect cultural and religious differences between Europe and Asia, as when Persian fleets and armies descended on the early Greek city states, or when the Knights of St John attempted to restore the Byzantine Empire. However, the present dispute between Greece and Turkey is a break with history in that both countries are, however uncertainly, members of a 'European' alliance (NATO). Turkey in particular, forming a bridge between the two continents, has for sixty years sought to resolve her problem of identity by facing westwards. Yet it would be unrealistic to ignore past events and their continuing influence both on popular opinion in the two countries and on Western attitudes towards them.

For this reason this study gives more space to history, albeit fairly recent history, than is customary in an Adelphi Paper. It reflects both the enmities of the past and the spirit of the years between 1923 and the late 1950s when Greece and Turkey lived in amity. It also notes the role played by individual political leaders, for it is they, rather than any doctrines, who have determined (and remain likely to determine) relations between the two countries.

This Paper occasionally goes out of its way to try to describe each side's perception of the other's intentions. This is in the hope that, by comparing such perceptions with the facts as they appear to an impartial observer, it may be possible to unravel the knot of mutual suspicions that has contributed to the difficulties of the present situation. It also seeks, by analysing each side's suggested procedures for reaching a settlement, to identify issues which may be beyond the capacity of the parties themselves to resolve.[1] Finally it looks at a number of formulae that could be used by an arbitrator.

It is a Turkish complaint that Western attitudes towards Greek–Turkish differences are frequently coloured by philhellinism, reflecting both the romantic tradition of the nineteenth century and also ignorance of what modern Turkey stands for. There may be justice in this complaint, but it is also possible that many commentators of the opposite persuasion fail to understand the basic sense of insecurity that pervades Greek politics – a legacy of the years of Ottoman rule no less than of Greek suffering in World War II and more recently.

Both governments have generously given facilities, and individuals their time, for the purpose of this study. They have done so in the belief, which I have tried to fulfil, that it will help to narrow, not widen, their differences. The reflection and interpretation of their views in the following pages is, of course, unofficial and my own.

I. HISTORY, GEOGRAPHY AND INTERNATIONAL LAW

The 'Aegean dispute' is a composite term covering three separate but related issues between Greece and Turkey:
1. The dispute about sovereign rights over the Aegean continental shelf.
2. The question of the territorial sea limits claimed by each country.
3. A dispute over military and civil air traffic control zones in the Aegean area.

Three other questions are intimately involved and must be considered in connection with the Aegean dispute: the remilitarization of the Greek islands of the eastern Aegean, whose demilitarization was ordered by the Treaties of Lausanne and Paris; the problem of minorities (the Greek Orthodox minority in Istanbul and on the islands of Gockeada (Imbros) and Bozcada (Tenedos), and the Muslim minority in Western Thrace); and – overshadowing all else – the Cyprus question.

Greek–Turkish Relations up to 1947

Throughout the nineteenth century the Greeks had fought for their freedom from the Turkish Sultanate. Starting in the Peloponnese in 1821, the War of Independence spread first to Attica, then to the islands of the Western Aegean, and finally to Crete. Subsequently, after the Russo-Turkish war of 1877–8 and a conference in Constantinople in 1881, nearly all central Greece was brought under the Greek flag. But until the Balkan wars of 1912–13 the north, including the second largest city, Salonika, remained Turkish, with a large Turkish population, as did the islands of the Eastern Aegean. At the same time, Greeks dominated and administered many of the cities of Asia Minor, including Izmir (Smyrna), as well as the commercial life of Istanbul (Constantinople).

During this time Greek irredentism was aimed at territories under Ottoman rule inhabited by Greek Orthodox Christians. Beginning in the early 1850s, while Turkey was at war with Russia, the notion grew of a partial revival under Greek rule of the Byzantine Empire, known as 'The Great Idea'. The Great Idea became a national obsession, reaching a climax after the defeat of Turkey in World War I.

In 1919 Greek troops landed in the Smyrna region of Asia Minor to enforce a mandate given to Greece by the victorious Allies to occupy the mainly Greek areas of western Anatolia. Under the Treaty of Sèvres (1920) the region's population was to decide in five years' time whether to become part of Greece or remain with Turkey. But this plan was upset in 1920 by the successful revolt of Kemal Ataturk against the weak government of the Sultan and by the defeat, in the Greek elections, of the level-headed prime minister Venizelos (who had brought Greece into the war on the side of the Allies). Venizelos was ousted by his Germanophile opponent, King Constantine.

Faced with Ataturkist resistance to the Greek occupation and gravely misjudging the reaction of the Allies, the King's General Staff decided in 1921 to launch an attack against Ataturk's stronghold in Ankara. Advancing from Smyrna, the Greek armies came within sixty miles of Ankara, where, caught with greatly overextended communications in a terrible winter, they were crushingly defeated by the rejuvenated Turkish forces under Ataturk in early 1922. Thirty thousand died, Smyrna was destroyed, and 1,350,000 refugees were expelled from Asia Minor to fall on the resources of the impoverished Greek homeland.

The events of this period left a trauma in both countries, and not least Turkey, where even today there is a tendency to see a revival of the Great Idea in any Greek move thought hostile to Turkish interests. But they also led to a new and stable relationship which lasted until the onset of the present Cyprus dispute.[2] The basis of this relationship was the Treaty of Lausanne (signed in 1923) under which Greece, Turkey, Great Britain and France determined the frontier and created a balance between the two countries. The land frontier, which as late as 1912 had run through Central Greece, just south of Volos, was now fixed on the present line running northwards through Thrace to Edirne (Adrianople). The whole of Anatolia was recognized as belonging to Turkey. At the same time Turkey recognized as Greek the islands of Lemnos, Lesbos, Chios, Samos and Icaria, which had been wrested from Ottoman control between 1878 and 1913. A corollary of the frontier settlement was the exchange of populations agreed in the 1923 Treaty. Under it the entire Greek Orthodox population remaining in Asia Minor, with the exception of those in Istanbul and on the islands of Imbros and Tenedos, was transferred to Greece and the Muslim population, except that in western Thrace, to Turkey. An international commission supervised the move and the payment of compensation for property. Although by modern stands, the exchange paid little attention to human rights, it helped to defuse more than a century of tension, and the spirit of the 'Venizelos–Ataturk era' is today recalled approvingly in both countries.

A further settlement underlying today's frontiers was the Treaty of Paris (1947). This was the peace treaty between Italy and the Allies, including Greece, after World War II, which disposed of Italy's overseas possessions. Among these were the Dodecanese islands: Astypalaia, Rhodes, Telos, Chalki, Karpathos, Kasos, Megisti (Kastellorizo), Nysiros, Kalymnos, Leros, Patmos, Lipsos, Syme, Cos 'and adjacent islets'.

These islands had in most cases been Turkish from the sixteenth century until taken by Italy in the Italian–Turkish war of 1912. Their Italian ownership had then been confirmed in the World War I peace settlement by the Treaty of Lausanne. Turkish commentators sometimes argue that Turkey 'agreed to' their transfer to Greece thirty-five years later as a token of her joining the post-war Western alliance. But this is not so. The Dodecanese, with an overwhelmingly Greek population, were awarded to Greece in compensation for her sufferings under wartime Italian and German occupation. Turkey, a neutral in World War II, was in no position to obstruct the transfer, even if she had wished to do so.

The Geopolitical Balance

Since the settlements of 1923 and 1947, non-territorial developments have established the economic and military balance of the Aegean region. The statistics can be read in two ways: as supporting each side's claim to an equitable share of the resources of the region, or as indicators of each side's ability to exert pressure for a favourable settlement.

The current principal statistical elements, shown in Table 1, gain significance when projected in time and considered in greater detail. Thus a projection based on current birth rates

Table 1

	Greece	Turkey
Population	9,245,000	40,130,000
Area	131,990 sq. km	780,576 sq. km
GNP (1978)	$32·3 bn	$45·3 bn
Army	145,000	470,000
Fighting ships*	72	124
Combat aircraft	259	303
Merchant marine (million gross registered tons)	49	1·3

* Including submarines, excluding landing craft.

would give Turkey a population of about 71 million by the end of this century, and Greece a population of 10·6 million. Of the present population of Turkey, about 5 million (12·5%) are concentrated within 100 kilometres of the Aegean coast, compared with a Greek population of about 3 million (30%) in the Aegean islands and the Aegean-facing areas of the Greek mainland. In other words, while in absolute figures the population balance in the area favours Turkey, a substantially larger proportion of the Greek population is likely to depend on the Aegean for its livelihood.

The place of the Aegean in Greek life and in the Greek economy is also reflected in the number of ports. In addition to the two main Greek ports, Piraeus and Thessaloniki, with an annual combined trade of 15,742,883 tons,[3] there are three smaller ports on the Greek coast (Alexandroupolis, Kavala and Volos) and some ten ports of varying size on the islands: Vathy (Samos), Kalymnos, Mytilene (Lesbos), Rhodes, Syros, Halkis (Euboea), Chios, Heraklion, Souda and Chania (the last three in Crete). Turkey, in addition to Izmir (and, at a distance, Istanbul), has five smaller ports on the Aegean coast – Canakkale, Edremit, Cesme, Kusadasi and Bodrum. Although the Aegean is a greater source of livelihood to Greece than it is to Turkey, the latter, of course, depends on free movement across the Aegean for an important part of her trade and communications.[4]

The military balance, apparently favouring Turkey, is also more complex than mere force strengths suggest. Forces must be kept available for internal security purposes, as is the case in every country, and furthermore, even allowing for some redeployment as a result of detente with the Soviet Union, a large part of Turkey's army must continue to guard her frontiers in Asia, particularly with Iran and with the troubled Kurdish area in Iraq.

In air power, Greece's three F-4E *Phantom* squadrons, three A-7H *Corsair* II squadrons and two F-104G *Starfighter* squadrons face Turkey's three F-4E, three F-5, three F-100 and two F-104G squadrons. Turkey has additionally suffered setbacks to the modernization of her forces as a result of the American arms embargo imposed after the Cyprus landing of 1974 and conditionally repealed by Congress in August 1978. Army conscripts, for example, have had to be released before the end of their 20-month term for want of equipment.

The Legal Background
It could be argued that Turkey would never have signed the Treaty of Lausanne if the Ataturk government had been able to foresee the developments that were to take place in regard to the Law of the Sea in the latter part of this century. As Barry Buzan has pointed out, the old ocean regime, in which anyone could do what he liked outside a three-mile territorial sea limit, was bound to decay as pressure increased by a multitude of states on what are now recognized as limited maritime resources.[5] At the same time certain of today's disputes are the results, not of pressure, but of attempts to produce a system for avoiding disputes. The Aegean dispute could be said to fall into this category.

Until 1973 there was no hint of competition to explore the mineral resources of the Aegean. Hopes of finding large oil deposits, prompted by the Greek find off Thasos that year, proved to be short-lived (see Appendix 2). Neither government has published plans for exploiting other mineral deposits, and fishing rights have not been an issue. The Aegean dispute, apart from being a complex projection of other conflicts, is therefore over two main questions: freedom of navigation (the territorial seas question) and sovereign rights in the continental shelf *per se*.

Both these issues were the subject of conventions drawn up by the First United Nations Conference on the Law of the Sea (UNCLOS I) in 1958, which, by providing a new legal definition of the continental shelf and the sovereign rights of states therein, has been the cause of many arguments since. A Convention, dealing with territorial seas, defined a so-called Contiguous Zone, up to 12 miles from the shore, in which coastal states would have jurisdiction over customs, fiscal, sanitary and immigration arrangements. It did not define a maximum limit of territorial seas within the zone, though many states extended their territorial waters as a result of it.[6] Neither Greece nor Turkey have signed the Convention.

Another one, on the Continental Shelf and otherwise known as the Geneva Convention, was signed by Greece but not by Turkey, whose abstention was understandable in view of the advantages the Convention confers on archipelagic states at the expense of others in a confined sea. The Convention provides *inter alia* that:

– 'Continental Shelf' shall refer (*a*) to the seabed adjacent to the coast but outside territorial seas to a depth of 200 metres or, beyond, to a depth where exploitation is technically feasible and (*b*) to a similar submarine area adjacent to the coasts of islands.
– The rights of the coastal state over the continental shelf do not affect the legal status of the waters above as high seas, or the airspace above those waters.
– Exploration and exploitation of the shelf must not result in unjustifiable interference with navigation or fishing or with oceanographic or other scientific research for open publication.
– Subject to the provisions on non-interference with navigation, the coastal state may construct and operate installations for the exploration and exploitation of natural resources, with safety zones of up to 500 metres radius.
– Where the shelf is adjacent to the territories of two or more states whose coasts are opposite each other, the boundaries of the shelf, unless agreed otherwise, shall normally be the median line. But another line may be justified by special circumstances.[7]

In addition to objecting to the definition of the continental shelf as including the submarine area adjacent to islands (Article 1b) and the right of coastal states to exploit such areas, Turkey has put forward her own definition of the Aegean continental shelf as the 'natural prolongation' of Anatolian lands. Under this formula the Turkish continental shelf would extend to the west of the Greek islands adjacent to the Turkish coast, while sovereign rights to exploit the sea bed round such islands would extend no further than the present territorial sea limit, i.e. six miles.

What is at issue in the Aegean dispute is whether the Geneva Convention can be regarded as the 'last word'. Turkey appears to hope that the convention will be overtaken by a new one arising from the current law of the sea conference (UNCLOS III). But Greece can cite opinions to the effect that the 1958 Convention is declaratory of international customary law and thus, by implication, 'final'. This was the opinion of the International Court of Justice in the *North Sea Continental Shelf* case.[8] The principle that islands have a continental shelf is also confirmed in the Informal Composite Negotiating Text of UNCLOS III[9] and conforms with bilateral State practice as exhibited in numerous treaties.[10]

If *both* principles are accepted as having validity (which seems to be the case in a variety of International Court judgements), the task in the Aegean dispute is to find a compromise based on equity – though equity, as the International Court ruled in 1969, does not necessarily imply equality.[11]

Territorial Seas

It is here appropriate to say a further word about territorial sea dispute which, unlike the dispute over the continental shelf and air traffic control (covered in the following chapters) has remained latent rather than active.

At present both Greece and Turkey continue to observe the six-mile territorial sea limit adopted by most maritime countries in the 1920s.[12] Both follow general practice in recognizing that territorial sea limits apply equally to islands, of which Greece has more than 3,000, including 2,383 in the Aegean. Because of the enclosed nature of the Aegean, the effect of this is to designate some 35% of the Aegean as Greek territorial sea and only 8·8% as Turkish territorial sea. It also gravely restricts the number of points at which shipping may enter or leave Turkish territorial sea from international waters (see Map 1 on p. 36).

The position appears to have been acceptable to Turkey for two reasons. First, at the time the six-mile limit was adopted, Turkey took relatively little interest in maritime matters. Secondly, the Geneva Convention, which, although not signed by Turkey, is the current treaty on the subject, leaves untouched the right to innocent passage of all ships, including warships, except for the requirement that submarines transit on the surface and show their flag, and except for the right of the coastal state to expel warships which break its regulations.

The threatened dispute arises from the possibility that Greece might follow most other states in extending her territorial waters to twelve miles. Were she to do so, and Turkey to follow suit, the Greek share of the Aegean would rise to 63·9% and the Turkish to only 10%. The proportion remaining High Sea would fall from 56% to 26·1%, and all ships sailing westwards from Turkish Aegean ports to the Mediterranean would be obliged to pass through Greek waters (see Map 2 on p. 37).

Despite the right of innocent passage, Turkey considers that in these circumstances she would be vulnerable to total enclosure and has said that she would regard a Greek extension as a *casus belli*. Early in the present dispute Greece advised Turkey that she had no intention of announcing an extension, though she reserved the right to do so if occasion arose.

II. DEVELOPMENT OF THE DISPUTE

The Voyage of the Candarli

Although Turkey maintains that earlier Greek activity (the granting of exploration licences in 1970) precipitated it, the dispute about the continental shelf began on 1 November 1973. On this date Turkey awarded mineral exploration rights in the Eastern Aegean to the Turkish State Petroleum Company, TPAO. On the same day the Turkish *Official Gazette* published a map giving the limiting line of the Turkish continental shelf as being west of the Greek islands of Samothrace, Lemnos, Aghios

Efstratios, Lesbos, Chios, Psara and Antipsara. The area thus designated overlapped with the area of the continental shelf claimed by Greece, and in some cases the Turkish awards were in areas where Greece had already granted licences to foreign companies.

When Greece protested, partly to preclude a finding of acquiescence in international law,[13] the first Turkish response, on 28 February 1974, was to propose negotiations. This Greece accepted on 25 May 'in accordance with international law as codified in the Geneva convention' – a step described by the Turkish Prime Minister, Mr Ecevit, as a 'positive development'. Three days later, however, Turkey announced that a survey ship, the *Candarli* was to make magnetometric studies in the Aegean in preparation for oil-drilling. The area of the survey, according to the Minister for Power and Natural Resources, Mr Cahit Kayra, was to be 'in the Turkish continental shelf'.

The *Candarli* entered the Aegean on 29 May and, accompanied by 32 warships of the Turkish navy, spent six days exploring and sailing along the western limit of the areas in which Turkey had granted mineral exploration concessions. In the ensuing tense situation Greece sent a new protest, which Turkey rejected. A month later Turkey granted more exploration licences, extending further west and south including the waters around all the Dodecanese Islands.

At this point (in mid-July) the continental shelf dispute was overtaken by a sequence of outside events: the Samson coup in Cyprus, the Turkish intervention, and the fall of the Greek military junta in Athens and the return of Mr Karamanlis. The landing of Turkish troops, which was to lead to the occupation of nearly 40% of Cyprus, put Turkey in a position of strength in the island, with the possibility of trading concessions in Cyprus against concessions in the Aegean. The Cyprus crisis also introduced a new element – the dispute over air traffic control zones.

In 1952 a regional conference of the International Civil Aviation Organization (ICAO), with Greece and Turkey participating, had decided that, except for the narrow band of Turkish national airspace off the Anatolian coast, Aegean controlled airspace over the Aegean should form part of the Athens Flight Information Region (FIR) for air traffic control purposes. The arrangement, which was purely technical, meant that all aircraft flying west from Turkey, whether civil or military, were required to file flight plans and report position as they crossed the FIR boundary a minute or so after leaving the Turkish coast (see Map 1 on p. 36). They then came under orders of the Athens flight control centre, which was responsible for providing meteorological and other information. Aircraft flying eastwards from Greece were similarly required to report to the control centre in Istanbul as they entered the Turkish FIR. To have placed the FIR boundary further to the west would have obliged Greek aircraft to pass through a Turkish control zone on flights to the Greek islands. To this extent the arrangement was consistent with geography and seems to have worked well for 22 years. But in the tension following the Cyprus landing it broke down.

On 4 August the Turkish authorities issued NOTAM 714 (a notice to ICAO for transmission to all air users) requiring all aircraft approaching Turkish airspace to report their position and flight plan on reaching the Aegean median line, which lay considerably to the west of the FIR line. The purpose, according to later Turkish explanation, was to enable Turkish military radar to distinguish between innocent flights and potential attackers bound for targets in Asia Minor.

Greece flatly refused to accept this instruction, saying that NOTAM 714 contravened ICAO rules by seeking to establish Turkish control measures in a region assigned to Greece. She noted that the proposed 'report line' appeared to have a political purpose, in that it approximated to the Western limit of Turkish claims to the continental shelf. On 13 September she issued her own NOTAM 1157, declaring the Aegean air routes to Turkey to be unsafe because of the threat of conflicting control orders. As Greece no longer accepted responsibility for safety measures or guaranteed traffic information, international airlines suspended all direct flights between the two countries – a situation that still exists at the time of writing.[14]

Tension and Initiatives, 1974–5

The tension following the Turkish landing in Cyprus on 20 July 1974, and more particularly the second landing, on 14 August, gave the whole Aegean dispute a very much more serious aspect. Within days of Turkey advancing her

95

occupation zone, Greece took steps to fortify the islands, the militarization of which was forbidden by the Treaties of Lausanne and Paris.[15] Though no figures have been given, it seems likely that she dispatched the equivalent of two divisions, laid mines extensively in some areas and prepared the civil airport in Rhodes to receive military aircraft.

Throughout the winter of 1974–5 Turkish leaders made numerous statements that caused Greece to fear an attack. This could have come either in Thrace (where heavy security measures were imposed) or against the islands, which Turkey appeared to see as springboards for Greek raids against Asia Minor.[16] In Greece, too, there were belligerent statements – particularly by Andreas Papandreou, leader of the Pan-Hellenic Socialist Union (PASOK) – which, if heeded nationally, could have increased the danger of war. But the Greek government itself adopted a restrained policy.

It was in this spirit that Greece proposed on 27 January that the two countries should jointly take the continental shelf issue to the International Court of Justice (ICJ). The Turkish Prime Minister, Prof. Sadi Irmak, welcomed the idea, and was attacked for doing so by the then Opposition leader, Mr Ecevit. Turkey accepted the proposal on 6 February. But almost at once there was a change in policy following the replacement of Prof. Irmak by the Justice Party leader, Mr Süleyman Demirel. On 6 April Mr Demirel declared that the boundaries of the continental shelf would have to be established 'through a negotiated settlement'. And on 16 April the Foreign Minister, Mr Ihsan Sabri Caglayangil, spelled out the principle that has dominated Turkey's approach ever since: 'Let us talk first – we may reach an agreement – and not go to the Hague'.

In spite of Turkey's preference for a political rather than a legal settlement, Mr Caglayangil met the Greek Foreign Minister, Mr Dimitrios Bitsios, in Rome on 19 May for preliminary discussions on a *compromis* for joint submission of the Aegean question to the International Court. Twelve days later Mr Karamanlis met Mr Demirel at a NATO summit in Brussels and they agreed to speed up the work of legal experts preparing it. This meeting later acquired legal significance when Greece cited the joint communiqué as evidence to the International Court that Turkey had agreed to submit to the latter's adjudication. The communiqué said that the two Prime Ministers had decided that their problems should be resolved peacefully by means of negotiations and, as regards the continental shelf of the Aegean Sea, by the International Court at the Hague. It also said that they had defined the general lines on which the forthcoming meetings of the representatives of two governments would take place.[17]

From now on the two sides' legal experts met at more or less regular intervals. But progress remained slow. In June there was tension when a Canadian hydrographic vessel, *Goel 1*, arrived at Izmir to prospect near Greek territorial waters on behalf of an American company, the Dorchester Gas Corporation, with Turkish experts aboard. More tension occurred in July when Turkey set up a new military command, the Fourth Army, with headquarters at Izmir. Dubbed the 'Army of the Aegean' by the Turkish Press, it was given the task of defending the Anatolian coast, and pointedly excluded from Turkey's commitment to NATO.

In September the Demirel government, under attack from the Opposition (and particularly Mr Ecevit) for agreeing to go to the International Court at Greek insistence instead of first 'creating Turkey's legitimate rights to the Aegean seabed', announced that it was postponing a further meeting of legal experts about to be held in Paris. It gave as its reason that Greece wanted the immediate drafting of a *compromis*, whereas Turkey sought the examination of 'every method' for a solution of the problem. It was, of course, perfectly true that the Greek government attached primary importance to the signing of the *compromis*. Its reasons were twofold. First, it believed that the two sides would never be able to resolve all their differences by themselves. Second, a handed-down legal decision would encounter less opposition from Greek public opinion than a negotiated one.

Hard-line pressure by the Turkish Opposition continued, with dramatic results the following year. In February 1976 Mr Ecevit accused Mr Demirel of allowing 'the balance of power in the Aegean to change against us'. Next day the government announced that a hydrographic research ship, the *Hora*, later re-named *Sizmik 1*, was being fitted out to prospect for oil near the Greek island of Thasos, the area of Greek discoveries three years previously. That the main purpose of the *Sizmik 1* was to assert Turkey's claim to the seabed seemed to be confirmed by Power and Natural Resources Minister Selahattin Kilic, when he said the issue of exploration licences for 8 million hectares covered all Turkish claims to the continental shelf.

While the preparation of the *Sizmik 1* went ahead, Greece made a proposal for a non-recourse-to-force pact. This was initially welcomed by Turkey but rejected when Opposition leaders described it as a Greek manoeuvre in preparation for extending territorial waters from six to 12 miles.

The Voyage of *Sizmik 1*

On five occasions between March and August Greece expressed anxiety to Turkey about the *Sizmik 1*'s intended operations. She also announced that if the vessel entered the area of the Greek claim it would create a dangerous situation. Turkey replied that if Greece interferred with the vessel, she would be forced to retaliate. The *Sizmik 1* sailed from Canakkale and entered the disputed area on 6 August, accompanied by a Turkish minesweeper and naval co-operation aircraft. For three days she prospected on the Greek-claimed continental shelf west of Lesbos.[18] Though she was closely observed and her movements plotted by the Greek navy, there was no attempt to interfere. Exact details of her position appear to have been temporarily concealed from the Greek media so as not to further inflame public feeling.

Although Greek sources affirm that there was a danger of war between Greece and Turkey on this occasion (and clearly the possibility of an accident existed), the episode appears in retrospect as evidence of both sides' determination to stop short of the brink. Thus Turkey severely restricted the size of the *Sizmik 1*'s escort (a single warship, compared to the 32 units that had accompanied the *Candarli*) and Greece at no time showed any sign of using force against an intrusion into her claim area. At the same time the *Sizmik 1*'s short voyage abruptly raised the level of the Aegean dispute and accelerated legal and political developments.

Greek Appeal to the Security Council

On 10 August 1976, within hours of the *Sizmik 1*'s return to Canakkale, Greece asked for an urgent meeting of the United Nations Security Council on the ground that 'repeated violation by Turkey' of Greek sovereign rights in the Aegean continental shelf had created a dangerous threat to peace and security. She also started proceedings against Turkey in the International Court and filed a request for interim measures of protection. The appeal to the Security Council cited Article 35 of the United Nations Charter and was accompanied by an Explanatory Memorandum referring to the 'already very serious' Greek–Turkish dispute, Turkish naval and air manoeuvres preceding or accompanying the movement of the *Sizmik 1*, and Turkey's insistence on continuing exploration of the seabed.[19]

In the Council the Greek representative asked members to instruct Turkey to suspend her 'provocative acts' and to prevent in the Aegean the kind of tragedy it had been too late to stop in Cyprus.[20] He also delivered a statement, made a few days earlier by Mr Karamanlis, reiterating Greece's interpretation of the Geneva Convention as binding countries, such as Turkey, that had not signed it. The statement recalled Turkey's February 1975 acceptance of the Greek proposal to refer the continental shelf question jointly to the International Court and accused Turkey of adopting inflexible positions in negotiations on a *compromis* for joint submission.[21]

Turkey had responded to the Greek request for a Security Council meeting by restating her position on the continental shelf question: that, in the absence of an agreed delimitation, the Greek claim that she had violated Greek sovereign rights was unfounded. She said the *Sizmik 1* was conducting researches outside Greek territorial waters, where the continental shelf had yet to be delimited, and that while engaged in this lawful pursuit the vessel had been harrassed by the Greek navy and air force. She also complained that Greece had violated the treaties of Lausanne and Paris by militarizing the East Aegean islands.[22]

In the Council the Turkish representative repeated Turkey's claim to sovereign rights where the continental shelf was a natural prolongation of the Anatolian land, adding that a Greek vessel, the *Nautilus*, was 'at this very moment' conducting researches similar to those of the *Sizmik 1* in a neighbouring region. She hoped that the Council would invite Greece to enter into 'meaningful negotiations' and that it would also examine Greek violations of treaty obligations regarding demilitarization of the islands. Other points were that:

- Turkey did not exclude recourse to the International Court to settle certain relevant aspects of the problem, but the dispute must first be negotiated between the two parties. Only then should aspects that could not be resolved be submitted to the Court 'or any other legal or judicial instance'.
- The Geneva Convention was not applicable to the Aegean, whose shape made it a special case; and in any case legal doctrines on the continental shelf were in a state of flux, particularly in the light of UNCLOS III, which had been discussing the subject since December 1973.
- The task of *Sizmik 1* was to collect scientific data necessary for conducting negotiations with Greece, whose government had been kept fully informed about the preparations for the ship's voyage.[23]

The Security Council did not assess blame for the Aegean situation attributable to either party or attempt to deal with the substance of the dispute. Instead it adopted Resolution 395, offering a procedural framework for seeking a settlement.[24] After referring to various provisions for the peaceful resolution of disputes in Chapter VI of the UN Charter, it appealed to the two parties to 'do everything in their power to reduce present tension in the area so that the negotiating process may be facilitated'.

The operative paragraphs of the resolution were Nos 3 and 4. Paragraph 3 called on the governments of Greece and Turkey to resume direct negotiations over their differences and appealed to them to do everything in their power to ensure that these resulted in mutually acceptable solutions. Paragraph 4 invited them in this respect to continue to take into account the contribution that appropriate judicial means, in particular the International Court of Justice, were qualified to make to the settlement of any remaining legal differences which they might identify in connection with their present dispute.[25]

The wording of Paragraph 4 was, of course, extremely ambiguous. Some authorities considered that it conformed to the Turkish position in envisaging that the two parties should decide through negotiations what issues should be submitted to the Court.[26] Others argued that it endorsed Greece's unilateral application by inviting the parties to '*continue* to take into account' the potential contribution of the court – a course since ruled out by the Court's decision that it lacks jurisdiction on the matter.[27] From any point of view the Security Council resolution must be considered indefinite and unsatisfactory. It did, however, manage to take some steam out of the dispute.

Greek Appeal to the International Court

Greece's application to the International Court was in two separate actions. The first instituted proceedings against Turkey over delimitation of the continental shelf and the rights of each country to explore and exploit it. The second, a request for interim measures of protection, asked the Court to direct both countries to 'refrain from all exploration activity or any scientific research, with respect to the continental shelf area in which Turkey has granted such licences' and also from any further military measures or actions which might endanger the two countries' peaceful relations.[28]

Greece based her request for interim protection on two grounds: first, that the grant of licences to the Turkish State Petroleum Company and the activities of *Sizmik 1* constituted an 'irreparable prejudice' to Greece's right of exclusivity of knowledge about her continental shelf and to the Court's future judgment on the merits of the case; second, that any continuation of the grant of licences and of exploration would undermine friendly relations between the two countries. Turkey opposed this on the grounds, *inter alia*, that her exploration activities did not prejudice any of Greece's rights in the disputed areas, and that even if they did, compensation would be given and the Court would not be prejudiced.

The Court refused the Greek request for interim protection because it could not find enough risk of 'irreparable prejudice' to justify exercising its power to grant an interim injunction. However, the request gave rise to an interesting argument as to the Court's jurisdiction in the case. In contentious cases the jurisdiction of the International Court is dependent, under its Statute, on the consent of the parties. In this particular case Greece alleged two independent expressions of Turkish consent. The first was the General Act on the Pacific Settlement of Disputes of 1928. This, she argued, gave the Court jurisdiction, since under Article 37 of its Statute it had inherited the function of the former Permanent Court of International Justice, to which the General Act refers. The second was the joint communiqué issued after the Brussels meeting of the Greek and Turkish Prime Ministers on 31 May 1975.

Article 17 of the General Act (to which both Greece and Turkey acceded) says that all disputes over which the parties are in conflict shall be submitted to the jurisdiction of the Permanent Court, unless the parties agree to arbitration. Turkey raised two objections to its application to the present case. The first was that the Act might no longer be in force, the second that its application was in any case precluded by a Greek reservation. A similar argument about the desuetude of the General Act had been made by France in the *Nuclear Tests* case (in which Australia sought relief from French nuclear tests in the Pacific), but had been rejected by four judges upon whose opinion Greece relied heavily. She also adduced evidence of the General Act's continuing vitality, based on the fact that the UN Secretary-General, having for several years dropped the Act from his list of multilateral treaties, reinstated it in 1974.[29]

The Greek reservation on which Turkey based her second objection had been made at the time of Greece's accession to the treaty. It withheld from the Court disputes 'relating to the territorial status of Greece, including disputes relating to its rights of sovereignty over its ports and lines of communications'.[30] Greece argued that this use of the phrase 'territorial status' covered only land territory (the reservation was directed at a dispute with Bulgaria) and that 'sovereignty' was quite separate from the sovereign *rights* claimed in the seabed. Turkey contended that there could be no such distinction, citing a ruling in the *North Sea Continental Shelf* case in support of this.

The Brussels communiqué offered a fall-back position for Greece. The communiqué said that at their meeting the Prime Ministers had agreed that Greco–Turkish problems 'should be solved peacefully by means of negotiations and as regards the continental shelf of the Aegean Sea by the International Court at the Hague'. Greece contended that this amounted to a 'joint and several' acceptance of the Court's jurisdiction, and that the communiqué, being a juxtaposition of two binding unilateral statements, was sufficient to endow the Court with responsibility to adjudicate under Article 31 of its status. Turkey contended that, since the two countries had never been able to define the scope of their dispute over the Aegean, they could not have reached an agreement to submit it to the Court at the Brussels meeting, and that, by agreeing to speed up a proposed meeting of experts on the question of the continental shelf, the Prime Ministers had given priority to political negotiations.

In January 1979 the Court ruled that it lacked jurisdiction in the *Aegean Sea Continental Shelf* case. This foreclosed one of the three avenues open for the peaceful solution of the dispute. The others remain political negotiation (which shows signs of being insufficient), or some form of non-judicial arbitration, which has yet to be explored.

III. ATTEMPTS AT A SOLUTION

The effect of Security Council Resolution 395, followed on 11 September by the International Court's rejection of the Greek request for a temporary injunction, was to throw the parties back on their own resources. In November experts from both sides met in Berne and, after 10 days of talks, signed a declaration establishing a code of behaviour to govern future negotiations on the continental shelf.

The most important points of the declaration (see Appendix 1) were that such negotiations should be sincere, detailed and confidential with a view to reaching a settlement based on mutual consent; that both parties should abstain from anything that might prejudice the negotiations; and that both agreed to study state practice and international rules 'with a view to educing certain principles and practical criteria that could be of use in the delimitation of the continental shelf between the two countries'. For further talks a method of work was also accepted by the two Secretaries-General of Foreign Ministries. The declaration was released in Athens and Ankara on 20 November. Despite some lapses in respect of the paragraphs on prejudicial initiatives, it remains the recognized framework for bilateral discussions.

Attempts to Solve the Air Question
One of the first areas to benefit from the spirit of the Berne Declaration, though the subject was technically beyond its scope, was the FIR dispute. The interruption of air services had been more damaging for Turkey than for Greece, whose main air routes, lying westwards, were unaffected;[31] but the consequences were general, since other countries' air services had also had to be re-routed, resulting in increased fuel costs and longer flight times. First attempts to restore the situation had been made by ICAO, through personal missions by its Secretary-General, Mr Binagi, in October 1974 and April 1975. On each occasion ICAO proposed the simultaneous withdrawal of the Greek and Turkish NOTAMS. Greece agreed, but Turkey declined, citing security reasons.

When talks were begun on the continental shelf question, following the Brussels Prime Ministers' meeting of May 1975, parallel talks were started on the air question also. Officials from both countries met in Ankara (June 1975), Athens (July 1975), Istanbul (December 1975) and again in Athens (January 1976). At the start of these talks Turkey raised a new issue. Her original demand for a mid-Aegean report line had been taken to apply only to international commercial flights. Now she insisted that *all* aircraft, including Greek military aircraft flying in the international airspace of the Aegean, should notify their position and flight plans to the Turkish military authorities.

In spite of misgivings, the Greek government authorized its experts to continue the talks, with the result that by the end of the July 1975 meeting it was agreed that captains of civil aircraft should report (for information purposes) when reaching certain points on either side of the FIR boundary line. The only obstacle now standing in the way of a simultaneous withdrawal of both NOTAMS was the question of military flights.

It was agreed early on to exclude flights by single military aircraft from the proposed agreement. Discussion thus centred on what constituted a formation of aircraft (how many, what distance between them, etc.). At the same time Greece insisted on a reciprocal undertaking that Turkish military planes would report to Greek control on entering a zone east of the FIR boundary. Shortly after agreement had been reached on this point, there was a sudden near-breakdown, at the January 1976 meeting, when Turkish experts, having agreed on arrangements, received different instructions from their government. The two sides came together again in Paris in July and November. But at the November meeting, when everything appeared to have been settled, disagreement over the drafting of a preamble caused the talks to collapse, this time for good.

Accounts differ as to the reasons for this breakdown. Greek sources say that Turkey refused 'at the last minute' to accept the inclusion of a reference to ICAO and FIRS which would have confirmed that the bilateral agreement was temporary and without prejudice to the existing regime. Turkish sources say that it was Greece which 'at the last minute' insisted on inserting the reference to ICAO. What is clear is that Greece made a number of concessions[32] but that in the end Turkey, despite the easing of the military situation that had originally prompted her NOTAM, and despite being the chief loser from the interruption of air services, was ready to go on arguing in the hope of changing an international arrangement which she felt (and still feels) to be incompatible with her status.

Although precise details of the airspace negotiations have been kept confidential, Turkish officials have circulated an account of alleged abuses of the ICAO FIR system,[33] according to which the core of the Aegean airspace conflict is Greek abuse of FIR responsibility. The account alleges five cases of Greek contravention of ICAO rules:

– Greece has consistently hindered Turkish military exercises by refusing to issue

NOTAMS necessary for air safety, or has required changes in the timing or place of such exercises 'according to Greek desire'.
- Greece, without consulting and co-ordinating with Turkey as a coastal state, in accordance with ICAO rules, has set up around the island of Lemnos a 3,000-square mile 'control zone', most of which is in international air space.
- Greece, without consulting Turkey in accordance with ICAO rules, has unilaterally set up air corridors in Aegean airspace, thus reducing free international airspace and obstructing Turkish entry thereto. (Airway W-14, running north–south near the Turkish coast, is given as an example).
- Greece has further narrowed international airspace by setting up two training areas within the Athens FIR region.
- The Turkish account further accuses Greece of 'serious arbitrary action' in claiming, for 'civil aviation and air policing purposes', a national airspace limit of 10 nautical miles beyond her coast – i.e. extending four miles beyond the limit of her territorial sea. According to Turkey, if applied to all 3,054 Greek islands and islets, such a claim 'could reduce international airspace in the Aegean by 50 per cent'.

As for NOTAM 714, Turkey affirms that this in no way created a dangerous situation 'nor did it violate Greek FIR responsibility', as it only requested position reports of aircraft flying in the vicinity of the Turkish coasts. 'As on the radar screens civil and military aircraft cannot be differentiated, Turkish NOTAM 714 was meant to provide necessary information as to the identity and position of an approaching aircraft, thus providing a partial security measure.'[34]

The Greek response to Turkish allegations is as follows:[35]

- Greece has never exercised her FIR responsibilities for any purpose other than the safety and facilitation of international air traffic.
- She has never required the Turkish authorities to alter the location or the timing of a military air exercise without serious reason. The reason for such changes was that the exercises, which also involved naval movements and firing practice, would have either completely cut off certain islands from the mainland or, at the time requested would have interrupted scheduled sea and air services between the Greek mainland and islands.
- The air limit was fixed at 10 nautical miles for the purposes of air policing by Presidential Decree, issued in 1931. This was never challenged by Turkey until 1975. The Lemnos terminal control area occupies only a small part of Aegean international airspace, and, during the negotiations, Greece offered to reduce it very substantially.
- Any change in the existing FIR system that involved placing Greek islands within a Turkish FIR would be contrary to international practice and quite unacceptable.[36] Greece had made major concessions to meet Turkish demands. But there could be no change in the regional arrangements which had been agreed on by Greece and Turkey and carried ICAO sanction.
- NOTAM 714 did in fact endanger the safety of aircraft and passengers, since the Turkish Authorities did in practice try to take over flight control of aircraft crossing the Aegean median line.

It seems clear from each side's presentation of its case that, although military security considerations may originally have been a factor in the airspace dispute, they are no longer the major one. The dispute appears rather to be about national status which, however regrettably from the point of view of ICAO, has come to be identified with the FIRs. To this extent the painstaking negotiations of 1975–6 were an evasion of the main issue.

Since the breakdown of talks in November 1976 further efforts have been made through diplomatic channels to find a wording for a preamble to an agreement acceptable to Turkey. In March 1977, and again in September, Turkey presented a new draft agreement, its main point being a proposal for joint control of the whole of international air space over the Aegean. This proved unacceptable. In 1978 each side accused the other of obstruction, while at the same time saying that the remaining problems should not be too difficult to solve. In the last half of the year there were two further meetings of experts and a review by the two Secretaries-General, but without concrete results.

The Continental Shelf

The Berne declaration led to a resumption of bilateral meetings by experts on the continental shelf question. But, although these were again a focus of attempts at a settlement, they were no longer the only one. The Hague Court's refusal of a temporary injunction did not affect the main Greek application requesting the Court to delineate the continental shelf in accordance with the principles and rules of international law. Nor did it have any bearing on the Court's jurisdiction on the substance of the dispute (on which the Court would decide later); this was stated explicitly by the President of the Court, Eduardo Jiménez of Uruguay. The Court also rejected a Turkish request that it should remove the case from its list.

Even before the Berne declaration the readiness of Greece to pursue diplomatic means for settling the dispute had been emphasized by Mr Karamanlis. In a speech in Thessaloniki on 4 September he urged all Greeks 'to follow his example of patience', and to accept that he was no less sensitive than any of them to questions of national honour. The recent dangerous state of Greek–Turkish relations had been brought about 'not so much because Turkey makes claims – which may be debatable to a certain extent – but rather because Turkey attempts to impose them by the use of violence'. Recent events had created dangerous tensions, he said, but they also seemed to open the road for a dialogue.

This conciliatory note was much needed; but it did not necessarily reflect national opinion. The Berne agreement was criticized by even moderate Greek opposition leaders. George Mavros, leader of the major opposition party, the Centre of the Democratic Union (EDHK), referred to 'open threats' and lack of good faith by Turkey, whose government would be unable to negotiate seriously until after elections due to be held in 1977. Under these conditions any dialogue with Turkey could only harm Greek national interests, he said. The PASOK leader, Andreas Papandreou, deplored the intention to hold secret negotiations with Turkey and accused the Government of virtually giving up Greece's 'internationally recognized rights' under the Geneva Convention. The Communist Party also opposed the secret talks, and only Elias Eliou, Chairman of the United Democratic Left (EDA) expressed general agreement with the action the Government had taken.

The Berne Declaration also produced a mixed reaction in Turkey. According to the Foreign Ministry, the procedural agreement was important because, (a) it would create the climate of trust suitable for negotiations between the two parties, and (b) the two sides had expressed their political will to find a solution through negotiations. But Mr Ecevit, in opposition, condemned the declaration outright, saying he would not recognize any agreement that might emerge from it.[37]

The numerous meetings of officials which have followed the Berne declaration have been kept confidential by both sides under Paragraph 2, but it is not difficult to identify their general substance from ideas expressed by sources close to each government. Discussion appears to have centred on technical formulae that might somehow meet at least part of the Turkish claim, while preserving the Greek position with regard to the islands. At the same time, each party has stuck to its claim with a tenacity explicable only in terms of its perception of its national identity and of the other's intentions.

Greece, which most foreigners see as a protuberance of the European mainland, with a multitude of islands as a decorative appendage, is seen quite otherwise by Greeks. The islands are as much 'Greece' as the mainland. One might even say more so, since a high proportion of Greeks now living on the mainland have their roots in the islands, regard them as home, endeavour to retain some property on them, and visit them at intervals as an almost religious duty. It is necessary to this Greek view of Greece that every island is immediately accessible from the mainland and *vice versa*, and that nothing should intervene, or threaten to intervene, between the two. In the official phrase the islands form a 'political continuity' with the Greek mainland.

Turkey's claim to an area of continental shelf extending well to the west of the East Aegean islands strikes Greeks of nearly every persuasion as in some degree sinister – if not immediately, then potentially. At worst they fear that claims to the seabed will one day become claims to sovereignty over the superadjacent sea and air space. In the meantime they fear that the rights now recognized in the Geneva Convention – to explore and exploit the seabed, and to set up installations protected by 'security zones' for that purpose – could be used to interfere with sea communications. In either case, the political continuity of the islands would be compromised.

Turkey, too, fears that sovereign rights in the continental shelf (in this case those of Greece) will develop into claims to full sovereignty over sea and air space, and that Greek claims to the continental shelf on the lines of the Geneva Convention will lead to the Aegean becoming quite literally a Greek sea, in which no amount of guarantees of Turkish navigation rights will safeguard her access to the high seas. Fundamental to Turkey's position is her concept of herself as a modern state which has voluntarily joined the West and which aspires in due course to full membership of the European community. To have access to the latter's ports only through Greek waters would be precarious and humiliating.

Formulae for Delimitation

Two kinds of formula could be used to try to find a compromise between the two countries' positions. Those which envisage a joint regime in the disputed area (broadly the approach favoured by Turkey), and those in which a compromise would be achieved by simple delimitation.

Proposals for a joint regime seem to have received less attention, at least in academic discussions. But they remain a valid approach. The simplest model envisages limiting each country's exclusive rights in the continental shelf to an area contiguous with the territorial sea limit. The rest of the seabed would be placed under the joint regime for exploration and exploitation. Such operations could be conducted by a joint international company, or by national companies under a joint authority. The attraction of such a formula is that, by retaining the international character of the seabed, it would avoid both the 'enclaving' of the Greek islands (the fear of Greece) and the hellenization of the continental shelf feared by Turkey. The objection raised by Greece is that such an arrangement would be difficult to tie up legally and would leave scope for disputes in the future.

The most promising basis for the second type of formula is the 'maritime facade' concept.

Maritime facade, as the name suggests, is the frontage a coastal state presents to the sea. It is possible, where two or more states have overlapping claims to a sea area, to appeal to their respective lengths of maritime facade as a means of apportioning it. A delimitation of the Aegean on this basis would give Turkey an area of continental shelf appreciably greater than that due to her under the formula provided by the Geneva Convention. Even more conveniently, it would be possible, using this formula, to assign her 'fingers' of continental shelf extending westwards between the Greek islands; and since no Turkish area need actually intervene between the islands and the Greek mainland, the political continuity of Greece would remain unaffected (see Map 3 on p. 38).

Turkey's hitherto negative reaction to this formula may stem from the fact that the specific proposals in which it has been put to her do not offer her anything like the share of continental shelf (at times stated as 'half the Aegean seabed') to which she aspires. Her opposition may have been further increased by the fact that Turkish experts seem to have interpreted one proposal as offering her some 13% of the total Aegean seabed, only to find, after further computations, that what she was being offered was only 8%. Obviously any further proposal based on the maritime facade or any other 'mathematical' formula needs to be accompanied by clearly marked maps.

In addition to these two basic types, a hybrid solution could be found in the so-called 'Bay of Maine' formula adopted to settle the continental shelf dispute between the United States and Canada in the Bay of Maine. In the Aegean this would mean delimiting the continental shelf according to the Geneva Convention (thus avoiding possible legal ambiguities) but reserving exploration and exploitation outside territorial sea limits to companies or organizations licensed by a Joint Authority. At the end of each year the profits – or, alternatively, the physical product (oil or other minerals) – would be shared under a formula reflecting each State's claim on the area's resources.

The 'Bay of Maine' formula would permit a fair sharing of economic resources without incurring difficulties (for Greece) over political continuity. However, it ignores the major problem that what Turkey is mainly concerned about is not mineral resources (though these are of potential secondary interest) but future areas sovereignty.

The Status of Islands

Failing agreement on some form of joint regime, an equitable delimitation of the Aegean continental shelf can hardly avoid the de-emphasis of islands and a departure from the principle of equidistance laid down by the Geneva Convention. The need for a departure from this principle in a variety of 'special circumstances' is recognized by numerous authorities, who do not, however, dispute that *in general* islands are entitled to their area of continental shelf. Thus Andrassy points out that: 'if, like the Channel Islands, the island or group of islands is located near the coast of the claiming state but yet nearer the coast of another state, it is doubtful whether the island's continental shelf should be recognized and the principle applied.'[38] And Gutteridge argues that: 'Where the continental shelf underlies an area of shallow sea ... which has many islands and is surrounded by coasts of opposite or adjacent States, the drawing of the boundary in strict principle of the median line could, it is clear, result in many curious and inequitable deflections of the median line. There may, for instance, be a very small island which lies approximately in the middle of the shallow sea; or there may be islands which are so close to the mainland as to be justifiably considered part of the mainland for the purpose of working out the boundary of the continental shelf. Again there may be islands which, although near the coast of State A, are under the Sovereignty of State B. All these circumstances ... show the difficulty of a uniform application of the median line principle.'[39]

Various criteria can be used for deciding whether particular islands should be given effect on continental shelf boundaries. Thus Hodgson, suggests that *full effect* should be given to:

(a) islands larger than 1,000 square miles in area;
(b) islands so close to the mainland as to constitute a cohesive part of it;
(c) islands forming part of situation in which the insular geography of adjacent or opposite States is almost identical;
(d) islets within 24 miles of the coast of the owner's mainland or of one of his major islands;

that *no effect* should be given to:

(a) islands in dispute;
(b) small and uninhabited islands in enclosed seas;
(c) isolated rocks and islets which support only caretakers or tokens of the owner's sovereignty;

and that others, such as sparsely inhabited islands some distance from the sovereign state's mainland, should be given only *partial* effect.

An Analytical Model

An article in the *American Journal of International Law* of October 1977 described an analytical model of continental shelf delimitations based on the premise *inter alia* that a 'reasonable degree of proportionality' should exist between the effect to an island and the island's coastline.[40] The model includes four 'zones of distortion' in which an island's location, if used as a basepoint, would have varying effects on equidistance, depending on its proximity to the mainland of the sovereign state and that of neighbouring states.

Normally only islands situated in the territorial sea of the sovereign state would be given an area of continental shelf, the principal exception being where an island forms a substantial part of the sovereign state's territory. According to the article 'this does not mean that it should be used as a basepoint, but that a way should be found to give it maritime space that takes the interest of all parties into account'.

The author refers to the North Sea cases in which the Court stated that an equitable delimitation should involve a 'reasonable degree of proportionality' between the continental shelf area of a coastal state and the length of the state's coast.[41] It is argued that this approach is adaptable to the continental shelf of islands and that 'proportionality of coastline' (roughly expressed as the *length* of an island) can be used to determine which islands are substantial and what effect should be given them.

The model, which, with the inclusion of Crete, would divide the continental shelf of the southern Aegean two-to-one in favour of

Greece, is rejected by Greek analysts as being without basis in international law or state practice. It is interesting, however, as a bold attempt to solve the problem of delimitation systematically, and as illustrating the difficulties thereby raised.

IV. RELATED QUESTIONS

Militarization of the Islands

The militarization of the East Aegean islands took place only after the Turkish landings in Cyprus in 1974. Both before this and afterwards there were statements by Turkish leaders that could have justified apprehension on the part of those responsible for Greek defence,[42] and accusations that Greece was preparing the islands as the base for offensive action have been made frequently in the Turkish press. Greek offensive preparations were given as the reason for setting up the Turkish Fourth Army ('The Army of the Aegean') in 1975. Yet it is noteworthy that the militarization, which Turkey holds to be in breach of the treaties of Lausanne and Paris, has never appeared on the published agenda of bilateral talks, nor has it been brought before the International Court.

From the standpoint of international treaties, the islands can be divided into three groups:

Lemnos and Samothrace came under the demilitarization clause of Article 4, Point 3, of the Treaty of Lausanne, which also ordered the demilitarization of the Turkish islands of Lagoussai, Imbros (Gockeada) and Tenedos (Bozcada). In 1936 the Treaty of Lausanne was replaced by the Treaty of Montreux, to which both Greece and Turkey are signatories. Although Turkey insists that the original demilitarization clauses remain legally applicable, Greek sources argue that they lapsed with the change of treaty and that the abolition was explicitly recognized. The Turkish Foreign Minister at that time is on record as saying: '...the provisions regarding the island of Lemnos and Samothrace, belonging to our neighbour, friendly Greece, islands which were demilitarized according to the Convention of Lausanne in 1923, are also abrogated by the Treaty of Montreux'.[43]

Lesbos, Chios, Samos and Ikaria were also subjected to militarization restrictions under the Treaty of Lausanne, but with a modified formula. Article 13 of the Treaty provided that they 'should not be used for the establishment of any naval base and the construction of fortifications'. It also stipulated that the stationing of military forces there 'should be confined to persons locally recruited for their military service and to a force of gendarmerie proportionate to the total strength of the Greek security forces'. Since, during the preparation of the treaty in 1923, a Turkish proposal for complete demilitarization was rejected,[44] it would seem that some form of local defence for this group has always been permitted.

The Dodecanese Islands were ordered to be disarmed by Article 14 of the Treaty of Paris (1947). But this provision does not apply to members of the internal security forces. Since 1974 advantage has been taken of this exclusion to increase the strength of the gendarmerie in the islands to a point at which it is barely distinguishable from a regular Army force. Greece argues that Turkey has no legal right to protest at Greek military measures in the Dodecanese since Turkey is not a party to the Treaty of Paris, and that, according to a principle of international law, a treaty creates rights and obligations only among signatories (*pacta tertiis nec nocent prosunt*). She also contends that the demilitarization of the Dodecanese cannot deprive her of her natural right to defend the islands if their security is threatened.[45]

The military situation presents the commentator with something of a challenge if he is not to seem to underplay its importance. On the one hand the stationing of Greek forces in the islands, with the Turkish Fourth Army only a few miles away across the water, creates a wasteful and dangerous military confrontation, the implications of which are discussed in Chapter IV. On the other hand, the legal arguments advanced by both sides remain largely academic so long as they have not been submitted to the International Court of Justice, and very little would be achieved here by attempting to pass judgment on them.

In April 1978 the author asked the Turkish Prime Minister, Mr Ecevit, if the demilitarization of the islands and a corresponding redeployment of the Fourth Army could profitably be made the subject of a joint declaration of intent by both sides as a step to improve the atmosphere following his recent return to the premiership. Mr Ecevit answered that such a point would be unnecessary since (1) Greece was committed to disarm the islands by existing treaties, and (2) progress on other questions, i.e. the Cyprus and general Aegean questions, would lead to the solution of the problem as a matter of course.

Minorities

Allegations of discrimination against ethnic minorities have played a smaller part in the recent troubled period of Greek–Turkish relations than the larger questions of the Aegan and of Cyprus. But any general settlement will need to include the removal not merely of discrimination but also of any suspicion of discrimination, if the minorities question is not to be material for future discord.

The criterion of the minorities' identity is basically religious, and follows from the text of the Treaty of Lausanne and the minutes of the Lausanne Conference relating to the exchange of populations. It is therefore technically inaccurate to call them 'national' minorities, though they are generally referred to as such.

The Greek Orthodox minority remaining in Turkey is largely confined to Istanbul and now numbers only 10,000 compared with 110,000 in 1934 (the first year for which impartial figures exist).[46] In contrast, the Muslim minority in Western Thrace numbers 130,000, compared with 106,000 in 1934.

It is felt in Greece that these figures speak for themselves. But Turkey could point out that the increase in the number of Muslims in Thrace is considerably less than would be expected from the minority's high birth-rate, and that large numbers of Muslims have, in fact, emigrated. Such emigration (illegally at 120 a month according to 1975 figures) is not necessarily or simply the result of discrimination, however.[47] Emigration to Turkey could be a natural outcome of ethnic and religious affiliation, or of a belief that Turkish cities provide more opportunities than Greek cities for Turkish-speaking Muslims.

Ethnic and religious affiliations may also have contributed to the exodus of Greeks from Turkey. But there have also been harsh political factors behind this exodus. The good relations which had existed between the communities in the Ataturk years were marred in 1942, when Turkey imposed a capital tax, aimed nominally at those who had made profits from war conditions – the farmers (mainly Muslims) and the merchants (mainly Orthodox Christians, Jews and Armenians). For a majority of those in the latter category, assessments were made arbitrarily by 'special commissions'. Payments were required in 15 days, no appeals were allowed, and thousands of defaulters were arrested and deported or sent to labour camps. Although this measure, which had been encouraged by xenophobic pro-Axis elements in the Turkish press, was rescinded and remissions made in 1943–4, the injury to many victims was irreparable.

A second historic factor behind the exodus was the Istanbul riots of 6–7 September 1955, organized by anti-Greek factions under the Menderes Government in the context of the tripartite talks on Cyprus in London.[48] A third factor was the expulsion in 1965 of virtually all Greek *nationals* (as distinct from the 'minority') after Turkey denounced the Agreement of Establishment, Commerce and Navigation which had been signed in Ankara in 1930 as part of the Ataturk–Venizelos Pact. This was said to be justified by 'new circumstances' in the form of Greek popular support for union of Cyprus with Greece. In the same year strict financial and administrative control was imposed on Greek cultural foundations[49]

The difficulties of the Turkish minority in western Thrace arise principally from the land question. Though forming only about 35% of the population, the Turks, who live largely by agriculture, once held about 60% of the land in the area. The Greek authorities have reduced the latter figure to 20%, and this has inevitably produced social and economic problems.

Chief among the measures used to achieve this reduction has been the grant of long-term loans at very low interest rates to Greek families who come to settle in the area from other parts of Greece. The loans have been used to acquire Turkish land at what, it must be emphasized, are quite generous prices. Turkish land has also been requisitioned in some areas for defence purposes.

In others it has been compulsorily purchased for civil projects, such as the university colleges of Western Thrace.[50] Owners in such cases have been compensated.

Intentionally or not, the effect of these measures has been to create a growing pool of landless labourers – mostly young people who are obliged either to work for Greek farmers at low rates of pay or else to emigrate to Turkey, where they find themselves at a disadvantage because of their lack of industrial skills.[51]

Two other practices alleged by the Turkish minority are said to involve linguistic discrimination. This, if it were true, would contravene Articles 37–45 of the Treaty of Lausanne, which guarantees Muslims the same civil and political rights as non-Muslims (equality before the law, the use of Turkish before the courts, and Turkish and Muslim religious instruction in schools). The first is alleged discrimination against non-Greek-speakers in the granting of driving licences, which are very important for farmers dependent on tractors and farm vehicles.[52] The second is alleged discrimination against Muslims seeking admission to the universities, where the medium of instruction is Greek.

For the Muslim minority the problem of landless workers is paramount. Many Turks believe it will get worse until the land holdings of the two communities have been brought into line with their share of the population. If this is so, the Greek authorities have a clear and urgent duty to speed up industrial investment in the area. As to allegations of linguistic discrimination the visitor might find cases about which he feels strongly but, as a practical matter, it seems unlikely that injustices (and suspicion) can be removed until there is a settlement of other matters. The same is true of the anxieties of the Greek Orthodox minority in Istanbul.

Both governments have a self-interest, quite apart from any moral obligation, in restoring the spirit as well as the letter of the guarantees of equality laid down in 1930.[53]

Cyprus

The Aegean and Cyprus questions are technically separate, a division that has been recognized by both sides. But, as the dominant issues in Greek–Turkish relations, they are bound to be examined for evidence of interaction. (A comparative chronology is given in Appendix 3.)

The Cyprus question developed through the demand of Greek Cypriots under British rule, for *Enosis* (union) with Greece. After the EOKA guerrilla campaign in Cyprus and the eventual conclusion of the Zurich and London agreements, Cyprus became independent in 1960. The constitution gave 35 seats in the House of Representatives to the Greek community (some 450,000 strong) and 15 to the Turkish community (some 150,000 strong). Treaties with the three Guarantor Powers (Britain, Greece and Turkey) precluded both *Enosis* and partition. Communal clashes occurred when, in 1963, Greek Cypriots took armed action against the Turkish Cypriots and President Makarios tried to impose changes in the Zurich and London agreements. Peace was restored with the help of a British-backed UN peace force, and in 1968 Greek- and Turkish-Cypriot leaders (who since 1963 had stayed out of Parliament and the Cabinet) began talks aimed at finding a solution.

Failure to make progress in this direction was due not so much to intercommunal differences as to a split on the Greek-Cypriot side between the Makarios government, intent on preserving the island's independence, and former EOKA supporters (soon to emerge as 'EOKA B') who were again plotting for *Enosis*. Between 1969 and 1974 the split increased in bitterness and violence as EOKA won backing from the Athens Junta and Makarios set up contacts with the Soviet bloc. In July 1974 a coup by the EOKA B leader, Nicos Sampson, backed by the Ghizikis Junta in Athens, forced Makarios to flee, whereat the Turkish government, which had always feared such a coup as a prelude to *Enosis*, invaded the island in the Kyrenia area on 20 July.

For several days Greece and Turkey were on the verge of war as Greece mobilized and clashes occurred between the Greek and Turkish military contingents stationed in Cyprus under the Treaty of Alliance. Tension was relaxed when, on 22 July, the Athens Junta ordered a cease-fire, and Sampson was ousted by the legal Cyprus vice-president, Glafkos Clerides. Next day the Junta, long hated and now totally discredited for having created a crisis it had no means to handle, decided to hand over to a civilian government, and Mr Karamanlis returned to Athens from self-exile in France.

The collapse of the Junta was welcomed by the Turkish Prime Minister, Mr Ecevit, and prospects of a settlement looked momentarily encouraging. They clouded, however, when Greece and Turkey took opposing views of UN Security Council Resolution 353 calling for a military withdrawal (Turkey believing that a withdrawal before a settlement would lead to a return to the situation that had existed before the coup).

On 30 July the Guarantor Powers' Foreign Ministers, meeting in Geneva, agreed on a cease-fire, the non-extension of occupied areas, the evacuation of Greek forces which had occupied Turkish enclaves in response to the Kyrenia landing, and an exchange of civilian detainees. They also noted the existence of two autonomous administrations and called for a military buffer zone and for talks, involving both communities, to restore peace and constitutional government.

Greek Cypriots saw the agreement as a capitulation, since the Turks were under no commitment to withdraw their troops from the territory they had occupied. As a result they did not evacuate the Turkish enclaves, and the situation worsened with the daily arrival of further Turkish reinforcements and the occupation of new military positions. When a second Geneva conference opened, amid sharp recriminations, on 8 August, the Turks controlled the approach roads both east and west of Nicosia and there was no sign of their retirement to the 30 July cease-fire line.

Greece now made concessions, giving up her demand for a Turkish withdrawal to the cease-fire line while herself withdrawing National Guard units from the Turkish enclaves. But disagreement arose over future constitutional and territorial arrangements. The Greeks and Greek Cypriots proposed a unified Cyprus on the basis of the 1960 constitution, while the Turks demanded autonomous areas within a federal state. When the former asked for a 36-hour adjournment to consider the Turkish proposals, the Turks refused to extend the deadline for a settlement. On 14 August fighting was resumed, and within three days Turkey had occupied 40% of the island. Some 200,000 Greek Cypriots, a third of the island's population, became homeless as they fled before the Turkish advance.

Whereas the first Turkish invasion had won widespread international sympathy (it was also described as 'justified' by several Greek observers consulted in the preparation of this paper), because of the threat to the Turkish community by EOKA and because Turkey had acted within the terms of the Treaty of Guarantee on Cyprus independence, the second invasion was almost universally condemned as a direct breach of the Zurich agreement. Since the invasion, the two parts of Cyprus have remained under independent administrations, the Turkish one backed by a considerable military force (currently 25,000 strong), the Greek one recognized internationally (except by Turkey) as the legal government of Cyprus.

The Turkish 'Federated State of Cyprus' was proclaimed unilaterally in 1975 and held parliamentary elections the following May. It now administers about 36% of the island's territory, into which the Turkish-Cypriot community (about 18% of the island's population) was consolidated in 1974. It has not received any recognition as an independent state, nor has it sought seriously to claim it.

Some progress towards a settlement was made in February 1977, at a meeting in Nicosia between President Makarios and the Turkish-Cypriot leader, Rauf Denktash, in the presence of UN Secretary-General Waldheim, when the following guidelines were agreed for talks to be held in Vienna:

—The aim was to establish an independent, non-aligned bi-communal federal republic.
—The size of the territory under the administration of each community would be negotiated in the light of economic viability, productivity and property rights.
—Questions of principle, such as freedom of movement, freedom of settlement and property rights, would be open to discussion, taking into account the fundamental principle of a bi-communal federal system and certain practical difficulties which might arise for the Turkish-Cypriot community.
—The powers and function of the central federal government would be such as to safeguard the unity of the country, having regard to the bi-communal character of the state.

Within these guidelines the Greek-Cypriot Administration, having accepted the concept of a federation of two states, has since continued to press for a strong federal government and for significant concessions to permit the resettlement of Greek refugees from the territory now administered by the Turkish community.

The Montreux 'Summit'

The latest phase of Greek–Turkish relations, in respect of both the Cyprus and the Aegean questions, began with the return to power of Mr Ecevit in January 1978. This was followed by a meeting in Montreux between Mr Karamanlis and Mr Ecevit on 10–11 March. The initiative for the meeting came from Mr Ecevit, after Mr Karamanlis had congratulated him on his appointment.

The Turkish Prime Minister's first proposal was for a meeting 'to establish a dialogue that may clear the way for finding mutually satisfactory solutions to our problems'. To this Greece replied positively but cautiously, suggesting a meeting in the spring and stressing the need for thorough preparation. Mr Ecevit, however, came back with a proposal for an earlier meeting, with a slightly different emphasis from his first suggestion. The idea, he said, was not to seek actual solutions to the problems, but to exchange views on them with no fixed agenda and 'to try to create a climate of confidence'.

The meeting took place in amicable circumstances, in contrast to four years of almost unbroken tension. This was the more remarkable in view of Mr Ecevit's record in opposition, where he had frequently spurred Turkish governments, such as Mr Demirel's in 1976, to take a harder line than they had intended. Both leaders emphasized that no spectacular results were to be expected from the meeting. A communiqué afterwards said simply that they had discussed bilateral problems and established a 'friendly and sincere dialogue' which they hoped to continue at a subsequent meeting. In the meantime matters should be reviewed through normal channels.

In a further elaboration on the Greek part in the meeting, Mr Karamanlis told the Press that on the Aegean question 'we gave priority to the question of procedure on the basis of internationally accepted methods ... Today 61 countries are involved in continental shelf disputes, which they are solving through negotiations. From the moment when procedures are determined, the matter will go forward smoothly. This may happen at our next meeting'. Asked whether Cyprus had been discussed at the meeting, Mr Karamanlis said he had told Mr Ecevit that if he wanted a dialogue, reasonable proposals would have to be made in the context of the inter-communal negotiations.

On 3 April the two Foreign Ministries announced that there would be a meeting of Secretaries-General on 14 April. But, by an unfortunate coincidence, later the same day the US State Department announced that Congress would be asked to lift the Turkish arms embargo. So violent was Greek public reaction that Mr Karamanlis had to ask for a postponement 'for technical reasons'. This was immediately seized on by Turkish spokesmen as foot-dragging. A further setback developed on 13 April, when the Turkish-Cypriot Administration delivered to the UN Secretary-General in Vienna the proposals for which all were waiting. By offering only small territorial concessions, and by providing weaker powers than are to be found in other contemporary federal systems in the world, these fell so far short of Greek and Greek-Cypriot expectations that all movement on both the Cyprus and the Aegean questions came to a halt. (A similar failure attended an attempt by Mr Waldheim to restart talks thirteen months later.)

A further step in the threatening political chain reaction came when the US House of Representatives Foreign Affairs Committee approved the lifting of the arms embargo but the Senate Committee (acting, the Turks believed, under pressure of the Greek–American lobby) voted to continue it. The continuation now became a critical source of friction, since it was believed in Ankara that Greece hoped to use the embargo to weaken Turkey to a point at which she would be forced to lower her demands on major issues. This caused the Ecevit government to adopt new defence objectives with implications for the regional arms balance.

Turkey's New Defence Concept

Mr Ecevit addressed the IISS on the principles of the New Defence Concept (reprinted in *Survival*, September/October 1978). Though its details remained unclear when he lost the October 1979 election, it seemed to have three elements:
 (a) Smaller but more efficient armed forces.
 (b) Indigenous defence industrial capability.
 (c) A flexible deployment plan, enabling forces to be switched from the northern to the western frontier.

Fears in Athens that this meant a move to escalate the Aegean dispute were not substantiated. For one thing, external considerations were only one constituent of the new Turkish defence thinking, which also had industrial and economic objectives. But clearly, if relations were to deteriorate, any reorganization could place larger Turkish forces in the area of confrontation with Greece.

A graver complication arising from the arms embargo was a belief on the part of the Ecevit government that Greece was trying to isolate Turkey diplomatically and to frustrate her efforts to secure future arms supplies from NATO partners in Europe, particularly West Germany. It was also feared in Ankara that Greece might use her forthcoming entry into the European Community to isolate Turkey yet further.

At the end of April 1978 a new chance for a meeting of the two Prime Ministers was provided by a NATO summit in Washington. Though short of the second 'summit' originally envisaged, it enabled each Head of Government to reassure himself about the other's position and opened the way to a renewal of bilateral contacts at a variety of levels.

Problems for NATO

The Turkish invasion of Cyprus had serious consequences for NATO when, because of the Alliance's failure to intervene, Greece withdrew all her forces from NATO command. The reorganization necessitated by this action became belatedly effective in 1978.

Up to this time the NATO structure in the Eastern Mediterranean had provided for two NATO headquarters in Izmir: Land Forces South-East Europe, and the Sixth Allied Tactical Air Force, each under an American general, with Greek and Turkish deputies.[54] In December 1977 the Supreme Allied Commander Europe announced that the two headquarters would be taken over by Turkish generals with American deputies, since, with the withdrawal of Greek forces, it was anomalous for US generals to command only Turkish forces. Thus in July the two commands became 'Turkish–NATO' headquarters, the land command being directly subordinate to the C-in-C Allied Forces Southern Europe (CINCSOUTH) in Naples, and the air command coming under CINCSOUTH's subordinate, Commander Allied Air Forces Southern Europe, also in Naples. At the same time proposals were made for the creation of a 'Greek–NATO' headquarters at Larissa in Greece, where Greek army and air force commands are already located.

The division of the commands, particularly the air command, could cause serious problems in war. The settlement of Greek–Turkish differences and the restoration of a logical command structure can therefore be considered a NATO priority.

A further problem has arisen in the case of US electronic 'listening posts' in Turkey – a problem aggravated by the dismantling of US listening posts in Iran. Two of the largest outposts engaged in electronic intelligence collection are at Sinop, on the Black Sea coast, and Karamürsel, on the Sea of Marmara. Sinop, manned by the US National Security Agency, collects data on Soviet naval and air activities in the Black Sea area as well as on missile tests. Associated with Sinop is the Samsun communications site manned by the US Air Force Security Service. In east-central Turkey a long-range radar and communications complex at Diyarbakir tracks Soviet missile launches. At Balbasi, near Ankara, a US seismographic detection base monitors Soviet nuclear tests. Together these sites are believed to provide about 25% of all US first-hand information on missile tests. In addition there are numerous US Defence Satellite Communications System (DSC) terminals and 14 NATO air defence early-warning sites throughout Turkey.

Other important installations used by the United States include Incirlik air base, near Adana in south-eastern Turkey, and storage depots at Iskenderun and Yumurtalik, on the Mediterranean coast near the Syrian border. Incirlik is the major tactical fighter base in Turkey and houses USAF aircraft on rotation from Torrejón air base in Spain. Kargaburun, on the Sea of Marmara, is a US Navy LORAN station assisting US military aircraft to fix their positions in the Mediterranean. Ankara is the site of an air station and of TUSLOG, the US Logistics Group, Turkey, which supports US military supply services throughout the country.

V. CONCLUSIONS

Current Positions

It is the purpose of this chapter to evaluate the prospects of a peaceful solution and suggest procedures for reaching it. Before doing so it may be useful to summarize each side's position on the three main issues.

The Continental Shelf: The Turkish Position

The main points of the Turkish position on the continental shelf question are as follows:

The question of the continental shelf is not essentially a legal issue but a politically charged aspect of relations between Turkey and Greece. Turkey has constantly sought to maintain the balance established by the Treaty of Lausanne and to find a mutually acceptable solution to Aegean problems through negotiation. The principle of a negotiated settlement was upheld by the International Court in the *North Sea Continental Shelf* Case and by the United Nations in Resolution 395. The Berne Agreement of November 1976 also demonstrated the possibility of reaching a settlement by negotiation.

A look at the map is sufficient to demonstrate the importance of the Aegean – a semi-enclosed sea – for Turkey's political, security and economic interests. Within the context of the equilibrium established by the Treaty of Lausanne, Greece and Turkey have been using the Aegean on an equal footing. Turkey believes that the same principle of equal sharing within the framework of that treaty should apply to delimitation of the Aegean continental shelf.

Greece, by her claims to the continental shelf, is seeking *de facto* sovereignty over the whole Aegean Sea.

Greece has violated the Treaties of Lausanne and Paris by militarizing the Eastern Aegean islands which, lying only a few miles off the Anatolian coast, are of great importance to Turkey's security. This shows that she seeks to extend her control over the air space, the sea, the seabed and the subsoil of the Aegean.

Turkey believes that a fair and lasting solution for the Aegean problem could be found through meaningful negotiations. For the continental shelf, equity, natural prolongation, equal partition of the shelf and an appropriate method of delimitation (for instance, an equitable median line) would be necessary. Turkey, which is not a party to the 1958 Geneva Convention, does not believe that islands have their own area of continental shelf. Moreover the islands of the Aegean do not form a continuation of the Greek mainland, because there are intervening High Seas. However, Turkey could provide guarantees to satisfy Greek needs in respect of the islands. Her position on the continental shelf issue does not constitute any claim to the superadjacent waters affecting the free movement of international shipping.

The Continental Shelf: The Greek Position

The Greek position is as follows:

It is an internationally accepted principle, inscribed in the Geneva Convention and in the revised Composite Negotiating Text of UNCLOS III, that islands have their own area of continental shelf. Moreover the islands of the Aegean form a political continuum with the Greek mainland, and it would upset the balance established by the Treaty of Lausanne to interfere with this continuum.

The continuum would be threatened if Turkey were granted sovereign rights in any area between the islands and the Greek mainland. Such rights would entitle her to establish installations and associated security zones in an area from which, if she wished, she could now or later interfere with Greek internal sea and air communications. Furthermore, enclavement of a large number of islands (over 500) in a Turkish zone of exclusive economic rights would threaten Greek sovereignty over these islands, which are inhabited by over 330,000 people.

Greece's position contains no threat to Turkey, since her claim to the continental shelf carries no claim to the superadjacent waters, in which Turkish and international shipping may move freely. The militarization of the islands was undertaken in accordance with the right of legitimate self-defence recognized by the UN Charter.

Though believing that the character of the dispute necessitates a legal settlement, Greece has always been ready to enter into political negotiations as a parallel course, and her record of proposals in meetings, at expert and ambassadorial level, is proof of her seriousness on this point.

Turkey's action in sending *Sismik 1* to explore in an area where Greek claims accord with international usage (the Geneva Convention), and where for three years Turkey raised no objection to Greek activity, was provocative and threatening to Greek interests.

Security Council Resolution 395 supported the Greek position by calling on the parties to settle their differences within the framework of international law.

This call remains valid despite the decision of the International Court of Justice in December 1978 that it lacked jurisdiction in the case brought by Greece – a case in which Turkey's failure to submit a counter-memorial was at variance with the pledges contained in the Brussels communiqué.

It is in the application of international law that Greece continues to seek an equitable settlement.

Territorial Sea: The Turkish Position

The main points of the Turkish position on the territorial sea are as follows:

The Aegean is a semi-enclosed sea in which international practice in regard to other seas is not applicable. Already the application of the six-mile limit restricts Turkey to only three places where shipping may enter or leave Turkish territorial waters from international waters.

Any extension of the territorial sea limit to twelve miles (following general world practice) would deprive the Aegean coast of Turkey of all direct exits to international waters. It would also cut into the area of the continental shelf claimed by Turkey, reducing the area covered by TPAO exploration licences from 16·3% of the total Aegean seabed to 9·27%.

Turkey needs equitable access to the waters of the Aegean for the same reason that she needs an equitable share of the continental shelf: to support the large population of her Aegean coast and its immediate hinterland.

She welcomes the assurance that Greece, while reserving the right to extend her territorial waters to twelve miles, has no plans for doing so. Any extension would be regarded by Turkey as a *casus belli*.

Territorial Sea: The Greek Position

The main points of the Greek position are as follows:

Greece has the right, in accordance with international law and the practice of other maritime States, to extend her territorial sea limits from six to twelve miles. She has indicated to Turkey that she has no intention of doing so, in the interest of good relations. However, she would not consider surrendering a right which already accrued to her under international law and practice.

There is no question of Greek territorial sea 'enclosing' Turkey, since it offers no obstacle to innocent passage. As owner of the world's largest investment fleet, Greece has no incentive to institute measures that might lead to a restriction of this freedom of the seas.

The demographic argument used by Turkey to support her claim to an 'equitable' share of the resources of the Aegean can be more forcefully invoked by Greece, four-fifths of whose population of 9·25 million live in, on or near the Aegean coast and islands.

Air Traffic Control: The Turkish Position

On air traffic control the Turkish position is as follows:

The arrangement to which Turkey agreed in 1952 was intended to be purely technical. But Greece has used it to establish *de facto* sovereignty over Aegean airspace, just as she has sought to establish sovereignty over the continental shelf.

While the two countries enjoyed normal relations, the placing so close to the Turkish mainland of the boundary between the Athens and Istanbul FIRs presented no problem. The report line specified in NOTAM 714 became necessary for reasons of national security in the strained situation resulting from events in Cyprus (the Sampson coup and the Turkish intervention).

However, the 1952 arrangement had become unsatisfactory before this for other reasons.

First, Greece used her position as control authority to impose restrictions or alterations on Turkish military air exercises in Aegean controlled airspace (for which, under the agreement, plans had to be submitted to Athens control centre in advance).

Secondly, the airspace available for this and other purposes was significantly reduced in 1931, when a presidential decree unilaterally extended Greek airspace round the Aegean islands from six to ten nautical miles – four miles more than the territorial sea limit.

A further reduction in usable international airspace was effected by Greece's declaration of a 3,000 square-mile 'control zone' round the island of Lemnos.[55]

For security purposes Turkey foresees a system giving balanced reciprocity as well as sufficient mutual early warning for military areas of prime importance to both sides. FIR responsibility is technical and does not endow the responsible state with sovereignty rights over the FIR area. Greece is abusing FIR responsibility by acting as if it entailed sovereignty.

Turkey's NOTAM 714 did not create a dangerous situation, nor did it violate Greek FIR responsibility, since it merely requested, for security purposes, position reports by aircraft flying in the vicinity of the Turkish coast.

Air Traffic Control: *The Greek Position*
The Greek position on air traffic control is as follows:

Greece has never exercised her air traffic control responsibilities for any purpose other than the safety and facilitation of international air traffic.

She has never required the Turkish authorities to alter the location or timing of an air exercise without compelling reasons. The reason for such time changes, which were never by more than 1–2 hours, was that the exercises, usually combined with sea exercises, would have interrupted scheduled sea or air traffic.

The ten-mile national airspace limit round islands is necessary for policing purposes and needs to be greater than the sea limit because of aircraft speeds. The Lemnos terminal control area (for both civil and military purposes) occupies a small part of Aegean controlled airspace.

Any move to put Greek islands within a Turkish FIR would be contrary to international practice. Greece has made important concessions to meet the Turkish call for a mid-Aegean reporting line. But there can be no change in regional arrangements without her agreement and that of ICAO.

It was necessary to declare the air corridor to and from Turkey unsafe because of the confusion caused to flight crews by conflicting instructions from the Turkish authorities.

How Urgent is a Settlement?

The delay in coming to either 'meaningful negotiations' or a joint legal approach might suggest that the parties themselves see the need for a settlement less urgently than do western observers worried at the situation on NATO's southern flank. The latter, indeed, may sometimes wonder whether the parties have been tempted to prolong and exploit Allied anxieties for their own purposes.

These are understandable reasons why both sides might want to delay. Turkey, for instance, could have come to the conclusion that economic and other forms of aid flow more generously to unpredictable partners than to reliable ones. Another hypothesis is that she is hoping for a more favourable definition of the continental shelf to come out of the continuing third Law of the Sea Conference. Or a real or supposed threat from Greece could be a convenient means of diverting attention from internal problems. Greece, on the other hand, could have decided it was better to delay a negotiated settlement until she had completed her entry into the EEC (where she could hope for political backing); or she might have calculated that Turkey's economic difficulties, and (until its recent lifting) the American arms embargo, would weaken Turkey to a point at which, sooner or later, she would have to drop her demands. All these considerations must have occurred, at one time or another, to officials of the two governments. Whether, and how far, they may have influenced policy is beyond the scope of this study. One can only observe that the arguments against such unfavourable interpretations are considerable and take note of the evidence pointing to the seriousness of both sides in reaching an early settlement.

In Turkey, one of the most thought-provoking developments during Mr Ecevit's 1978–79 premiership was his move to restructure the country's defence policy. Some remarks by Ministers and officials caused the concept of a more flexible, self-sufficient defence to be seen in some quarters as a threat to leave NATO and aim Turkey's forces against Greece. But in May 1978 Mr Ecevit declared: 'We have taken the initiative also to try and establish a friendlier atmosphere with our neighbour and ally, Greece.' He went on, 'this new concept of national defence which we are trying to evolve should be compatible with our continued membership of NATO.... In spite of everything we do not intend to leave NATO'.[56] It is to be hoped that this will continue to be Turkey's policy.

Certainly logic is against continuing the quarrel with Greece. To restore her economy and modernize her armed forces, Turkey urgently needs NATO's help. The Alliance's first acknowlegment of this was a decision by member governments in May 1978 to examine the problems of the weaker members. In early 1979 it was taken a step further by the agreement of the Guadeloupe summit on an emergency aid package. The aid has been pledged mainly by the United States and Germany and will be administered partly by the OECD and partly by the International Monetary Fund. And although the total proposed – $1·45 billion in all – falls well below the $1 billion a year reportedly requested by the Turkish Finance Ministry, the Turkish government will need to weigh its continuation against that of a costly dispute which NATO would like to see settled.

Admittedly Mr Ecevit has occasionally alluded to an alternative policy: that of neutrality between East and West through the development of association with the non-aligned countries, particularly Arab ones, in the Mediterranean basin. In July 1978 the Turkish Foreign Minister, Mr Gündüz Ökçün, attended the non-aligned Foreign Ministers' meeting in Belgrade as an observer. But three factors make a policy of neutrality unlikely: the Arab states' uncomfortable recollection of Ottoman rule, the inability of non-aligned countries to provide Turkey with much-needed technological assistance, and, not least, Turkey's historical fear of her northern neighbour the Soviet Union.

In short, Turkey, by past choice and present necessity, is a Western-looking country, but one which understandably wants to emerge from her position as a mere provider of NATO manpower and bases. In this she looks for help to her European partners, and in particular to West Germany.[57]

The more obvious consistency of Greek efforts towards a settlement may be partly due to the continuity of government in Athens. There have been five Turkish governments since 1974, compared with the unbroken premiership of Mr Karamanlis. A further factor has been the priority given in Athens to gaining full EEC membership, which the quarrel with Turkey at times threatened to jeopardize. (Turkey, quick to recognize this point, sought to persuade EEC members not to admit Greece so long as the dispute continued.)

Turkish officials could here point out that Greek initiatives, beginning with the original proposal for a *compromis* to the International Court in January 1975, have nearly all been directed to securing a *judicial* settlement, in opposition to Turkish initiatives aimed at securing a *political* one – a difference over procedures that has attracted as much discussion as the conflict between the two sides' actual claims. They believe Greece is using her legal initiatives to delay a settlement in the hope (referred to earlier) that in time political factors will move in her favour.

There can, however, be a quite different explanation for Greek insistence on a judicial solution, to which the internal political situation in Greece lends support. This is that, in the context of an issue such as the Aegean question, which arouses deep national emotions, a handed-down judgement is much easier to put before public opinion than a negotiated settlement – assuming (as must certainly be the case in the Aegean) that the settlement involves concessions by both sides. If this is so, Greek concern with judicial procedure must be seen not as a delaying tactic but as evidence of sincerity.

Defence Aspects

A common factor ought to act as an incentive to an early settlement on both sides. This is the level of defence spending due to the Cyprus and Aegean quarrels. In 1976 defence cost Greece $1,249 million, or 26% of total government expenditure. Between 1974, the last year of the military junta, and 1975, the first full year of confrontation with Turkey, it rose from 4% to 6·9% of GNP. Turkish figures were even higher. In 1976 Turkey spent $2,800 million on defence, or 29·4% of total government expenditure, while between 1974 and 1975 the defence budget rose from 3·7% to 9% of GNP.[58] The latest figures show a return to more sustainable levels, but 4·7% of GNP (Greece) and 4·5% (Turkey) could still be thought high in the context of the countries' overall economic situation.

Scarcely less important is the potential for mutual destruction represented by this excessive spending, and the danger that confrontation on political issues could, through miscalculation or accident, lead to war. Officials are understandably reluctant to elaborate on ways in which hostilities could develop, but it was put to the writer in Ankara that 'although we can probably go on living with the present situation for some time, the danger is escalation, and escalation can be a very rapid process'. The opinion was offered in Athens that 'war, if it occurs, will be fought to the point of mutual exhaustion, say in three or four weeks'. Authorities on both sides were sure that, if hostilities once started, neither NATO nor any other body would be able to stop them.

Two *casus belli* have been explicitly stated: an extension of Greek territorial waters, and a Turkish landing on any of the Greek islands.[59] Such declarations, despite their alarming nature, have almost certainly made the feared actions less likely. A greater risk comes from confused information, for example about the movements of a survey vessel, plus the possibility of either government being forced by public opinion to adopt a position from which it cannot withdraw.

These risks of an 'unthinkable' war between NATO allies must be weighed against the capacity of Athens and Ankara for crisis management. It could be argued that in 1976 *Sizmik 1* crisis this capacity proved adequate. Greece, particularly, showed skill in her responses and in refraining from any action that could have led to military conflict. But could such restraint be relied on from a PASOK government, or from some of the more belligerent contenders for power in Ankara? Even a slight doubt about the answer to this question must be considered an argument for the urgency of a settlement.

Political Risks
One need not look to the danger of war in order to find reasons for settling the Aegean dispute with a minimum of delay. The Greek–Turkish quarrel has already produced major political changes on NATO's southern flank that will be hard to reverse. And although not all these changes are bad – it could be argued, for instance, that regional Alliance members have long needed greater independence – there is clearly a point at which the shake-out must stop if it is not to lead to a dangerous regional imbalance.

A most serious imbalance would result if Turkey, for real or imagined reasons, were to decide that she had been rejected by the West. The cataclysmic changes referred to earlier might then indeed take place, and while Turkey groped blindly for a new destiny in Asia, NATO would be left with the almost impossible task of rebuilding its right flank. A situation only slightly less serious would arise if Greece, reacting to a Western refusal to give her unqualified backing in the dispute, were to transform her present policy of temporary non-participation in NATO military activities into total withdrawal – the declared policy of PASOK.

The time remaining for a peaceful settlement could well be limited by the availability of individuals. The problem is seen with particular concern in Greece, where many people believe that the one person capable of carrying the country with him in acceptance of a settlement involving significant concessions is Mr Karamanlis. Mr Karamanlis is now 72, and it is by no means certain that he will want to stay in office till the next elections, perhaps not due until 1981. At this stage it is difficult to see a successor from within his New Democracy party who could carry a difficult settlement through. If, on the other hand, his government were to be succeeded by a PASOK government – a real possibility if the present electoral trend continues – that party's militant line on Cyprus and the Aegean would make any compromise settlement extremely unlikely.[60]

The time-scale imposed by Mr Karamanlis' premiership is well enough perceived in Ankara, despite the tendency of officials to deny that a single personality can play such a crucial role. It must now be extremely questionable, in view of Mr Ecevit's 1979 mid-term election defeat, whether things can be carried forward before the middle of 1980 at the earliest.

Arbitration versus Negotiation
The solution of the continental shelf dispute falls into two parts: reaching an equitable formula, and reaching it in a forum that will ensure acceptance of the formula by opinion in both countries.

The fact that the two sides have been willing to talk at expert level is an indication that neither stands immovable on the conflicting claims over the seabed with which the dispute originated. The most satisfactory solution, economically and politically, would be some form of joint ownership of the disputed area. Turkey believes this should be further discussed. However, since it appears to have been conclusively rejected by Greece, attention must be focused on simple delimitation.

To offer a quasi-mathematical prescription for resolving a multitude of unmeasurable claims would be simplistic. It makes better sense to list certain conditions which (from what is known of the problems in bilateral talks to date) appear to be essential to a fair and acceptable settlement.[61] These are that:

1. The settlement must involve some de-emphasis of islands as base points for apportioning shares of the seabed.
2. There must be no interposing of 'foreign' continental shelf between the Greek islands and the Greek mainland (enclaving).
3. Delimitation must bear some relationship to each state's geographical presence, probably on the basis of maritime facade.
4. The agreement must provide, like the Geneva Convention (not recognized by Turkey), that rights over the continental shelf do not affect the legal status of the waters above as High Seas.

A settlement based on these points could produce a roughly 'hand-shaped' Turkish area with fingers of the hand extending *between* the most easterly Greek islands but not behind them (see Map 3 on p. 40).

By this means Turkey could receive considerably more than the 2·4% of the total area of the Aegean continental shelf that she would receive under the Geneva Convention (though considerably less than the half she claims) without compromising the continuity of the Greek state.

However, the choice of forum is extremely important. Any compromise settlement is almost certain to be condemned by large sections of public opinion in both countries as a betrayal of national interests. But it is felt by many observers, particularly in Greece, that a compromise would encounter less opposition if it were handed down by an external authority. (A similar conclusion was apparently reached by Argentina and Chile in the Beagle Channel case, arbitrated by the Vatican.) The best arbitrator in the Aegean Sea Continental Shelf case would have been the International Court. Had the Court decided that it had limited jurisdiction, it could have combined the political and legal approaches by holding that the two parties had an obligation to negotiate, while reserving jurisdiction for issues referred to it by special agreement or on which deadlock was reached.

Since the Court has decided that it has *no* jurisdiction, some other authority must be found. This may not be easy, since the two organizations best placed to offer their sevices, NATO and the European Community, are vulnerable to accusations of bias – pro-Greek bias in the case of the Community (on account of Greece's recent accession), pro-Turkish in the case of NATO (because of the American interest in Turkish installations). Apart from such objections, whether or not they have any basis in fact, neither the Alliance nor the Community might wish to risk the complications arising from an unpopular judgment – a doubt which must assail any other organization or State asked to arbitrate.

This leaves expert rather than State arbitration as a possibility, on the lines of the three 'wise men' called on to arbitrate between British and French claims to the continental shelf surrounding the Channel Islands.[62] Not only is this likely to be the most easily available method, but the verdict of a small panel of international lawyers, visibly without bias and with a clear comprehension of the complexities of the Law of the Sea, could well carry greater authority than some of the alternatives mentioned. Though NATO and the European Community may have no direct part in such an arbitration, they have the strongest possible interest in promoting it (as Britain and France have done, by their example in submitting the Channel Islands dispute to arbitration).

Airspace Problems
Progress on the continental shelf dispute could be a catalyst for progress on the others. But there is no reason why on one of these, the air traffic control dispute, the process should not be the other way round. The simplest course would be to go back to the abortive agreement of November 1976 and work out a preamble without prejudice either way to the existing ICAO regime. For the sake of international air communications, and to prepare the way for an ultimate decision on the existing FIR pattern, the immediate need is to rescind unilateral declarations and get

air traffic moving again. If, as a condition for restoring the FIR system, Turkey were to seek guarantees that Greece would not use her authority to impose unjustified restrictions on Turkish air exercises, it would be reasonable to give these, however unnecessary they might seem to Greece.[63] But if she insists on re-drawing FIR boundaries in consonance with what she regards as her international status, the problem will be much more difficult. The only way to solve it will be through a regional conference of ICAO. In either case, any settlement must reaffirm the international character of non-territorial airspace and the fact that air traffic control is a technical responsibility without hint of future sovereignty claims.

Territorial Sea
The present quiet over the territorial sea issue does not mean that the question of sea limits has been disposed of. On the contrary, Greece retains the option to declare an extension to twelve miles. She has said that she would not surrender this option although she has no intention of exercising it for the time being. This is a threat with dangerous possibilities which range well beyond the Turkish declaration of a *casus belli*. (Extension would most probably be seen as interfering with the passage of Soviet ships, especially subs, between Mediterranean and Black Seas. Nor is it likely that in these circumstances the USSR would be placated by the offer of a twelve-mile channel, which is sometimes discussed.) Greece and Turkey have lived comfortably with a six-mile limit for more than forty years. The surest solution would be a joint declaration establishing this limit in perpetuity.

The Islands
The militarization of the Greek islands and the 'Aegean' role of the Turkish Fourth Army are elements of a military situation that needs to be defused as quickly as possible, both to remove the danger of war and to restore NATO partnership in the overall defence of the region.

During the preparation of this Paper Greek and Turkish officials were asked their opinions about a proposal for a joint declaration in which Turkey would undertake not to invade the islands and Greece would undertake to demilitarize them. The proposition met with a negative response. On the Greek side it was said to carry no enforceable guarantee. On the Turkish side it was said to be redundant, since Greece was already pledged to demilitarize the islands under treaty.

Another way forward would be via a mutually agreed 'phased disengagement' from the islands and coastal areas. But, although this might seem to offer a basis for negotiation, it presents difficulties not unlike those of Mutual and Balanced Force Reduction (MBFR) in Central Europe, the chief being the ease with which Turkey could reintroduce forces, and the inhibiting effect this would have on Greek withdrawals.

It is difficult to quarrel with the proposition put to the author by Mr Ecevit, as well as by a number of Greek officials, that the question of the islands (and, by implication, the Turkish Fourth Army) should be 'allowed to take care of itself' after settlement has been reached on other issues. In this, as in other matters, much could be done to improve the situation by restraint on the part of the media of both countries.

Cyprus
Obviously progress on a Cyprus settlement can help in the Aegean and *vice versa*. But the opposite is also true: setbacks can have repercussions (witness the interruption of meetings on the continental shelf question as a result of the poor reception of Turkish-Cypriot proposals for a Cyprus settlement in April 1978). The objective, clearly, is to get Greek Cypriots and Turkish Cypriots into real direct negotiations. As to priorities, there can be no quarrel with Mr Ecevit's proposal that talks on Cyprus and the Aegean should be 'simultaneous but separate'. But there must also be no question of Turkey using her strong military position in Cyprus to try to force Greece into Aegean concessions beyond what is equitable. Instead she should use her substantial and indispensable economic aid as a lever to bring the Turkish Cypriots to the conference table, while on the Greek side Mr Karamanlis can be expected to bring his very great personal authority to bear on the Greek-Cypriot government. To allow the two Cypriot communities to become arbiters of Greek-Turkish relations would be a development that would help nobody.

Can Confidence be Restored?
This study has been largely concerned with political and legal niceties, since such things must play a part in any Aegean settlement. Yet there is a danger that some of the more fundamental reasons for the quarrel may be overlooked.

On the face of it, the dispute has revolved around sovereign rights in the seabed, national security, freedom of transit, and so on. These matters are important, but they are not necessarily the 'real' issues.

The more one studies the dispute and talks with those involved, the more one realizes that what is often largely at issue, apart from lack of confidence, is national pride. This is particularly noticeable on the Turkish side, where pride or self-respect (the preferred Turkish phrase) has come to mean almost literal equality in bilateral relations. It is a weakness in Greek policy not to recognize this fact – for example in supposing that Turkey might accept joint exploitation rights in a seabed that remained almost wholly Greek. But there are also blindnesses on the Turkish side, for example with regard to the place of the Aegean islands in Greek emotions, and to the impact of the Cyprus operation on Greek public opinion.

Unless there is greater understanding of these things, it is uncertain whether any political settlement can lead to a return of the co-operative spirit of the later 1920s. And without this spirit there can be no sure future.

Finally a word is needed about time. Enough has been said about the dangers of delaying a solution. When bombs were falling in Cyprus and tension was rising over the explorations of *Sismik 1*, this urgency was obvious. But more recently there have been fewer incidents provoking world newspaper headlines. This change is welcome as a sign of the two governments' efforts to avoid dramatic confrontations, of a possibly cooler attitude on the part of the media (which bear a heavy responsibility for aggravating tension in the past), and of better prospects for unravelling mutual suspicions.

But quiescence has its dangers. One is that, because there is no dramatic threat, the Aegean dispute will be allowed to rumble on in the background – a struggle that is liable to explode in all its force on some future provocation. It is important for the West that a settlement should be both speedy and complete, and that the Aegean dispute, like the Cyprus dispute, should not be allowed to become an institutionalized threat to peace.

APPENDIXES

Appendix 1: The Berne Declaration

'*On the procedure to be followed for the delimitation of the continental shelf by Greece and Turkey.*

(1) Both parties agree that negotiations be sincere, detailed and conducted in good faith with a view to reaching an agreement based on mutual consent regarding the delimitation of the continental shelf

(2) Both parties agree that these negotiations should, due to their nature, be strictly confidential.

(3) Both parties reserve their respective positions regarding the delimitation of the continental shelf.

(4) Both parties undertake the obligation not to use the details of this agreement and the proposals that each will make during the negotiations in any circumstances outside the context of the negotiations.

(5) Both parties agree no statements or leaks to the press should be made referring to the content of the negotiations unless they commonly agree to do so.

(6) Both parties undertake to abstain from any initiative or act relating to the continental shelf of the Aegean Sea which might prejudice the negotiations.

(7) Both parties undertake, as far as their bilateral relations are concerned, to abstain from any initiative or act which would tend to discredit the other party.

(8) Both parties have agreed to study state practice and international rules on this subject with a view to educing certain principles and practical criteria which could be of use in the delimitation of the continental shelf between the two countries.

(9) A mixed commission will be set up to this end and will be composed of national representatives.

(10) Both parties agree to adopt a gradual approach in the course of the negotiations ahead after consulting each other.

Signed in Berne: 11th November 1976.
Released in Athens and Ankara: 20th November 1976.

Appendix 2: Confirmed Mineral Resources

Although oil exploration licences were issued by the Greek government in 1970, it was not until 1974 that commercially significant deposits were discovered off Thasos by Oceanic Exploration of Denver, Colorado – part of a consortium including the Hellenic Oil and Wintershall companies and the White Shield (Greece) Oil Corporation. The original Oceanic contract, signed with the military junta, was revised in 1975 as being too favourable to foreign interests. The new terms put the state share in the field, now called the Prinos field, at 65% of production up to 200,000 barrels a day, and 80% beyond that figure. For the first five years this clause was not to operate until the licensee had recovered his full capital expenditure and operating costs from his share of gross income.

In May 1975, however, Oceanic ran into financial difficulties and was obliged to hand over its 67% share in the Prinos field to Wintershall.

Following the sinking of two exploration wells, it was first estimated that output from the Prinos field would rise to a maximum of 50,000 barrels per day. But the sinking of further delineation wells revealed a fault in the field; estimates have now been revised downwards to give an ultimate maximum output of 25,000 barrels a day and total deposits of about 65 million barrels. Production, originally expected to start in 1978, has also been put back and is not now due to begin until 1981, by which time Greece's domestic oil requirement is expected to be 200,000 barrels per day. In addition to the Prinos field, drilling has established the existence of a small natural gas field in the Thasos area, which has still to be delineated and which could be commercially exploitable.

These are the only commercially exploitable fields to be discovered after nearly eight years' exploration of the northern Aegean, and the faulty paleontological structure of the seabed is now seen as ruling out the likelihood of further exploitable fields.

It is not yet certain whether the same faulty structure exists in the southern Aegean. More promising indications have come from geological and seismic studies in the Ionian Sea, where the state-owned Greek Public Petroleum Company plans exploratory drilling.

Appendix 3: Greek-Turkish Relations 1973–1978

'Cyprus' events	*'Aegean' events*

1973

27 July: Cypriot Justice Minister abducted by EOKA (later freed). Incidents and security measures continue throughout the year.

1974

15 July: Sampson coup. President Makarios flees to London.
17 July: Turkish Prime Minister Ecevit flies to London for talks with Britain and US.
20 July: Turks invade Cyprus. Greece mobilizes. Security Council calls for cease-fire.
23 July: Athens military government falls. Karamanlis returns.
24 July: Sampson ousted by Clerides.
25 July: Peace talks between Britain, Greece and Turkey open in Geneva.
25 July: Ecevit expresses hope for improved relations. Greece and Turkey affirm endorsement UN cease-fire resolution.
30 July: British, Greek and Turkish Foreign Ministers sign Cyprus declaration providing for an end to Turkish advances and setting up of buffer zone.
4 August: Second Geneva Conference opens against background of continuing fighting. Greeks reject Turkish proposal for bi-communal federation.
14 August: Turks bomb Nicosia and Famagusta, advance on all fronts. Greece withdraws from military structure of NATO.
16 August: Turkish forces reach 'Attila line' (proposed by Turkey as dividing line in 1965); nearly 40% of Cyprus in Turkish hands. Security Council calls for cease-fire.
22 August: 'Autonomous' Turkish-Cypriot Administration declared.
30 August: Greece announces intention to renegotiate foreign military bases.

1 October: President Makarios in UN Assembly rejects geographical federation.
1 November: UN Assembly passes Resolution 3212, calling for withdrawal of all foreign troops. Announcement that Makarios will resume presidency.

1973

1 November: Turkey grants oil exploration licences.

1974

28 February: Turkey proposes negotiations on continental shelf question.
7 April: Greece and Turkey place troops on alert.
25 May: Greece accepts Turkish proposal.
29 May: Survey ship *Candarli* enters Aegean.
27 June: Greek and Turkish leaders meet to discuss Aegean dispute, without progress.

4 August: Turkey issues NOTAM 714, requiring all approaching aircraft to report to Turkish authorities.

13 September: Greece issues NOTAM 1157 declaring Aegean a danger zone. Air services suspended. Greece begins fortification of East Aegean islands.

'Cyprus' events	*'Aegean' events*
1975	**1975**
8 January: Greek and Turkish Cypriots agree to resume negotiations on basis of federal government.	
	27 January: Greece proposes joint approach to ICJ on continental shelf question.
5 February: US imposes arms embargo on Turkey. Turkey withdraws from Cyprus talks.	*6 February:* Turkey accepts proposal to approach ICJ.
10 February: Greek Cypriots propose multi-regional Federation.	
13 February: 'Turkish Federated State of Cyprus' declared.	
	17 March: Third session of UN Law of the Sea conference opens in Geneva.
	6 April: Demirel government, reversing its earlier 'ICJ' proposal, says boundaries of continental shelf must be established 'through negotiation'.
28 April: Intercommunal talks start in Vienna under UN Secretary-General. Agreement to set up committee on constitutional matters.	
	19 May: Greek and Foreign Ministers meet in Rome to discuss joint submission to ICJ.
31 May: Karamanlis and Demirel meet in Brussels, declare support for intercommunal talks.	*31 May:* Brussels Communiqué says the two sides will resolve problems peacefully 'by means of negotiations and as regards the continental shelf [through] the International Court'. Lines laid down for meetings of officials.
12 June: Greece applies for full EEC membership.	*15 June:* First meeting to resolve air traffic dispute. Turkey extends demands to cover reporting of Greek military flights.
	22 June: Tension over survey ship *Goel 1*.
	July: Agreement reached on commercial flight reporting.
25 July: Turkey takes over US bases in Turkey after US House of Representative votes to extend arms embargo.	
31 July: Third round of talks in Vienna. Greek-Cypriot negotiator Clerides agrees to allow 10,000 Turkish Cypriots in southern Cyprus to move to Turkish-held north. Number migrating from south to north of island after July 1974 reaches 65,000. Turkish-Cypriot negotiator Denktash promises comprehensive proposals for remaining problems before next talks.	
10 September: Fourth round of talks, in New York, called off due to lack of formal proposals.	*September:* Turkish government, under Opposition pressure, postpones further talks by legal experts in Paris. Objects to Greek pressure for joint submission of continental shelf case to ICJ.
	11 December: Inconclusive talks on remaining air traffic question.
29 December: Turkey and USSR sign friendship and co-operation accord.	

'*Cyprus*' events	'*Aegean*' events
1976	**1976**
	7 January: Near break-down of air talks.
17 February: Fifth round of talks in Vienna, agreement to exchange proposals simultaneously within six weeks.	
6 April: Greek-Cypriot territorial and constitutional proposals handed to UN Special Representative.	
17 April: Turkish-Cypriot plan for bizonal federation handed to UN Representative.	
30 May: Makarios rejects Turkish-Cypriot plan.	
	3 June: Greece orders partial mobilization of reservists in response to Turkish naval manoeuvres in Aegean.
	30 June: Negotiations over Aegean in Berne end without progress.
	23 July: Sizmik 1 leaves for Aegean despite Greek protests; stops short of disputed waters as talks are held (26 July).
	29 July: Talks break down. *Sizmik 1* enters disputed waters as Greece threatens military action and Turkey calls armed forces alert.
	3 August: Greece sends oceanographic vessels to northern Aegean; calls for UN Security Council meeting (9 August); Turkey offers to resume negotiations (15 August).
	25 August: Call to resume negotiations by UN Security Council Resolution 395.
	1 September: Greece mobilizes Aegean fleet after Turkey announces further exploration by *Sizmik 1.*
5 September: Centre–left alliance defeats Clerides' Democratic Rally Party in Cyprus elections.	
	6–8 September: Sizmik 1 prospects in disputed claim area.
	12 September: ICJ rejects Greek request for interim injunction to stop Turkish exploration.
21 September: UN Secretary-General fails to achieve resumption of talks when Turkish Cypriots refuse to commit themselves to further proposals.	
	25 September: Security Council recommends negotiations.
	3 October: Greece and Turkey agree to talks on Aegean demarcation boundaries.
	7 November: Air talks break down over wording of preamble to draft agreement.
	11 November: Berne declaration sets out agreed procedure for seeking settlement of continental shelf dispute.
1977	**1977**
27 January: Makarios holds first meeting with Denktash since invasion after 14-year refusal to meet the Turkish-Cypriot leaders.	
12 February: Second Makarios–Denktash meeting. Guidelines for a Cyprus settlement agreed. Agreement on resumption of intercommunal talks.	

'Cyprus' events

31 March: Sixth round of talks in Vienna. Greek-Cypriots propose two-region federation leaving 20% of island under Turkish-Cypriot administration. No Turkish-Cypriot territorial proposals. Turkish-Cypriot constitutional proposals appear to provide for confederation.
21 April: Carter administration seeks partial relaxation of US arms embargo.
20 May: Karamanlis says Greeks will not rejoin NATO until Turkey withdraws from Cyprus.

3 August: Makarios dies, succeeded by Kyprianou.
25 August: Denktash threatens to declare independence of Turkish-Cypriot state.

1978
2 January: Ecevit, again Premier, quoted as saying 'We will try to move things [in Cyprus]. We won't keep the problem suspended. We don't want to be stuck with this issue for ever.'
9 January: Ecevit says Turkey will take the initiative in making proposals to reactivate the intercommunal talks 'in a meaningful way'.
9 March: US government statement appears to link lifting of arms embargo to progress on Cyprus.
19 April: Nicosia (Greek-Cypriot) government rejects as inadequate recently-submitted Turkish territorial and constitutional proposals for Cyprus settlement.

9 November: UN General Assembly passes resolution to oust Turkish forces from Cyprus; insists Security Council implement it.

1979
10 January: Greek and Turkish Cypriots agree to accept UN formula for a resumption of negotiations.

'Aegean' events

3 July: Ecevit resigns after losing parliamentary confidence vote. Succeeded by Demirel.

2 November: In Greek elections PASOK wins 25% of vote, Government only 45%.
31 December: Demirel loses confidence vote. Ecevit returns.

1978

3 September: Greek–Soviet communiqué pledges closer bilateral ties and greater efforts towards detente.
26 September: US President Carter signs $2·8-billion International Security Assistance Act which ends US arms embargo against Turkey.
9 October: Turkey reopens 4 US military intelligence installations shut during arms embargo.

19 December: ICJ refuses to arbitrate Aegean dispute, calling it a domestic matter.

1979

14 January: Greece tells US that proposed increase in military and economic aid to Turkey threatens the regional balance of power.

'Cyprus' events	*'Aegean'* events
	18 January: Turkey and US open talks on new defence agreement.
9 April: Greece and Turkey start talks in Geneva aimed at resolving common problems.
1 May: Some Turkish forces withdrawn from Cyprus in preparation for Greek–Turkish summit talks.
19 May: Kyprianou and Denktash meet in Nicosia in attempt to resolve differences at meeting chaired by UN Secretary General.
15 June: Start of abortive attempt to re-start bilateral talks on Cyprus under UN aegis.	
	14 October: Turkish mid-term elections destroy Ecevit's parliamentary majority.

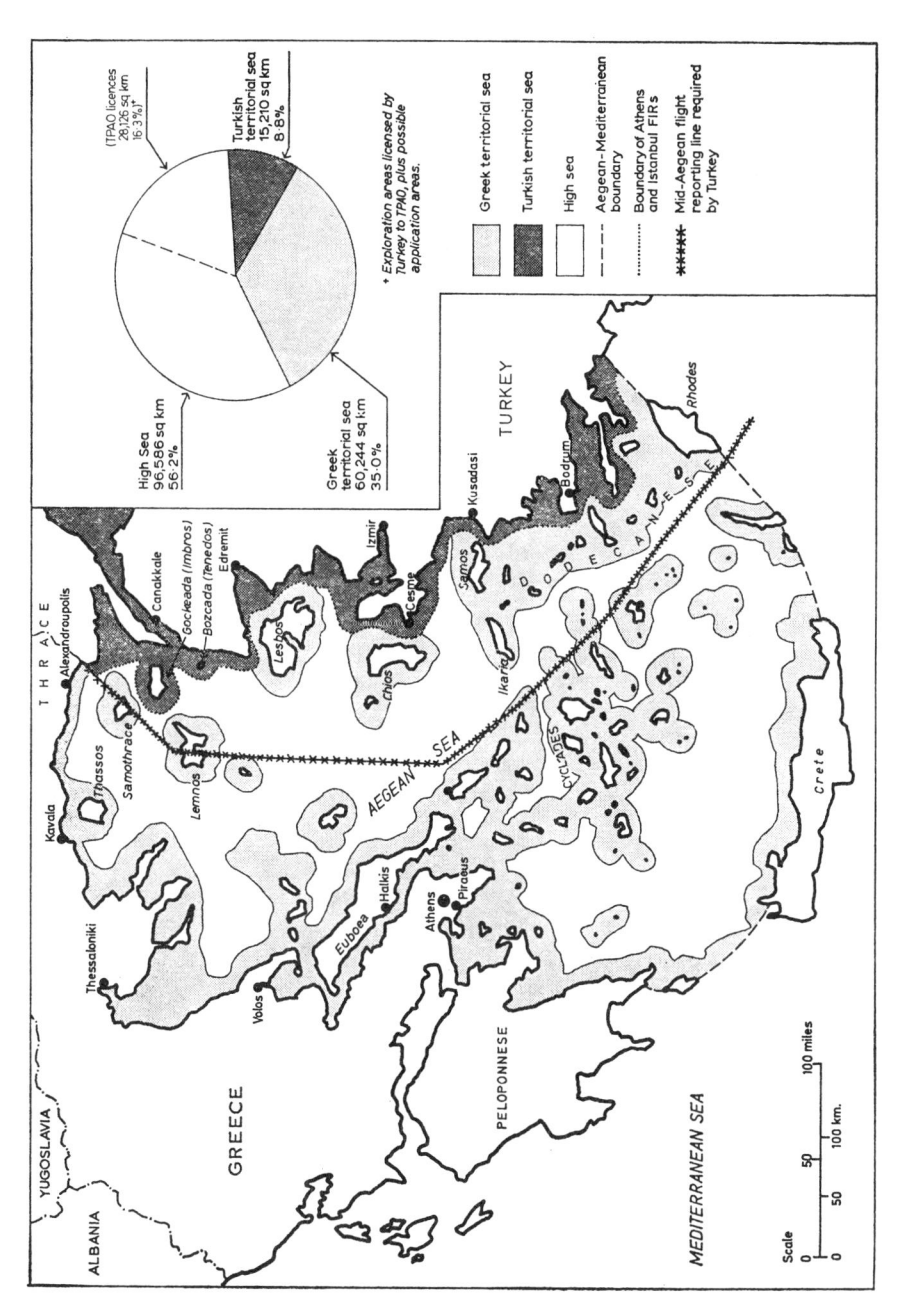

Map 1: Possible Distribution of Territorial Seas in the Aegean (16 nautical miles)

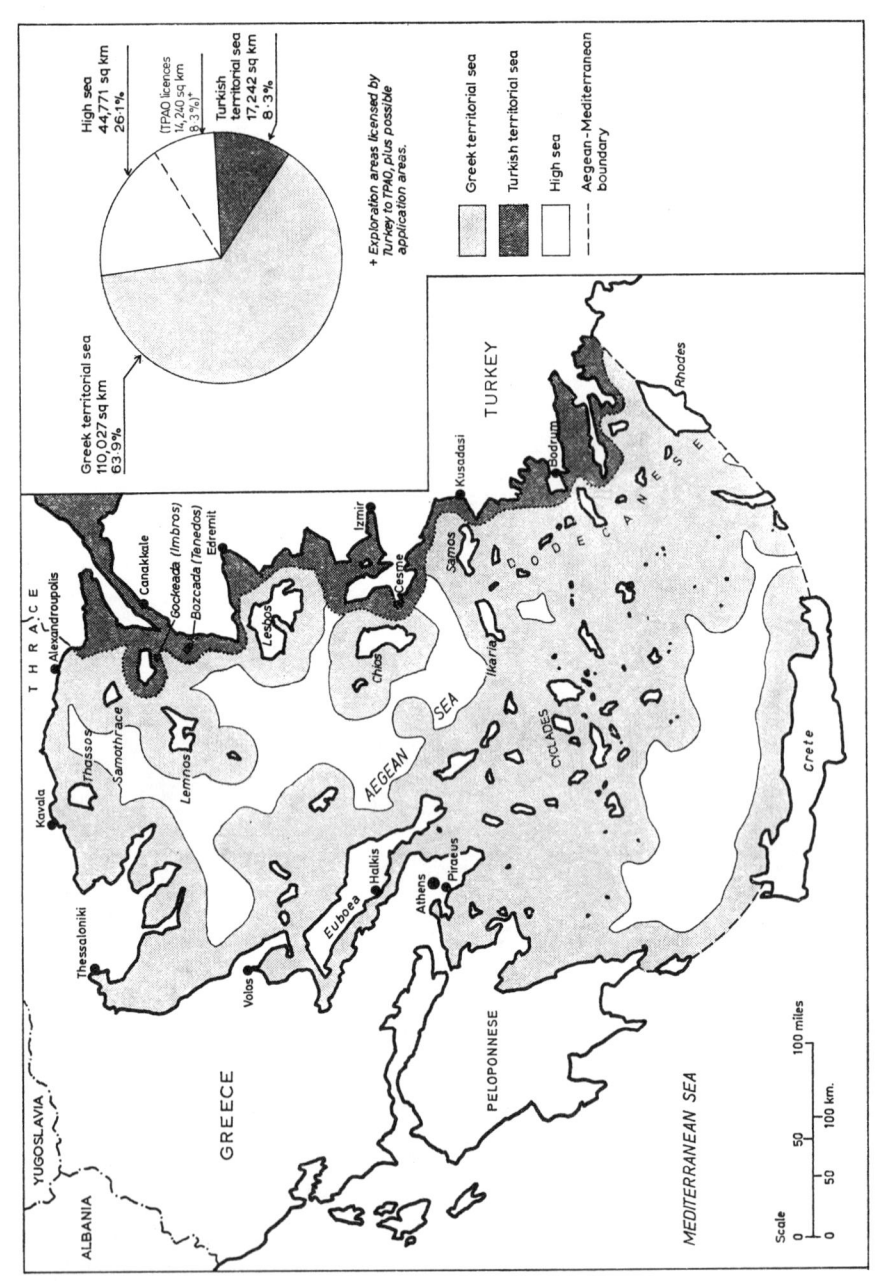

Map 2: Present Distribution of Territorial Seas in the Aegean (12 nautical miles)

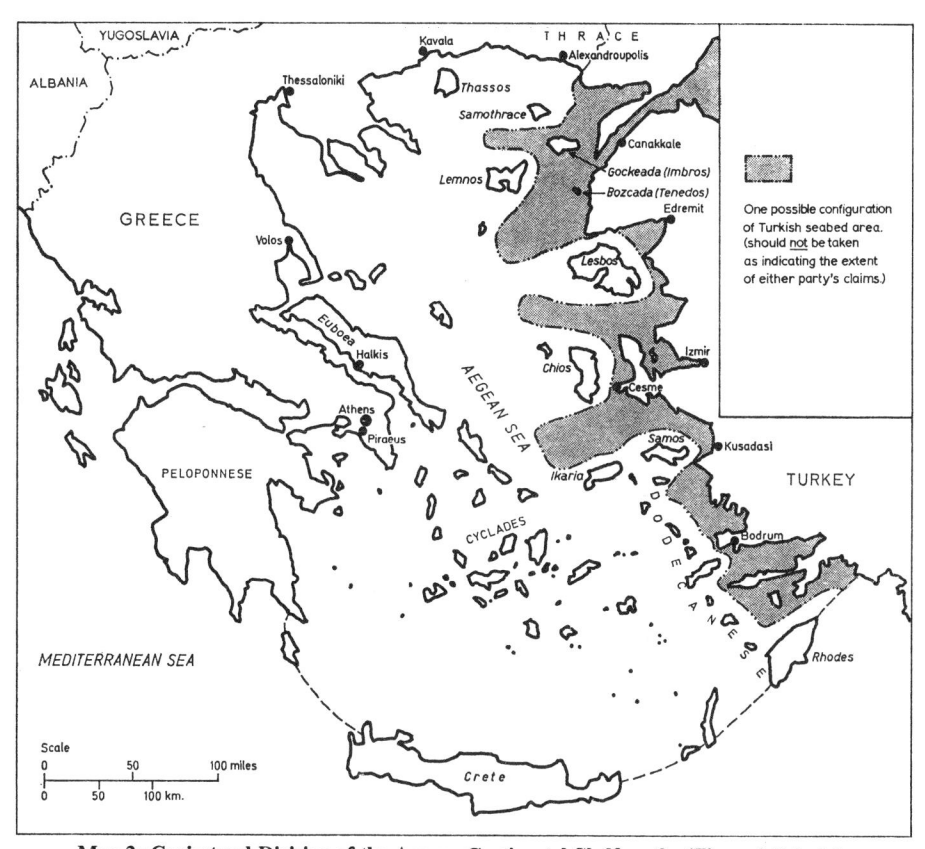

Map 3: Conjectural Division of the Aegean Continental Shelf on the 'Fingers' Principle

NOTES

[1] In a comment on this passage, Turkish officials said they believed that all issues between Turkey and Greece were still open to bilateral resolution.

[2] Although the 'Great Idea' died for good in the Greek defeat by Ataturk in 1922, its legacy might legitimately have been seen in the 1950s popular movement for the *enosis* of Cyprus with Greece.

[3] 1974 figures.

[4] It could be argued that Turkey's Black Sea ports should be taken into this picture, to the extent that they trade with the Mediterranean. This would not materially alter the situation, however.

[5] Barry Buzan, *A Sea of Troubles? Sources of Dispute in the New Ocean Regime*, Adelphi Paper No. 143 (London: IISS, 1978).

[6] At the time of writing some 23 states have declared territorial seas beyond 12 miles, and many more have expressed interest in security zones, economic zones and other formulae that would restrict the passage of shipping belonging to other states.

[7] Text available in *Report of the First UN Conference on the Law of the Sea* (London: HMSO, Cmnd 584, 1958).

[8] *I.C.J. Reports* 1969, p. 3 at p. 39, para. 63.

[9] Article 121 states that:

1. An island is a naturally formed area of land surrounded by water, which is above water at high tide.
2. Except as provided for in paragraph 3, the territorial sea, the exclusive Economic Zone, and the Continental Shelf of an island are determined in accordance with the provisions of the present convention applicable to other land territory.
3. Rocks which cannot sustain human habitation or economic life of their own shall have no exclusive economic zone or continental shelf.'

[10] Greek–Italian agreement providing for the delimitation of their continental shelf in the Ionian Sea (1977), Malaysian–Indonesian agreement (1969), Australian–Indonesian agreement (1971), agreement between Japan and Republic of Korea (1974).

[11] Judgment, *I.C.J. Reports* 1969, p. 3., para 90. In the following para (91) the Court ruled that 'there can never be any question of completely refashioning nature, and equity does not require that a State without access to the sea should be allotted an area of continental shelf, any more than there could be a question of rendering the situation of a State with an extensive coastline similar to that of a State with a restricted coastline.

[12] The Turkish six-mile limit applies only to the Aegean. On her Mediterranean and Black Sea coasts Turkey has a twelve-mile limit. The original global three-mile limit was determined by the range of naval and coastal guns. For a full treatment of the subject, see D. P. O'Connell, 'Transit Rights and Maritime Strategy', *RUSI Journal*, vol. 123, no. 2 (June 1978).

[13] Note verbale of 7 February and further note of 27 February 1974.

[14] Austrian Airlines and Sabena have since resumed restricted services between Athens and Istanbul and Salonika and Istanbul respectively, via Sofia FIR. But there are no direct flights across the Aegean, apart from domestic flights between the Greek mainland and islands, for the safety of which Athens accepts responsibility.

[15] Turkey has claimed that militarization started much earlier, in 1952. But this can relate only to NATO installations.

[16] On 13 January Turkish Prime Minister Irmak told the Innya Municipal Council: 'Half the Aegean is ours. Let the whole world know that this is so. . . . We know how to crush the heads of our enemies when the prestige, dignity and interests of the Turkish nation are attacked.' And on 19 January the Foreign Minister, Mr Essenbel, was quoted in *Cumhuriyet* as saying: 'The policy followed by the growing Turkey to safeguard her interest in the Aegean has to be different from the policy of the Turkey of 50 years ago. . . . The reason for this is not only a reaction to Greece's Great Idea policy. Turkey is not the Turkey of 1923 after the Lausanne treaty. It is a growing Turkey.'

[17] French original published in *Greek Application* [to the International Court] *Instituting Proceedings on the Aegean Sea Continental Shelf*, Filed 10 August 1976. Para 6.8.

[18] Co-ordinates given (by Greece), *Ibid*.

[19] UN Doc. S/12173, 12 August 1976.

[20] UN Doc. S/PV 1949, 12 August, 1976.

[21] Quoted in letter from Permanent Representative of Greece to UN Security Council, 10 August 1976. UN Doc. S/12168.

[22] UN DOC. S/12172, 11 August 1976.

[23] UN Doc. S/PV 1950, 13 August 1976.

[24] SC Res. 395, 31 UN SCOR, Resolutions and Decisions of the UN Security Council.

[25] SC Res. 395, 31 UN SCOR, Resolutions and Decisions of the Security Council 15, UN Doc. S/INF/32 (1976). The Resolution was based on a draft resolution (UN Doc. S/12187) submitted after consultations outside the Council by France, Italy, Britain and the United States. It was adopted by consensus, there being no unanimity in its favour, and no objection.

[26] See L. Gross, 'The Dispute between Greece and Turkey Concerning the Continental Shelf in the Aegean', *American Journal of International Law*, January 1977, vol. 71, no. 1.

[27] See T. R. Robol, 'Notes: Jurisdiction – Limits of Consent – The *Aegean Sea Continental Shelf* Case' *Harvard International Law Journal*, Summer 1977, vol 18, no. 3.

[28] Aegean Sea Continental Shelf, Interim Protection, Order of 11 September 1976. ICJ REP. 3.

[29] For a full discussion of this and other aspects of the International Court proceedings see the articles by Gross and Robol cited in notes 26 and 27.

[30] *Greek Accession to the General Act on the Pacific Settlement of International Disputes of 1928*, 14 September 1931, 111 L.N.T.S. 414 (1931).

[31] The height of absurdity was reached when overflight permission had to be obtained from Bulgaria for planes taking Turkish representatives to NATO meetings in Brussels.

[32] Greek officials finally offered to delete the word ICAO, leaving only a reference to FIRS.

[33] Background paper supplied to the author.
[34] Turkish background paper supplied to the author.
[35] Greek officials, verbally, to the author.
[36] The only ICAO state that has allowed part of its territory to be placed under a neighbour's FIR is Mauritania.
[37] *Pulse* (Ankara), 22 November 1976.
[38] J. Andrassy, *International Law and the Resources of the Sea* (New York: Columbia University Press, 1970).
[39] J. A. C. Gutteridge, ' The Regime of the Continental Shelf', 44 *Grotius Society Transactions 1958–1959*, pp. 77–89.
[40] Donald E. Karl, 'Islands and Delimitations of the Continental Shelf', *American Journal of International Law*, October 1977.
[41] ICJ REP. 54.
[42] Ilchami Sancar, Minister of Defence (*Yanki*, 20 January 1975): 'In the Aegean Sea the balance is obviously in Turkey's favour. This is true to such an extent that the eyes and thoughts of the Turks, former inhabitants of the islands, remained focused on islands a few miles from the Turkish coast, in hope of being able to re-establish themselves there one day.' Gen. Souat Atoulga, commander of the Turkish Second Army (*Gunaidin*, 25 January 1975); 'Greeks will never become friends of Turkey if they will not abandon the Great Idea. Consequently the question of the Dodecanese islands and Western Thrace must be raised.' Mr Demirel, Turkish Prime Minister (*Paris Match*, 5 July 1975): 'Till recently the islands of the Aegean belonged to whoever possessed Anatolia'. Mr Turkes, Turkish Vice-Premier (*Devlet*, 30 March 1976): 'The group of islands situated near the Turkish coasts, including the Dodecanese, must belong to Turkey. Among these we cite Samothrace, Lesbos, Chios, Samos, Kos, Rhodes and all others, small or large within a distance of 50 km.' Gen. Sunalp, Commander of the Turkish Fourth Army (*Politika*, 19 August 1976): "The Army of the Aegean has a striking capability. Its deterrent potential is very important to us. It now disposes of a force of 123,000 men.'
[43] *Record of the Turkish Grand National Assembly*, vol. 12, p. 309, 5th Parliamentary Period, 5th Session, 61st meeting.
[44] The conference preparing the Treaty was told by Lord Curzon on behalf of the Allies: 'The sub-committee recommended a milder form of demilitarization aiming at protecting the Turks in Anatolia against an attack from the Greek islands while allowing the Greek government the necessary forces for defending the islands and maintaining order'. *Documents diplomatiques, Conférence de Lausanne, premier volume, 21 novembre – 1er février 1923* (Paris: Imprimerie Nationale, 1923), p. 80.
[45] This view received support in a secret telegram sent to the US Embassy in Athens in 1948 by the then US Secretary of State, Gen. Marshall, in which he expressed the view that the demilitarization of the Dodecanese did not extend to the cases of the maintenance of public order and of the defence of Greek frontiers. (State Department Declassified Documents, 1974.)
[46] Report of the Mixed Committee on the Exchange of Populations. Greek sources claim that in 1923 the figure was over 200,000.
[47] Other factors causing emigration have been hardships at the hands of both the Bulgarians and the Germans in World War II, and at the hands of Greek guerrillas during the Greek Civil war. Turkish officials put the present number of Muslims in Western Thrace at 117,000 (not 130,000).
[48] At the trial of Menderes in 1961 the organization of the riots was one of the charges. A subsequent report on the riots by a mission of the World Council of Churches spoke of 'appalling destruction' and the hardships suffered by victims. Only 9 of the 80 Greek Orthodox churches remained intact, 29 being completely destroyed by fire. 'Four thousand shops were destroyed, their contents thrown into the streets, and 2,000 homes utterly ruined.' The psychological effect of the riots was such that in the following years approximately 40,000 Greek Orthodox (citizens and residents) left Istanbul, according to Greek figures.
[49] New taxes introduced in 1967 and 1972 put the foundations in danger of closing down. Following representations by the Greek government these taxes have not been collected yet, and it has been reported that the Turkish government has promised to alleviate them. Measures have also been taken to strengthen Turkish supervision of minority schools. The Greek nationals (who formed a separate community from those Orthodox Christians who had taken Turkish nationality) had already suffered a diminution of their privileges when in 1960 the Turkish government extended the list of professions and trades that could be exercised only by Turks.
[50] In the case of Komotini College, 83% of the land belonged to Turks (who are a majority in the area). But Greek authorities say that for the other college, Xanthi, 82% of the expropriated land belonged to Greeks.
[51] The Greek government has recently taken steps to introduce local industry, mainly in Komotini, Xanthi and Alexandroupolis, which could alleviate the employment problem.
[52] According to Greek records for Western Thrace 1960–68, 1,723 licences were given for driving tractors and similar vehicles (out of 2,367 applications) and 808 for driving cars (out of 1,053 applications).
[53] In an observation on the remarks above on the language question, Greek officials told the author that it would be impossible to introduce the Turkish language in Greek universities as a medium of instruction solely for their Muslim students, and that, similarly, citizens applying for driving licences could hardly be tested in any other language than Greek. They also considered that mention should be made of the establishment in Thessaloniki ten years ago of the Special Teaching Academy, exclusively as a centre where Muslim teachers can be trained to serve in the minority schools of Western Thrace. In February 1979 the Academy had 63 students, who enjoyed completely free education.
[54] In war the former would command the land forces assigned to NATO in Greece (First Hellenic Army, with headquarters at Larissa, concentrated mainly on the Bulgarian and Albanian borders), the Turkish First Army (headquarters Erzincan, defending the Eastern frontier), and the Turkish Second Army (headquarters at Konya, defending the south-eastern frontier). Similarly in war the air headquarters would command the Greek and Turkish air forces – the Helenic Twenty-Eighth Tactical

Air Force with headquarters in Larissa, the Turkish First Tactical Air Force with headquarters at Eskisehir, southeast of Istanbul, and the Turkish Second Tactical Air Force with headquarters at Diyarbakir in south-eastern Turkey. Both headquarters would form a joint operations centre in a protected headquarters complex which would include a liaison officer from the US Sixth Fleet.

[55] In a comment on the above passage, Turkish officials made the following additional observations, which Greece contests: (1) The 10-nautical mile air space limit remained almost a secret until mentioned in Greek air information circulars in 1974, when Turkey protested; (2) the Lemnos control zone, to enter which all aircraft must get prior permission, is unnecessarily large for civil terminal control purposes and contravenes ICAO rules.

[56] Statement in Bonn, 12 May 1978 (official transcript). The same statement gave three reasons for the new concept: the ending of the Cold War, advances in military technology, and the Turkish experience of the American arms embargo. Turkey, said Mr Ecevit, had become 'over-dependent on one source for most of its military equipment, and it has become obvious to us that this over-dependence on one source is quite risky, particularly if that source happens to be the United States [where] ethnic lobbies can be very influential.'

[57] Some observers have seen in the vigour of Islam in modern Turkey evidence of a popular sentiment which could one day lead to the rejection of the European idea. Certainly there are currents against Ataturkism, but the latter remains dominant in the sections of society that provide today's political and military leaders. Laicism remains an unspoken qualification for promotion to the higher ranks of the armed services.

[58] *The Military Balance 1977–1978* (London: IISS, 1977). The US, British and West German figures for defence spending as a proportion of GNP in 1975 were 5·9%, 4·9% and 3·7% respectively.

[59] According to Greek defence sources *all* the Aegean islands have now been put into a defensive state. In the case of the smallest islands this appears to mean that no island could be occupied without at least token resistance: a form of 'trip-wire' that would automatically lead to all-out hostilities.

[60] The Greek Left (with the exception of the small Alliance party) is more militant on Turkey, and thus on defence, than the Conservative Right. PASOK views on defence policy were outlined by Papandreou in an article in *To Vima* on 20 April 1978. Greece must leave NATO, which had supported the junta, dominated Greek policy-making and betrayed Cyprus to Turkey. In no case must Greece enter such alliances which put her under the influence of a foreign decision-making centre. For an independent foreign policy there must be a self-sufficiency in production of defensive weapons. Threatened areas, such as the islands of the Aegean, must be organized in a form of territorial defence, such as that in Yugoslavia in World War II. To meet the Turkish threat ('resulting from Turkey's socio-economic structure and dependence on the US') Greece should not only seek a balance of power in traditional weapons but should also anticipate Turkey's acquisition of nuclear weapons, if possible by securing a nuclear-free zone in the Mediterranean and Balkans, but if necessary by acquiring nuclear arms herself.

[61] In a comment on this passage Turkish officials observed: 'For a fair and acceptable settlement every single condition and detail must be carefully studied and taken into consideration. For example, while the second condition listed here indicates that there must be no enclaving of islands, there is no condition foreseeing the non-enclaving of the Turkish mainland.

[62] For fuller treatment see Robol, in *Harvard International Law Journal*, summer 1977, vol. 18, no. 3. The islands were awarded a 12-mile limit.

[63] The giving of 'unnecessary' guarantees may play a useful part in the solution of Greek–Turkish problems. The non-aggression pact proposed by Mr Karamanlis at his Washington meeting with Mr Ecevit in May 1978 falls within this category. He had also suggested a pact to Mr Demirel in April 1976.

4 Greek Security
IOANNIS PESMAZOGLOU

Instability in the Near East continues to focus attention on the disarray of NATO's *southern flank. Turkey's economic difficulties and political turmoil were no less acute after fresh elections brought Suleyman Demirel's Justice Party once more to power. A solution to Greek-Turkish differences remained as far away as ever. Ioannis Pesmazoglou, a post-dictatorship cabinet minister and President of the Party of Democratic Socialism, reviewed Greek perspectives at a meeting of the Institute on 25 October 1979. That review focused on relations with Turkey, then catalogued Greek concerns and set out an approach both to security arrangements in the Aegean and to broader links with Turkey.*

SUMMARY OF ADDRESS BY IOANNIS PESMAZOGLOU (EXCERPTS) 25 OCTOBER 1979

Foreign Policy Orientations

The reconstruction of democracy after the seven-year dictatorship in Greece has been associated with the pursuit of Greece's accession to the European Communities, the promotion of friendly relations with all countries and the active participation in the efforts to strengthen security and peace based on the respect of international order...

The problems of accelerated adjustment of Greece to the European Communities, although not insignificant, could certainly be coped with. It should be noted that in the fifties and sixties the long term annual rate of real growth of the Greek economy at about 7 per cent was among the highest in the world and was associated with a rate of inflation of about 2·5 per cent an average increase in productivity of almost 10 per cent in the secondary sector and an overall safe balance of payments ... A non-negligible opposition to Greece's accession to the European Communities is founded on the arguments that the fundamental interests of Greece are not in harmony with those of the industrially advanced western countries and that a Greek socialist society should be built on an autonomous economic and development policy combined with a non-aligned or neutralist Greek external orientation.

Closer relations with the Arab countries are of particular interest to Greece and consultations are being conducted with their governments on issues of significance to the area. In this climate, increased commercial relations and greater Greek participation in public and private projects are being sought. Greek initiatives in the Balkans aim at the establishment of a mechanism or network of relations leading to an increasingly close economic and political co-operation and detente. Trade, tourism and cultural exchanges could be expanded and investment projects of common interest advanced and implemented. Causes of possible friction should be controlled, weakened and ultimately eliminated on the basis of established international law and procedures, thereby reducing the probability of a local conflict.

Direct contacts between Greece and the Soviet Union at the highest political level were sought by both countries as a move towards the termination of the cold war for Greece. It is in this spirit that the recent visit by the Greek Prime Minister to Moscow was supported by the overwhelming majority of the Greek political parties. With the same objectives relations of friendship with countries of Eastern Europe are being promoted.

Greece has the possibility and the will to become a factor of peace and stability, co-operation and progress in Southern Europe and the Middle East. The respect of the existing international agreements and of the established international mechanisms and procedures are of vital interest to the Greek people. Small countries can and do contribute to world peace and detente. If the world is to become a safe place for every nation, whether large or small, to pursue its own goals in full cognisance and respect of everybody else's legitimate interests, better understanding between nation-states is urgently needed. Greece could contribute in these directions and in this respect an increasingly wide network of consultations is necessary. The promotion of relations with China, as an emerging world power, should be associated with this more general effort.

The particular aspects of Greek security are analysed in the following sections.

Developments in Greece's Relations with NATO

Greece's relations with NATO have rapidly deteriorated in recent years and appear to have reached a deadlock following General Haig's proposals concerning Greece's relations with NATO's military wing. These developments are the culmination of a series of actions and omissions by NATO, the American Administration and some European Governments, which have deeply affected basic considerations regarding Greek security. The belief that 'what is good for NATO is good for Greece' has been significantly weakened in Greek public opinion and could well be reversed on account of NATO attitudes and policies in the following matters of vital importance to the Greek people.

First, the 'coup d'état' and the seven-year dictatorship in Greece (1967–1974). The conviction that NATO is designed to defend a mode of living based on the respect of democracy and human rights has been profoundly shaken.[1]

Second, the 1974 Turkish invasion of Cyprus, an independent country with 80 per cent of her population having strong national ties with the Greek people. The use of American arms for this purpose was accepted by NATO, whether with indifference or acquiescence. The assumption that NATO bonds preclude[2] the use of violence was proved unfounded.

Third, the maintenance of a Turkish Aegean army – outside the NATO structure – and of a fleet of landing craft facing Greek territory, both evidently designed to operate in the Aegean, as well as statements[3] by senior Turkish officials laying claim to Greek islands in order to further Turkish aspirations in the Aegean, all (treated with indifference by NATO) constitute attempts to change the *status quo* in the area, as defined by the Peace Treaties which followed the two World Wars. The Greeks fought both wars on the side of the Allies at a high human cost.

The confidence gap between Greece and NATO, more specifically between Greece and the American Administration, has been widened by the realization that NATO is unprepared to prevent arbitrary and aggressive action by Turkey against Greece. At the same time American politicians and strategists are increasingly willing to sacrifice Greek rights in order to appease Turkish demands. The Greek islands, which are an integral part of Greek national territory, with a long cultural and historical hellenic tradition, are regarded as geopolitical oddities whose status should perhaps be reconsidered. These views disregard Greek sovereign rights and endorse the threat to Greece posed by a NATO member, which furthermore continues to be armed and assisted in ways directly strengthening its capability of using violence against Greece.

The theory expounded by some NATO officials that the North Atlantic Treaty does not cover potential conflict between its members is neither logically nor legally, let alone politically, acceptable. How could the Alliance be credible if the possibility of an armed conflict between its members were not completely ruled out? A cast-iron guarantee of the integrity and sovereign rights of each member state against any threat whatsoever is an essential element for the credibility of the Alliance. There is no Greek political force which could disregard the implication that NATO and the American bases in Greece are designed to safeguard the security of its members including Turkey but not the security of Greece against aggression by Turkey.

It should be emphasized that no-one in Greece underestimates the need for Turkey to enjoy social and political stability as well as the significance of Turkey in the area, which, however, would be minimized or even reversed if she continued to pursue policies designed to upset the established relations with Greece. It would be wrong to underestimate Greece's geopolitical importance and contribution to peace and security in Southern and Southeastern Europe and in the Mediterranean. There would be far-reaching consequences if Greece were forced to take action to prevent efforts aiming at, or leading to, the violation of the country's national rights, including the unimpeded exercise of security control in the Aegean.

Proposed Pact of Friendship and Co-operation

A reactivation of a NATO relationship could only be based on the operational responsibilities as defined before 1974. And this should be associated with the closing of the confidence gap, by effective and credible guarantees against the threat from Turkey. Such guarantees are not only fully compatible with the aims and principles of NATO but also serve the best interests of its members. The main elements of such arrangements would be the following:

First, the implementation of the UN resolutions on Cyprus. The continued military occupation of 40 per cent of Cyprus by Turkish forces, using NATO or specifically American arms, constitutes a grave violation of international law as well as of American legislation and a serious threat to peace. The way towards a permanent solution in accordance with the UN resolutions has been opened by the Cypriot government's acceptance of a genuinely federal solution as well as of a UN force guaranteeing the rights of both the Turkish and the Greek Community. The withdrawal of the Turkish occupation forces from Cyprus would lead to constructive negotiations between representatives of the two Communities for the determination of the details of the new Federal Constitution.

Second, a pact of friendship and co-operation between Greece and Turkey precluding the use of violence and including the withdrawal from sensitive areas of forces and landing vessels which could be used for aggressive action. The obligation to abstain from an aggressive or provocative action should be endorsed by NATO through the proper interpretation of the NATO commitment, defining the mutual obligations of all member-countries in accordance with the principles and the spirit of the North Atlantic Treaty.

Defence installations on Eastern Aegean islands, frequently invoked by Turkish officials as constituting violation of the Lausanne and Paris Treaties, were established in response to Turkish pressures and threats and are of a non-permanent and exclusively defensive character. No contractual or other provision could deny the right of self-defence to any country. The right to use military installations to defend the Greek frontiers was recognized by the American Department of State in 1948 specifically with respect to the Dodecanese islands.[4]

Third, procedures should be established for the maintenance of the balance of the military strength and for the progressive reduction of the arms race between the two countries. It should be noted that there is an actual American legal obligation 'to ensure that the present (1978) balance of military strength among countries of the region, including between Greece and Turkey, is preserved...'[5] It should also be noted that control of the naval arms race was established in a protocol attached to the 1930 Treaty of Friendship between the two countries. The respect for, and strengthening of, international law and corresponding procedures by arrangements of general application is of fundamental interest and importance to the whole international community.

Claims or other proposals presented by Turkey should be considered in the context of International Law. Failing agreement, the way is always open to the Hague International Court. The possibility of recourse to arbitrary unilateral action or force should be definitely and permanently excluded.

The following should be stated as constituting the positions of the overwhelming majority of the Greek people and of Greek political parties:

(a) Friendship and co-operation between the Greek and the Turkish people are deemed essential and to the advantage of both countries. Progress in this direction corresponds to a sincere desire of the Greek people. There are wide areas of joint action of benefit to both.

(b) Greece has no claims on Turkey but will not accept any violation, limitation or concession, open or tacit, of her own sovereign rights, as defined by the Treaties concluded after the two Great Wars and by international conventions. Attempts at unilateral action would be opposed by Greece and unless such action is made impossible through a well-defined framework of rules and obligations, a serious threat to peace will continue to exist in the area.

(c) Arguments challenging Greek sovereign rights betray certain long-term Turkish objectives which could in no case be accepted by any Greek government. Such arguments are mainly:

133

The view is put forward that Turkey is not bound by the Geneva Convention on the Law of the Sea and therefore does not accept the principle that the islands have their own continental shelf. But this principle has been embodied in the Geneva Convention as a codification of customary law binding on all countries, irrespective of whether they have or have not signed the Convention. The 'equity considerations' invoked by Turkey work both ways and include the full appreciation of the principle that continuous and unimpeded communications between Greek island – and mainland – territories is a fundamental security principle for Greece, as indeed it would be for any country.

'Geophysical' as well as 'Lebensraum' arguments have also been officially advanced by Turkish spokesmen. These views, if accepted, lead to the law of the jungle. Grave instability including the danger of a major conflict, as experience showed 40 years ago, would be the inevitable consequence.

It should be stated that freedom of navigation has always been respected by Greece and would continue to be guaranteed for all countries in all cases and under any circumstances, irrespective of when Greece exercises her right to extend her territorial waters to 12 miles. Correspondingly Greek security control in the Aegean is a vital security interest of Greece and is also essential for the respect of freedom of navigation in the Aegean.

Security Control in the Aegean

Recent proposals by NATO and American officials regarding the military arrangements on the south-east flank of the Alliance do not conform to these considerations. A connection of Greece with NATO's military wing could be envisaged only in conjunction with the re-establishment of respect for Greek security, which implies the clear recognition of Greek operational responsibility in the Aegean sea and air space. The recent proposals by NATO officials, usually known as 'Haig proposals', deviate from this principle since operational responsibility in an area vital for Greek security is taken out of Greek authority. In fact, these proposals correspond to the acceptance of unwarranted Turkish demands and are indicative of Turkish attitudes and aspirations.

It should be noted that an understanding had been reached in the spring of 1978 between NATO and Greek representatives on the return to the *status quo* valid before 1974 with regard to operational responsibilities. But proposals deviating from this understanding were subsequently made by General Haig in order to satisfy Turkish objections. These were associated with the argument that changes have occurred within NATO since 1974, which posed obstacles to a return to the *status quo ante* with regard to the respective areas of Greek and Turkish operational control. There is no foundation for this argument as can be deduced from the following:

Up to 1974 an American Commander Allied Land Forces Southeastern Europe (COMLANDSOUTHEAST) based in Izmir co-ordinated both Greek and Turkish land forces – each possessing operational responsibility within its own sovereign territory. An American (COMSIXATAF) Commander also based in Izmir (subordinate to COMAIRSOUTH in Naples) co-ordinated Greek and Turkish air forces – each maintaining operational control within the zones coinciding with the Flight Information Regions (FIR) of each country.

The south-east land and air commands were restructured with the establishment of Turkish commands in Izmir and separate commands are envisaged in Greece (Larissa). These changes were evidently intended to be of a technical nature, i.e., with no political implications, since otherwise they should have been approved by NATO's supreme political authorities. Such approval has never been sought.

A reconsideration of operational responsibilities between the two countries was in no way the logical consequence of this separation of commands. The fact that Turkey and Greece could not operate in joint headquarters does not entail a restructuring of zones of operational responsibility. Recent Turkish demands incorporated in General Haig's proposals, imply a westward expansion of the operational responsibility of Turkish air forces over an Aegean area studded with Greek islands. No Greek government could accept such an arrangement, which would amount to the submission of airspace vital to Greek communications and defence to the control of a foreign country.

With regard to the Naval Forces, before 1974 the Commander Eastern Mediterranean (COMEDEAST) was the Chief of the Greek Naval General Staff, while the Commander Northeast Mediterranean (COMEDNOREAST) was a Turkish Admiral. Both commands were subordinate to the Commander Allied Naval Forces Southern Europe (COMNAVSOUTH) and ultimately to the Commander-in-Chief Allied Forces Southern Europe (CINCSOUTH) in Naples. These arrangements have no connection with whatever changes may have occurred in the Izmir land and air NATO command. Any attempt to neutralize the COMEDEAST within his area of responsibility through a 'Task Force' concept – to be applied for the first time by NATO in the case of the Aegean – corresponds to an unwarranted acceptance of Turkish claims.

Perspectives from Greece's Accession to the European Communities

Greece's full membership to the European Communities is a development strengthening European and western co-operation. Greek official spokesmen have repeatedly stated that an increasingly close relationship between the EEC and Turkey, and ultimately her full membership of the Community in line with the principles and procedures applied for all European Countries, is welcomed by Greece. This position is based not only on principle but also on self-interest. We are indeed convinced that increasingly strong ties between Turkey and the European Community and the achievement of social progress and political stability in Turkey are of great value to Greece since they could contribute to respect for international law and order.

In the same spirit, Greece supports efforts to assist the rehabilitation and strengthening of the Turkish economy on condition that such aid does not lead to increased Turkish military preparations in support of pressures and aggressiveness against Greece.

Recent developments in many parts of the world have shown that possession of advanced military hardware does not constitute a guarantee against internal upheavals nor external threats, unless accompanied by the proper functioning of democratic rule. This is of particular significance for European political stability and defence. It would imply that no NATO global strategy would ever be credible or effective without a clear and consistent orientation towards the preservation of peace and democracy, respect for international law and procedures with exclusion of all arbitrary and aggressive action against any member. The proposals for closing the confidence gap between Greece and NATO are essential for strengthening the cohesion between NATO countries and promoting international peace and security in south-east Europe and the Mediterranean.

NOTES

[1] Cf. See the preamble and Article 1 of the North Atlantic Treaty. Also M. Goldbloom, 'American Policy in Post-War Greece', in Clogg and Yannopoulos *Greece Under Military Rule* (London: Secker and Warburg, 1978).

[2] Cf. See again the preamble and Art. 1 of the North Atlantic Treaty. Also Philip Noel Baker, *Turkish action in Cyprus*, a letter to *The Times*, 19 August 1974. L. Stern, *The Wrong Horse* (New York: Times Books, 1977).

[3] The following are only few, relatively recent indicative statements:

In an interview to the Associated Press on 14 October 1977 the Turkish Prime Minister Mr. Demirel stated: 'I never say "the Greek islands". They are Aegean islands. The reason is that they never belonged to Greece in the past . . .'.

Mr. Demirel stated also in an interview published in Tercuman on 20 and 21 December 1978: '. . . The Aegean islands have never been conquered by Greece. Besides, these islands throughout history belonged to those who possessed Asia Minor . . .'.

In a speech at the Turkish Senate on 13 February 1978, Mr. Okcun, the then Turkish Foreign Minister of the latest Ecevit Government, said: ' . . . The Turkish Nation should be united concerning the problem of the Aegean Sea against the Greek pressures aiming at incarcerating Turkey from the West and its strangling'.

[4] See Top Secret Telegram of the Secretary of State to the American Embassy in Greece of 20 July 1948, in *Foreign Relations*, 1948, Vol. IV, p. 116.

[5] 14 August 1978 Conference Committee of the US House of Representatives and Senate: Agreement on the final version of the legislation permitting President Carter to lift the arms embargo on Turkey under certain conditions. See Article 4 of Part B.

5 Turkey's Security Policies
BULENT ECEVIT

There have been great changes in the world in recent years, for better or for worse: some of these changes are directly relevant to Turkey and to Turkey's international relations and security forces, some are indirectly relevant. We cannot deny an interest in any of these changes, because Turkey is situated in such a critical part of the world geopolitically that she is bound to be influenced by events and developments taking place in the distant parts of the world as well as those nearer home.

During these recent years of rapid world-wide change – change involving international relations, technology and politics – many countries have been trying to adapt their foreign and security policies to these changes, and some in the meantime, by altering their postures, have caused other changes in the world.

Turkey has for some time lagged rather behind these changes, that is, she neglected for several years to gear her defence policies and international relations to the changes that started taking place in the world. Now we are trying to make up for lost time and trying to adapt Turkey in the international field and in the field of defence policies to the changing conditions. Because of her geopolitical position and history, Turkey is herself bound to become an agent of change in the world while trying to adapt herself to the changes that are taking place. The knowledge that the steps she will take, and that she may take, may influence the rest of the world to a great extent of course places great responsibility on the shoulders of a nation; being experienced people and being situated in a very critical part of the world, we are aware of this responsibility. Therefore, while adapting our policies to the changing conditions of the world, we shall take careful steps such that would not only strengthen Turkey's own security but also enhance her possibilities of contributing to world peace.

Mr Ecevit is Prime Minister of Turkey. The following is the text of an address he gave to the International Institute for Strategic Studies on 15 May 1978.

In trying to make these changes in Turkey's foreign and security policies we shall have to keep in mind that foreign and security policies are inter-related and that any nation's security is inseparable from her economy. We have to remind ourselves of that because for many years Turkey has been carrying too heavy a burden for NATO, allocating to NATO a proportionately greater part of her national income, her budget and her manpower than any other member country. Turkey has neglected her agriculture and industrialization as a result, and the defence burden that she took over largely for the sake of the collective security system has been too heavy a burden on our economy so that it has been kept at the so-called 'take-off' stage for too long.

Changing Conditions of Security

What are the recent changes that Turkey has particularly to take account of *vis-à-vis* international relations and her defence policies? We first have to realize the fact that the cold-war period ended and that detente started quite a few years ago, but Turkey's defence structure still largely dates back to the cold-war years and places a heavy burden on her economy. Because of her commitments to NATO, Turkey finds herself increasingly in a position where both her economy and her defence system must become more self-sustained.

Another change that we have to take into account is that the sources of imminent threat to Turkey have changed considerably in recent years. Her national security concept and defence structure ought to alter accordingly.

It has become obvious that Turkey has fallen into a very disadvantageous position because of her dependence throughout the years as a member of NATO almost exclusively on one source – that is the United States – for her military equipment. This has been creating increasingly greater problems because of a certain characteristic and peculiarity of American politics which became gradually more marked.

As I am sure you would appreciate, although the United States of America is a world power with world-wide responsibilities, there is too great an interaction, an inter-relationship, between her internal and her external politics. Her external politics are very much (too much for a world power) influenced by the ethnic lobbies so that when an allied country has problems with the mother country of one of those lobbies, she finds herself in a hopeless situation *vis-à-vis* her relations with the United States, and sometimes even the United States Administration itself cannot help such a situation. I am not mentioning this peculiarity of American politics as a criticism, I am just stating a reality of our present day world which we have to learn to live with.

In recent years there have also been great changes in military technology, most of which have not yet been sufficiently reflected in the defence structure of Turkey, so much so that as authoritative a person as General Haig himself has recently stated that much of Turkey's military equipment would become obsolete within two years, irrespective of those items which have already become obsolete.

Then, in revising and changing our international relations and defence policies, we also have to keep in mind the increasing isolation of Turkey in the European Economic Community, of which she is an associate member.

A forthcoming change of which Turkey has to take account is the expected full membership of Greece in the EEC. Of course it is not up to us to say anything as to whether Greece should become a full member or not if she feels that her stage of economic development is ready for it. It is up to Greece and the nine members of the European Community to decide that. But considering that there is a possibility of the right of veto being used in the EEC on many issues, Greece's inclusion as a full member when the veto system is still in effect might drag the other existing members of the EEC into such positions where they may find themselves, in spite of themselves, applying embargoes on Turkey similar to that which has been applied by the United States against Turkey for over three years. This is another expected change that we have to keep in mind.

The necessity of changing Turkey's security policy and structure has become particularly marked and inevitable because of the following additional reasons. Turkey's present defence policy and structure cannot function any more, even if we so wanted, because of the limitations that the American embargo has imposed on Turkey's military preparedness and also because our own economy is no longer in a position to sustain the defence policy and structure that has been in effect until now. We have reached the stage where we must concentrate more on Turkey's economic development.

When my government took over at the beginning of this year, Turkey had been passing through the gravest economic crisis of her republican history, with figures like a 50 per cent inflation rate, 16 per cent unemployment rate (20 per cent if disguised unemployment is included), a drastically falling production and exports rate, to such an extent that last year Turkey's export earning could not even meet her oil imports alone.

When you put all these factors together you can, I am sure, realize how serious the economic crisis in Turkey is. The American embargo is certainly not the factor which is solely responsible for this situation, but it has certainly contributed a lot to the economic crisis.

Over the years our infrastructure, particularly in the areas of energy and port facilities, has become very inadequate so that it cannot carry the weight even of our existing industries any more.

Turkey has also been passing through a stage of serious social and political crises which is also connected with the economic crisis, and the basic reason why these crises all take place together is, I believe, the following. For historical reasons, and also for the added reason that Turkey has been a free and democratic country since World War II – in fact the only developing country in the world where democracy has survived without interruption since World War II – for all these reasons, Turkish society can be considered to be highly developed in a socio-political sense, but the level of her economic development has remained far below. This created great tension which in turn resulted in social and political crises, and the way the governments have in recent years approached or reacted to these crises were rather anachronistic and therefore resulted in aggravating the crises.

The first condition for dealing with the social and political crises in Turkey would be to speed up our economic development in a healthy and balanced way and to meet more fully the demands that come from the people in an open and free society. This is essential for the continued survival of democracy in Turkey, and this is another reason why we have to give absolute priority to problems of economic development in Turkey.

In any case, a defence structure based on a weak and crumbling economy can certainly not be considered to be healthy or reliable, yet such is the case in Turkey. So this is another reason why we have to give priority to economic development in Turkey and devise our defence structure accordingly.

Principles of National Security
While formulating a new national security concept and new defence and foreign policies we feel bound to keep in mind certain principles and factors. One of them is that we should make our national security primarily dependent on good relations and on establishing an atmosphere of mutual confidence with all our neighbours, with all the countries of the region. Certainly a country always needs armaments and armies to ensure her security. But I believe, my government believes, that establishing an atmosphere of mutual confidence in our relations with the neighbouring countries is at least as protective as, and sometimes more protective than armaments. And we also believe that by basing her national security on such a principle, the principle of establishing a mutual atmosphere of confidence with her neighbours, a country can best contribute to peace.

In formulating a new national security concept and new defence and foreign policies we also feel bound to keep in mind the historical and geographical realities of Turkey. With changing times and conditions, alliances and other forms of co-operation may change. But the history and geography of a country do not change, so that the most permanent and sound basis of a country's international relations should, we believe, be her historic and geographical realities. Historically and geographically Turkey is primarily a Balkan, Middle Eastern and Eastern Mediterranean country. This certainly does not exclude the fact that Turkey is also a member of the community of Europe, but our starting point is the Balkan area, the Middle East and the Eastern Mediterranean. Therefore we should give greater emphasis to these historical and geographical realities. In any case, we believe that good relations and co-operation with regional countries are also essential for speeding up economic development and growth, because then we shall be able to embark upon co-ordinated efforts and markets to enlarge the possibilities for our respective economies in the area.

This attitude in a way indicates a return to a policy first adopted when the Turkish Republic started, that of peacefully establishing Turkey in her own region by forming very close ties with the Middle Eastern countries as much as possible, and with the Balkan countries, before opening up to the rest of the world, and this is what we are trying to do again now.

Another factor that we have to keep in mind in evolving a new national security concept and, based on that, a new defence policy is that our defence system and structure should not be a burden, but should rather be a spur to our economy. We should therefore try to develop such industries for our defence as would be compatible with the means of our economy and which would increase its productivity.

In preparing a new defence concept and policy we should also keep in mind the new order of urgency among threats towards Turkey because, as a result of the changes I referred to earlier, that order has changed quite considerably in recent years.

We should also keep in mind while trying to develop a new national security concept that we should not upset the delicate balance on which detente is based. We should instead make our own contribution to detente in a more effective way.

Our new defence system and structure should be compatible with our continued membership in NATO, but certainly our contribution to NATO in the future would be and should be commensurate with NATO's contribution to Turkey's security. At the same time we should see to it that our contribution to NATO in the future should not constitute a serious risk for Turkey by rendering her provocative in the region where she is situated.

These are the basic principles, rules and factors that we shall keep in mind while evolving a new national security concept and new defence policies with their side-effects on foreign policy.

At the same time, the complete contents of this new security concept and the new defence structure will vary to some extent according to two factors which are as yet rather uncertain. One of these is whether the American armaments embargo against Turkey is to be lifted or not. I am not very optimistic at the present stage that it will be lifted, but we are preparing ourselves, keeping in mind the greater possibility that it may not be lifted.

The second uncertain factor is the willingness or ability of our European allies to fill the gap left by the United States regarding the military and economic requirements of Turkey. There we have a problem which is beyond our control and to some extent perhaps beyond the control of some of our Western allies even, because they believe, in some ways correctly, that material would not be forthcoming to fill the gap created by the American embargo on Turkey. But certainly something ought to be done about it if all NATO members are anxious to preserve the cohesion and effectiveness of the Western Alliance, because in view of the peculiarities of American policy and the uncertainties affecting its credibility, internal as well as external, the European members of the Alliance ought to try to assume a greater degree of self-sufficiency in many respects and ought to take over greater responsibility than they have done thus far. Otherwise the incredibility of the United States will be reflected to the whole Alliance.

In the meantime we would wish the democratic countries of the West to bear in mind the following factors.

First, the Turkish contribution to democracy. If we are to adopt all the relevant articles of the North Atlantic Treaty then this contribution of Turkey ought to be taken into consideration, because the Treaty includes an article giving great importance to principles of democracy. And as I said, Turkey is the only developing country in the world which has been able to make democracy work uninterruptedly, with the exception of a few brief accidents, since World War II. To make Turkish democracy survive would offer hope for mankind. Turkey had led the way after World War I towards independence and liberation movements, and now, if we can prove to the world, if we can demonstrate to other developing countries that democracy and freedom can be made to survive even in developing countries with limited economic resources, then this might change the whole development of humanity and international relations in the future. We cannot be content any more with being evaluated as the armoured frontier guard of the Western Alliance.

We would also like our allies in the West to fulfil their commitments to support the defence and economy of Turkey to a more reasonable degree. This is another major obligation, another treaty obligation, to provide economic help to those members of the Alliance who need it, but this is often forgotten by the members.

In the meantime, if our Western partners are as interested as we are in seeing to it that Turkey does not feel utterly helpless within the Alliance and should not be forced to too radical changes in her defence policies, as a result of the American embargo, then efforts should be made by the European allies to bring Turkey into schemes of co-production which have been tried in Europe for several years. Turkey has been over-dependent on one source alone for her military equipment, whereas the European partners of NATO have been trying to replace such over-dependence by interdependence. We have not been included in such schemes of interdependence, yet industrialization in Turkey has already reached a level that could enable her to participate in some co-production schemes regarding military equipment.

We would also be interested in establishing closer economic co-operation with our Western allies and partners. We cannot long continue a partnership based solely on an increasingly unbalanced trade relationship. By itself, Turkey's is a very promising market; there is already a population of over 40 million, and this is growing rapidly. What is more, Turkey is adjacent to the most promising markets of the world, and she already has the outlook of an industrialized society even if it is not yet an industrialized society, and has good relations with all the countries of the region with the unfortunate exception of her only NATO ally in the region. So Turkey can be an ideal partner for some of her allies in the West or other members of the EEC. Turkey can be an ideal partner for establishing industries that would not only appeal to Turkey, not only meet the requirements of Turkey's own development, but can also appeal to other countries of the world, particularly those of the Middle East.

Cyprus

Turkey, in evolving a new national security concept and revising her defence and foreign policies accordingly, has also kept in mind her regional problems which, though very limited, have become rather acute in recent years, and these are her problems with Greece and also the problem of Cyprus. As soon as my government took over at the beginning of this year we took the initiative in approaching our neighbour and ally Greece to establish a friendly dialogue between the two countries and to restore our lost friendship. We also encouraged the Turkish Cypriot administration to take the initiative in coming up with concrete proposals to speed up a solution to the long delayed Cyprus problem. The Turkish Cypriot administration has complied with our wish and they came up with concrete proposals regarding both the geographical and constitutional arrangements. Dr Waldheim, who has the function of good offices for the Cyprus issue, reacted to these Turkish proposals in the following terms: 'they are concrete, they are substantial, voluminous and on time', he declared. However, the Greek side has rejected these proposals offhand and embarked upon such an effective publicity campaign throughout the world that many observers in the West, some of whom obviously did not have an opportunity to study the Turkish proposals, thought that they amounted to nothing. For instance, the Greeks claim that the Turkish proposal would involve only a one per cent change in the geographical arrangements, but what the Turks really did was to suggest that they were ready to discuss geographical arrangements in six different areas of the region under Turkish control without specifying how much land would be available. This attitude they adopted in order to be flexible and to sit around the table with an open mind. They also said that they would leave to the Greek side all the security zone separating the sections of the island, which amount to three per cent, apart from the geographical arrangements to be made in the six areas pointed to by the Turkish Cypriots. Besides, they suggested that Varosha, the richest part of Cyprus, could be resettled by the Greeks, which would mean that the resettlement problem for at least 30,000 Greeks would be solved, and economically the Varosha district would mean nearly half the island.

On the other hand, the Turkish side came out with a proposal that would establish a real federation from the start with several functions of joint responsibility, and besides it would be an evolutionary federation which would see to it that Cyprus becomes a more closely-knit political structure with time. Now the Greek Cypriots seem to have decided to reject all these proposals without even negotiating them. And the only reason, I believe, is that they are interested in seeing to it that American pressure on Turkey should continue rather than that a federal solution to Cyprus be found.

This has also adversely influenced relations with Greece. Earlier this year, as soon as we took over, I invited Mr Karamanlis, the Prime Minister of Greece, to establish a dialogue with Turkey on the prime ministerial level. He first hesitated and, after my second appeal, he accepted and we met in Montreux in mid-March; we had a very friendly talk and we decided to continue and institutionalize our dialogue, supplementing it with high-level technical discussions. The first high-level technical meeting was scheduled to take place in Ankara on 14 April. But as soon as President Carter approached the Congress to lift the arms embargo the Athens Government postponed this meeting indefinitely, so that the bridges seem to be broken for the moment at least (later the dialogue was resumed).

This shows that Turkey and Greece cannot solve their problems and the Cyprus problem cannot be solved under the shadow of others. History bears witness to that because whenever other countries were involved in the Turko–Greek differences the Turks and Greeks ended up in conflict. But whenever they were left alone to settle their own differences they showed great ability to do so. For instance, after the Turko–Greek war of the 1920s, even when the bitter memories of that war remained fresh, the Turks and the Greeks were able to come together under the leadership of Ataturk and Venizelos to establish friendly relations and co-operation because, at that time, the other powers, our friends in the West, were too occupied with their own problems to be concerned with ours. Again, after World War II, when other countries were too occupied with their own problems and left Turkey and Greece alone, excellent relations and co-operation between the two countries were established in the 1950s, and were only disrupted as a result of the events in Cyprus. So the elimination of outside influences is essential for a solution of the problems between Turkey and Greece and for a solution of the Cyprus issue.

From the moment we took over we have given a new impetus to Turkey's existing initiatives towards establishing increasingly good relations with all our neighbours. Unfortunately, we have failed only in the case of our NATO ally. But I am still hopeful that even there we may find the possibility of establishing a friendly dialogue and friendlier relations.

Index

Aegean dispute 5, 58–9, 90, 118
  Aegean Sea 59, 90, 112
    mineral resources 93, 119
  air traffic control question 5, 15, 32, 58, 91, 95, 116–17
    attempts to solve 100–1
    breakdown of talks, 1976 100, 101
    Greek case 101, 113
    Turkish case 100–1, 112–13
  continental shelf question 5, 14–15, 58–9, 91, 93–4, 95
    'Bay of Maine' formula 103–4
    Berne Declaration on 99–100, 102, 111, 119
    delimitation formula 103, 104–5
    Greek case 102, 103, 111–12
    Greek proposal to refer to ICJ, 1975 96
    Greek referral to ICJ 98–9
    Greek referral to Security Council, 1976 97–8
    joint regime solution 103, 115–16
    map 127
    'maritime facade' formula 103
    need for arbitrator 116–17
    oil prospecting by Turkish *Sizmik 1*, 1976 15, 96–7, 98, 112, 115, 118
    problem of islands' status 104
    prospecting by Greek *Nautilus* 97
    survey voyage of Turkish *Candarli*, 1974 94–5
    tension in mid-1970s 97
    Turkish case 102, 103, 111
    Turkish internal arguments over 96
    Turkish reply to Greek referrals 97–8, 99
  geopolitical balance 92–3
    military balance 92–3
    population 92

Greek-Turkish relations up to 1947 91–2
  Balkan Wars, 1912–13 2, 91
  distribution of islands 91, 92
  frontier settlement, 1923 91–2
  Greece achieves independence 1, 91
  Greek claims on Greek areas overseas 1, 91
  Greek invasion of Turkey defeated, 1921–2 2, 91
  refugees in Greece, 1920s 2, 91
Greek-Turkish relations, 1973–8 120–4
legal background 93–4
minorities problem 106–7
  exodus of Greeks 106
  expulsion of Greeks 106
  Greeks in Turkey 106
  Muslims in Thrace 106, 107
Montreux 'Summit' of 1978 109
need for settlement 114–15
  defence costs 114–15
  Greek viewpoint 113–14
  political risks and 115
  Turkish viewpoint 113–14
problem of islands' militarization 96, 105–6, 133
problems for NATO 110
territorial sea limits question 59, 91, 93, 94, 117
  Greek case 112
  maps 125, 126
  problems of islands 94
  Turkish case 112
Turkey's complaints of Western phil-hellenism 90
Turkey's New Defence Concept, 1978, and 109–10
Afghanistan
  effect of Soviet invasion 61, 82, 85, 86
Agnew, Vice-Pres. Spiro 19

Akmandor, Neset 68
Albania 8
  Greek relations with 8-9
American Journal of International Law
  on continental shelf delimitation 104
Andrassy, J. 154
Arafat, Yasser 25
Arsenis, Gerassimos 31
Atatürk, Kemal 2, 33, 45, 47, 49, 53, 77, 106
  defeats Greeks, 1921-2 2, 91
  goals 45
  secularist reforms 52, 52
Averof, Evangelos 25, 26

Baghdad Pact 60, 71, 78
Balkans
  Balkan Entente, 1934 79-80
  Balkan Pact 80
  Balkan Wars, 1912-13 2, 91
  Little Entente 80
  nuclear weapons in 38
Britain
  decline of influence in Greece 3
  occupies and gives up Cyprus 10, 11
  rift with Italy, 1935 2
  support for Greek monarchy 3
Bulgaria 58
  claims to Greek territory
  occupies Greek territory in WWII 6
  relations with Turkey 80, 81
Bulgarian Exarchate Church 2
Buzan, Barry 93

Caglayangil, Ihsan Sabri 96
Carter, Pres. James 14, 20, 140
Ceaucescu, Nicolae 9
Central Treaty Organization 71-2, 85
  achievements 72
  dissolution 61, 71
Churchill, Winston 3
Clerides, Glafkos 13, 107
Conference on Security and Co-operation in Europe 70, 73, 79
  Helsinki Document 80
  Helsinki Final Act 83
Constantine I, King of Greece 91
Constantine II, King of Greece 18

Council for Mutual Economic Aid (COMECON) 49, 80
Crawshaw, Nancy
  on Cyprus problem 12
Crete
  Iraklion air station 4, 20, 22
  Suda Bay complex 4, 20
Cuban missile crisis, 1962 62-3, 66
Cyprus 107-9
  becomes independent, 1959 11, 107
  British decide to relinquish control 11
  British occupation 10
  communal clashes 11, 65, 107
  coup of 1974 11, 66, 107
  deadlock in 13-14, 108
  demands for independence 10
  division of population 12, 13, 108
  Ecevit's belief in settlement 140-1
  enosis issue 10, 11, 59, 66, 107
  EOKA movement 11, 107, 108
  Graeco-Turkish confrontation begins 10
  Greek-Turkish relations 10, 12-13, 19, 58, 59, 120-4
  need for settlement 117, 133
  Turkish interest in 59, 71
  Turkish invasion of 1974 12-13, 19, 66, 74, 95, 107, 108, 132
    effect of 95-6, 112
  UN moves 11, 13, 14, 17

Dardanelles 36
  Montreux Convention on 3, 36, 53, 54, 57, 76
  Soviet right of passage 4
Davos, Gen. 19, 21
De Gaulle, Charles 73
Demirel, Süleyman 13, 50, 52, 66, 77, 85, 96, 109, 131
  economic measures in Turkey, 1979 48, 53
  forms government, 1979 49
Denktash, Rauf 12, 13, 14, 108
Dulles, John Foster 71

Ecevit, Bulent 12, 13, 15, 35, 50, 52, 66, 95, 102, 106, 107, 109, 115, 117
  confidence in Soviet friendship for Turkey 75

143

declares martial law, 1978 50
forms government, 1977 49
government's economic moves, 1978 47
introduces New Defence Concept 109, 113–14
meets Karamanlis at Montreux, 1979 108, 140
on Turkish security 136–41
  changing conditions and 136–8
  Cyprus question 140–1
  principles of national security 138–40
visits Libya, 1979 79
visits Romania, 1978 80
visits Yugoslavia, 1977 80
Eisenhower, Pres. Dwight D.
  visits CENTO countries, 1959 73
Eliou, Elias 102
Ellsworth, Robert 63
Erbakan, Mr 49, 51, 52, 66, 68
European Economic Community (EEC) 32, 34, 85
  Global Mediterranean Policy 48
  loans to Turkey, 1980–1 47
  trade with Turkey 48
Evran, Gen. Kenan 52

Faisal, King 78, 79
France
  withdraws from NATO 73

Gaddafi, Pres. of Libya 25
Geneva Convention on the Continental Shelf 93, 94, 97, 98, 102–3, 104, 111, 116, 134
George II, King of Greece 2, 3
Germany
  Ostpolitik in FRG 73
  overruns Yugoslavia and Greece, WWII 2
Goel 1 hydrographic vessel 96
Goldbloom, Maurice 18
Goodpaster, Gen. 19
Gorshkov, Adm. 57
Greece
  'Colonels' coup', 1967, *see* Greek armed forces
  defence role in NATO compared with Turkey's 33
  EEC entry 8, 32–3, 34, 131, 137

economic growth, 1962–78 30
economic problems 31
general compliance under Western pressure 32–3
Hellenikon air base 4, 20, 22
importance of sea to 5, 92
joins NATO, 1952 10
Marshall Plan in 16
NADGE sites 4
Nea Makri communications station 4, 20
relations with NATO 20–1, 32, 34, 37, 38, 84, 132–3
Treaty of Friendship and Alliance with Turkey and Yugoslavia, 1950s 7, 10
Greek armed forces 27
in post-war period 27–8
  abortive coup of 1951 28
  anti-communist and monarchist line 27
  'Holy Bond of Greek Officers' (IDEA) 28
  Supreme Council of National Defence (ASEA) 27, 29
  under Papagos as C-in-C 27–8
  US influence 27
intervention in politics, 1967 28–9
  conflict between throne and parliament 28
  dictatorship created 29
  failure during Cyprus crisis 29, 107
  nepotism during 29
  promotion problems 28
  reasons for 28
Military Academy 30
post-Junta 29–30
  parliamentary control 29
  problem of civilian control 27
Greek Communist Party (KKE) 3, 26–7
defeated in 1949 7
'Exterior' and 'Interior' divisions 26–7
legalized, 1974 26
policy on Macedonia, 1925–35 6, 7
Greek security 1, 6
address by Ioannis Pesmazoglou on, 1979 131–5
conditions of Greek security 3–5
regional 314

144

Soviet threat and NATO 4–5
Turkey 5
domestic factors 23–32
  Centre Union Party (EDIK) 17, 26
  Communist Party, *see* Greek Communist Party (KKE)
  economic aspects 30–2
  'New Democracy' Party 25–6, 31, 115
  PASOK Party, *see* Panhellenic Socialist Movement (PASOK)
  role of armed forces, *see* Greek armed forces
future prospects 36–8
  Greek defence industry 37–8
  Greek fears of Turkish expansionism 37, 38
  question for Greece of Spanish entry into NATO 37
  question of nuclear weapons 38
Graeco-Turkish relations 9–16, 35
  air traffic control question, *see* Aegean dispute
  Continental Shelf and, *see* Aegean dispute
  Cyprus problem, *see* Cyprus
  effect of WWII on 10
  friendly in 1930s 9–10
  friendly in early 1950s 10
  NATO framework 15–16
Greek relations with US and NATO 16–22
  Greek-American Agreement on bases, 1953 17
  negotiates special relationship with NATO, 1977 20–1
  PASOK and question of US bases 22
  problem of Cyprus 10, 11, 13, 17–20 *passim*, 110
  question of Aegean defence 21–2
  request for guarantee against Turkey, 1981 22
  strains in 1960s 17–18
  US commands in Greece 21
  US-Greek Defense Co-operation Agreement, 1977 22
  US-Greek-NATO agreements on military aid, 1976 20

  US post-WWII influence 16–17
  US relations with 'Colonels' 18, 19, 20
  withdrawal from military branch of NATO, 1974 20, 110
historical background 1–3
  achievement of Greek independence 1, 91
  Balkan Wars, 1912–13 2, 91
  British help for Greece, 1940 2
  defeat of communists, 1949 3
  defeated by Turkey, 1921–2 2, 91
  EAM-ELAS resistance movement 2–3, 6
  elections of 1946 3
  German conquest of Greece, WWII 2
  Greek accord with Turkey, 1930 2, 9, 106
  Greek claims on Greek areas abroad 1, 91
  Italian attack on Greece, 1940 2
  monarchist-communist conflict, post-WWII 2–3
  refugees in Greece, 1920s 2, 91
  religious struggle with Bulgarian church, late 19th c. 1–2
  US influence supplants British, 1946–8 3
  World War I 2
link with West and Turkey in 1980s 32–4
  admiration of Turkish 'independence' 33–4
  easing of relations with Turks, 1980–1 32
  EEC membership and 34
  non-aligned tendencies 34
  rejoins military arm of NATO 32, 37, 84
need for closer relations with Arab countries 132
problem of relations with Balkan states 6–9, 132
  Greek relations with Soviet Union 7, 132
  Macedonian problem 6–9 *passim*
  with Albania 8, 9
  with Bulgaria 6–9 *passim*

with Romania 8
  with Yugoslavia 6, 7, 8
 Soviet and communist threat 35-6
  Greece and Soviet-Turkish *rapprochement* 35
  in event of war 36
  thaw in Greek relations with Moscow, from 1977 35
Grivas, Gen.
 role in Cyprus 11
Gürsel, Gen. 56
Gutteridge, J.A.C. 104

Haig, Gen. Alexander 21, 22, 66, 132, 134, 137
Hill-Norton, Sir Peter 69
Hitler, Adolf 54
Hoxha, Enver 8–9

Indönü, Ismet 11, 65, 66
International Civil Aviation Organization (ICAO) 110, 116
 defines control of Aegean airspace, 1952 95
 tries to solve airspace dispute, 1974–5 100
International Court of Justice (ICJ) 96, 105, 114
 Aegean dispute before 98–9, 102, 116
 North Sea Continental Shelf ruling 94, 111
International Monetary Fund (IMF)
 credit for Turkey, 1978–9 47, 114
Ionnides, Col. 19
Iran
 concern with Gulf security 72
 coolness to Turkey, 1970s 72
 leaves CENTO 71
 pursues Kurds into Turkey, 1975 60
 revolution's effect on Turkey 44, 61–2, 82, 86
Iraq
 relations with Turkey 58, 78, 79
Irmak, Prof. Sadi 96
Islamic Conferences 78, 79
Israel
 relations with Turkey 78, 79
Italy 2

 invades Ethiopia, 1935 54
 invades Greece, 1940 2

Jiménez, Eduardo 102
Johnson, Pres. Lyndon B.
 warns Turkey about intervention in Cyrpus 11, 65, 66

Karamanlis, Constantine 8, 10, 13, 15, 20, 31, 37, 96, 97, 102, 114, 115, 117
 as leader of New Democracy Party 25
 becomes Greek President, 1980 25
 co-operates with Menderes to form independent Cyprus 11
 meets Ecevit at Montreux, 1978 109, 140
 political views 25–6
 returns to office, 1974 12, 95, 107
 visits Moscow, 1979 25, 35
 visits Romania and Bulgaria, 1975 9
Kayra, Cahit 95
Kennedy, Pres. John F. 17
Khrushchev, Nikita 62, 73
 desire for Turkish neutrality 56–7, 74
Kiev 57
Kilic, Selahattin 97
Kissinger, Henry 18
 attitude to Turkish invasion of Cyprus 19
 opposes arms embargo on Turkey 20
Konstantopoulos, N. 30
Korean War 62
Kosygin, Alexei 76
Kutchuck, Dr 11
Kuwait
 relations with Turkey 79
Kyprianou, Greek Cypriot leader 14
Kyrkos, Leonidas 27

Labouisse, Henry 17
Laird, Melvin 19
Lausanne, Treaty of, 1923 2, 5, 58, 59, 91, 93, 96, 105, 106, 107, 111
Lenin 77
Libya
 friendship with Turkey 79

Macedonia
  Bulgarian occupation, WWII 6
  Greek policy towards 7, 8
  Greek preponderance in population 6
  Pirin district 6, 7
  Yugoslav-Bulgar plan for, 1947 6
  Yugoslav-Bulgar quarrel over 9
Makarios, Archbishop 17, 74, 107, 108
  conservative attitudes 19
  death 13
  Greek coup against, 1974 10–11, 66, 107
  joins non-aligned movement 18
  President of Cyprus 11
  urges Cypriot independence 10, 11
Mavros, George 26, 102
Mediterranean
  extent 3
  importance to NATO and US 3–4
  NATO exercise, 1982 22
  Soviet navy in 4–5, 57, 71
  Soviet threat to 36
  US Sixth Fleet in 4, 19, 57, 71
Menderes, Turkish PM 11, 63, 73, 106
Metaxas, Ioannis 2
Mitsotakis, C. 26
Mussolini, Benito 54
Mutual and Balanced Force Reductions (MBFR) negotiations 70, 117

Nasser, Pres. of Egypt 71
Nixon, Donald 19
Nixon, Pres. Richard M. 73
Non-Proliferation Treaty, 1968 73
North Atlantic Treaty Organisation (NATO) 17, 32
  Aegean dispute and 110, 115
  command structure in E. Mediterranean 64, 110, 134
  Cyprus controversy and 10, 11, 13, 17–20 *passim*, 132
  element in Turkish security 82
  'flexible response' strategy 63, 68
  'forward strategy' 62
  Greek bases 1, 4
  Greek 'Colonels' loyalty to 19, 132
  intention to base cruise missiles in Sicily 5
  intra-alliance problems 73
  Izmir HQ 21–2, 110, 134
  Larissa HQ 32, 110, 134
  view of E. Mediterranean theatre 36, 132

Ôkçün, Gündüz 114
Organization for Economic Co-operation and Development (OECD) 48, 49
  economic assistance to Turkey, 1979 47, 114

Pakistan
  relations with Turkey 72
  scorn for CENTO 71
Palestine Liberation Organization (PLO)
  Turkish relations with 78, 79, 84
Panhellenic Socialist Movement (PASOK) 23–5, 30, 36, 37, 38
  divisions in 24, 34
  foundation 23
  programme 23, 24, 31
  wins Greek elections, 1981 1, 22, 23
Papadopoulos, Col. 19, 29
Papagos, Marshal 10, 16–19 *passim*
Papandreou, Andreas 1, 16, 17, 23, 38, 96, 102
  attitude to EEC and NATO 24, 25, 32, 34, 37
  attitude to US bases 22
  Balkan visits 9
  political stance 23–4
  support for Iraq 25
  view of Greece's position 23, 24, 31
  visits Cyprus, 1982 14
  welcome to PLO 25
Papandreou, George II, 17, 26, 28
  dispute with Greek king 18
Paris, Treaty of, 1946–7 5, 6, 92, 96, 105, 111
Partial Test Ban Treaty, 1963 73
Partsalides, Greek communist leader 7
Pesmazoglou, Ioannis (John) 26
  on Greek security, 1979 131–5
    foreign policy orientations 131–2
    Greek relations with NATO 132–3
    perspectives from Greek accession to EEC 134–5

proposed Pact of Friendship and
    Co-operation with Turkey 133–4
  security control in Aegean 134
Peurifoy, US ambassador to Greece 16
Plastiras, Gen. 16
Platias, A.G. and Rydell, R.J. 38
Powers, Gary 77

Rallis, George 24, 32, 37
  on Greek concern with Aegean 16
  visits Moscow, 1978 35
Rogers, Gen Bernard 21
Rogers, William 19
Romania
  at odds with Moscow 73
  relations with Greece, 1957–9 8
  relations with Turkey 80

SALT talks 63, 73, 77, 82, 85
Sampson, Nicos 12, 66, 107
Saudi Arabia
  relations with Turkey 78, 79
Sèvres, Treaty of, 1920 91
Shear, Adm. 66
Sisco, Joseph 12
Smyrna (Izmir)
  destruction of, 1922 91
Soviet Union
  Backfire bombers covering Mediterranean 5, 36
  credits for Turkey 49, 53
  navy, *see* Mediterranean
  rapprochement with Turkey, 1978 35
  relations with Greece 35, 36
  rift with China 73
  supports independent Cyprus 18, 35
  thaw in relations with Turkey 43, 74, 75, 76, 78
  treaties with Syria and Iraq 61
  view of Turkey's role 81–2
Stalin, Josef 3, 6, 43, 54
  death, 1953 7
Stavrou, N. 9
Syria
  relations with Turkey 59, 78, 79

Tito, Pres. of Yugoslavia 3, 7, 8, 80
  breaks with Cominform, 1948 6

death 8, 9
To Vima daily 22, 24
Tsaldaris, P. 2
Turkes, Alpashan 49, 66, 77
  forms Turkish NAP 51
Turkey
  Armed Forces Industries 68
  'Army of the Aegean' (Fourth) 64, 96, 105, 106, 117, 132
  Aselsan Military Electronic Industries 68
  Belbasi base 65, 110
  claims on Greek islands 5
  defeats Greek invasion, 1921–2 2, 91
  democracy under strain in 49–52
    deaths from ideological radicalism 49–50
    Democrat Party 45
    elections of 1977 49
    Federation of the Revolutionary Youth 50–1
    Justice Party 48, 49, 50, 52, 75
    multi-party democracy in 49, 50, 139
    National Action Party (NAP) 48, 49, 51, 77
    National Salvation Party (NSP) 48, 49, 51, 61
    Organization of the Hearts of Idealists 51
    Republican People's Party (RPP) 45, 48, 49, 50, 52, 75
    Socialist Revolution Party 75
    struggle between 'fascism' and 'communism' 52
    terrorism 51
    Turkish Workers Party (TWP) 50, 51, 53
  Diyarbakir communications complex 110
  Incirlik air base 60, 64, 65, 78, 110
  'independence' in international affairs 33–4
  joins NATO, 1952 10, 44, 53
  Karamürsel base 65, 110
  Kargaburun LORAN station 110
  Kurds in 50, 60, 61, 62, 77, 79
  Machinery and Chemical Industries (MCI) 68
  Marshall Plan recipient 63
  National Security Council 53

post-WWII growth of population 44, 47, 58
present problems 44–5, 47, 137
relations with Iran, 1970s 72
relations with Libya 79
relations with Pakistan 72
religion in 51
role of military 52–3
   army coups 49, 51, 52
   Junta of 1980 52–3
   loyalty to Atatürk 52
   modernizing role 52
Samsun communications site 110
Sinop radar base 65, 110
socio-economic transformation since WWI 45–9
   association with EEC 48, 63, 85
   economic activity of 1950s 45–6
   economic growth, 1960s–70s 46
   effect of 1970s world recession 46–7
   foreign currency remittances, 1970s 46
   government economic moves, 1978–9 47, 48
   ineffective coalition governments 48
   international assistance for, 1978–9 47
   legacy of Atatürk 45
   markets 48, 49
   oil supplies 46, 48, 61, 79–80
   overseas workers 46, 48
   secularization 45
   trade unions 46
stance in WWII 10
Treaty of Friendship and Alliance with Greece and Yugoslavia, 1950s 7, 10
Turkish Aircraft Industry (TUSAS) 68
view on NATO responsibilities with Greece 16, 37
Turkish Petroleum Co. 59
Turkish security 43–4, 85–6
   alliances and Western integration 62–5
      stationing of US missiles in, 1957 62
      Turkey's role in NATO 62–5
   background to security policy 53–5
      fears of Fascist aggression, 1930s 54
      fears of Soviet Union, post-WWII 54–5

      neutralism of 1920s and 1930s 53, 55
      relations with Soviet Union, 1920s and 1930s 53–4, 55
      turns to US, post-WWII 55
      War of Independence, 1919–22 53, 55
   Bulent Ecevit on 136–41
   Central Treaty Organization, *see* separate entry
   co-existence with Soviet Union 43, 53, 56–8
      contiguity problem 56
      Declaration of Principles of Good Neighbourliness, 1972 75
      friendliness in 1920s 53–4
      Pan-Turkism and 77–8
      Political Document on the Principles of Good Neighbourliness and Friendly Co-operation, 1978 75
      press views on 75
      problem of Straits 54, 56, 57, 73, 76
      problem of Turkey's geographical position 57
      problem of US U-2 flights 77
      public attitudes on 75, 76
      reduction of US presence and 75
      Soviet desire for Turkish neutrality 56–7, 75, 76
      Soviet economic aid 74
      Soviet naval power and 57
      Soviet support for Turkey over Cyprus 74
      thawing of relations 43, 74, 75, 76, 78
      Treaty of Mutual Friendship, 1921 53
      Treaty of Neutrality and Non-Aggression, 1925 53
      union views on 75–6
      vulnerability of Turkish Thrace 58
   co-operation with NATO 69–70
      problem of cost of defence 70, 136
      problem of meeting NATO arms standards 69–70, 137
      refusal to base NATO nuclear weapons, 1979 85
   effects of Iranian revolution 44, 61–2, 86
   Kurdish question 60, 61, 62

future prospects 81–3
　credibility of NATO defence 82–3
　defence of sovereignty 82
　development and security 81
military budgets 67, 70
military integration in NATO 64–7, 138–9
　'bilateral agreements' with US 64–5, 83
　chain of command 64, 110
　co-operation with US 64, 136
　deterioration of relations over Cyprus intervention 65, 66–7
　NADGE sites 64
　relations with Soviet Union and 66
　Turkish forces 64
　US bases 60, 65, 110
new approaches to security 73–4
post-WWII policy 43, 53
relations with Balkan countries 79–81, 138
　public indifference over 80–1
　with Bulgaria 80, 81
　with Romania 80
　with Yugoslavia 80
relations with Greece 5, 58–9
　continental shelf problem, *see* Aegean dispute
　control of airspace, *see* Aegean dispute
　Cyprus issue, *see* Cyprus
　early conflict 58
　recent revival of rivalry 43
　territorial waters issue, *see* Aegean dispute
relations with Middle East 43, 44, 86, 138
　historical memories 78
　oil supplies 46, 48, 61, 79–80
　pro-Arab position today 60, 78
　problem of Middle East instability 60
　Syrian-Iraqi *rapprochement* and 60–1
　Turkey denies US airlift facilities, 1979 60, 78, 84
　with Iraq 59, 78, 79
　with Israel 78, 79
　with Kuwait 79
　with PLO 78, 79, 84
　with Saudi Arabia 78, 79

roads to security examined 83–5
　dependence on US 83
　inapplicability of French model 83
　non-alignment 83–4, 114
　return to Middle East 84–5
　settlement of Cyprus problem 84
security environment 56
super-power detente and 70–1
Turkish-American Defence Co-operation Agreement, 1980 85–6
weapons acquisition 67–9
　effect of US embargo 68
　from US 136
　national arms industry 67–8
　need for arms from NATO 139

UN Conference on the Law of the Sea (UNCLOS) 59, 93, 94, 111, 113
　defines Contiguous Zone 93
UN Security Council
　Aegean dispute before 97–8
　resolution on Aegean dispute 98, 99, 111
United States of America
　arms embargo on Turkey, 1975 20, 63, 65, 66, 68, 70, 71, 82, 113, 137, 139, 140
　attitude to Cyprus problem 17, 18, 19–20
　commands in Greece 21, 110
　Defence Co-operation Agreement (DCA) with Turkey, 1976 20
　Greek-American agreement on bases, 1953 17
　Greek bases 1, 4, 19, 22
　Marshall Plan 10, 16, 63
　military aid agreement with Greece, 1976 20
　opinion of Greece and Turkey as allies 32–3, 37
　relations with Greek 'Colonels' 18, 19, 20
　role in Greece, 1947–53 17
　strained relations with Greece, 1960 17–18
　takes over British presence in Greece, post-WWII 3, 16
　Truman Doctrine, 1947 3, 62
　Turkish-American Defence Co-operation

Agreement, 1980 85–6
Turkish bases 60, 110

Venizelos, Eleutherios 2, 53, 91, 106
Vietnam War 73

Waldheim, Dr Kurt 13, 14, 108, 109, 140
Warsaw Pact
   forces on NATO's southern flank 5
   possible action in E. Mediterranean theatre 36
Wilson, Andrew 15
Wohlstetter, Prof. Albert 63
World Bank
   loan to Turkey, 1979 47

Yugoslavia
   drops support for Greek communists 6–7
   'Macedonian' policy 6
   relations with Greece, 1967–70 8
   Treaty of Friendship and Alliance with Turkey and Greece, 1950s 7, 10

Zachariades, N. 7
   'Ten Years of Struggle' 7
Zhivkov, Pres. Todar, of Bulgaria 9
Zigdis, John 26

DATE DUE